THE END
of the
SHERRY

THE END
of the
SHERRY

Bruce Berger

An Aequitas Book from
Pleasure Boat Studio: A Literary Press
New York

Casebound ISBN 978-1-929355-95-2
Paperback ISBN 978-1-929355-99-0

Library of Congress Control Number: 2013947906

Author's photo by Deb Milligan
Cover design by Laura Tolkow
Interior design by Susan Ramundo

Parts of *The End of the Sherry* have appeared in the following:
*The Yale Review, Traveler's Tales: Spain, Mountain Gazette,
American Way*

Certain people, of whom I am one, thrive in an atmosphere of uncertainty. It is not that we have the gambler's spirit, that we challenge chance for the sake of the game. We are not so dashing. If we take risks, we take them because we are lazy. We delegate our responsibilities to fate. In any situation, the more you are obliged to leave to chance, the less you are obliged to do yourself. Being for the most part inefficient, incapable of foresight, and rather irresponsible, we like best those situations in which a great deal has to be left to chance.

Peter Fleming, Brazilian Adventurer

For Bruno Aguilar Lozano

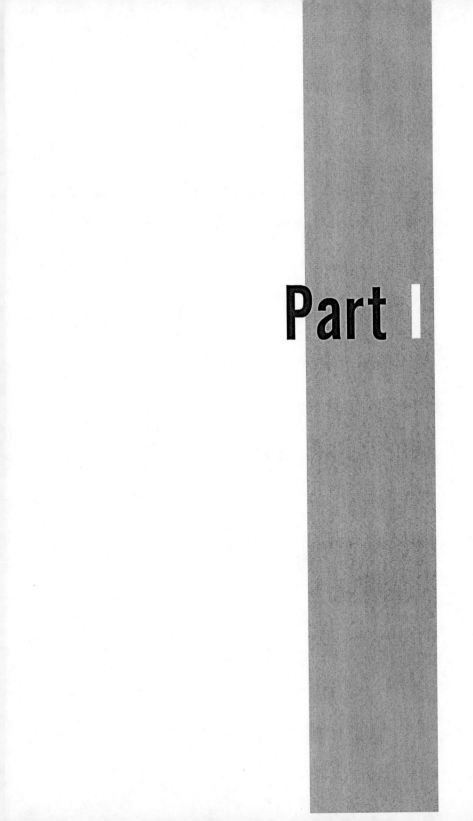

Part I

1

I learned Spanish by immersion, mainly in sherry.

I had always associated that viscous fluid with the lady bridge players who filled our living room on Wednesday afternoons, sippers who called each other's hats *darling* and *cunning* as their nails flamed against my mother's crystal. Andalucia's sherry drinkers, anno 1965, were male, bareheaded and serious. Instead of sitting at folding card tables, they stood tirelessly at a zinc bar in dark trousers and threadbare suit jackets. The sherry they tossed back was not the honey my mother's friends left unfinished, and which I polished off as she showed them to their sedans; it was as astringent as paint thinner, a taste I was acquiring more slowly as I washed down a new language. My German shepherd, drinking beside me from a saucer, preferred beer.

"Why are you living in Spain?" asked the sherry drinker beyond the dog.

The answer required more self-knowledge than I had. "I like it here."

"Nobody comes to live in Puerto Real," said a man to the other side of me.

"That's the perfect reason to do it."

"Foreigners never venture past the campground," he continued, naming the place I was living.

"The campground gets boring," I replied with enthusiasm. Having learned the word for *boring* that very morning, I was pleased to put it to immediate use.

"Is your dog from Spain?" asked the man beyond him.

"No, he was born in the States."

"Then how did he get here?"

"He flew."

The man backed up and looked at the dog sardonically. "Sure, lifting his leg on the clouds."

I was meanwhile monitoring, as best I could, a conversation farther down the bar. "I wonder if he's married," I heard a man say.

"I'm not," I said, leaning forward to answer the question directly.

"A three-eared American with a drunken dog that flies." A new voice. Normally I couldn't follow more than one conversational thread at a time, even in English, but voracity for the new language extended my reach.

"Another round," commanded the man next to the dog.

This conversation in the Bar Central replicated itself several times a week. A couple of months back I had dropped in for the first time, ordering a beer and inflicting that morning's vocabulary on Manolo, the eighteen-year-old bartender. The next morning Manolo, along with his twin brother Luis, a fifteen-year-old companion named Skinny and a forty-five-year-old named Sparkplug, appeared at my tent site to wish me good morning. I fired my butane burner, borrowed cups from the campers next to me and served instant coffee. We traded sounds for three hours.

The quartet was patient with my stabs at meaning, my ears were tuned to their salvos and we established a few basics. The twins' father owned the Bar Central, school had let out for Skinny, Sparkplug had been idled from the drydock. Drifts of free time washed them daily to my tent, sometimes bearing bread and cheese. We dissected life in the United States, life in Puerto Real, life. Often they lured me afterward to the Bar

Central, a kilometer along the railroad tracks that doubled as the perfect dog walk.

The zinc bar, it turned out, was Puerto Real's village green. Swelling the core clientele was a full complement of outsiders, some passing through on business, others in town for supplies. In a hub of compulsive socializing, where every topic had been exhausted, word quickly spread of the foreigner and his alcoholic dog. They could be encountered early afternoons in the Bar Central. I was never allowed to buy a round, for as soon as I signaled to Manolo I was outshouted and viscous gold fell into the narrow, short-stemmed *copa*. The astringency grew on me while facilitating, up to a point, my pronunciation. The repetitive, identity-establishing conversations, forgettable in themselves, consolidated some casual vocabulary and grammar, clichés from which I could eventually branch into more interesting specifics. On this particular occasion the banter had already grown a third ear for me and wings for the dog. "Manolo," said the man who had invited me, "I said a *round*. That's seven sherries plus a beer." He paused. "With a change of saucer."

A young American living among strangers outside a small Andalusian town in 1965, in the twenty-sixth year of Generalísimo Franco's dictatorship, might be considered adventurous—yet I had arrived in that situation quite passively. Rather than initiating my own plans, I had merely selected the more colorful alternative among options generated by others. Even the dog was a kind of inheritance. It was risk by default, by multiple choice, by valor among binaries. I said yes instead of no, then took the consequences.

I began by saying no to the Chicago suburb where I grew up, a childhood I thought of as boredom under the elms. I took refuge in the family Steinway, waiting impatiently for the teacher who showed up once a week to teach me classical music and memorizing his assignments as soon as he was out the door, whether I liked them or not. I filled the time between lessons by playing by ear all the pop standards and concerto themes from my parents' huge stack of 78 RPMs, and when I referred to the teacher's demonstrations beyond sight of the keys, he told me I had an unusual quality called perfect pitch. I trailed my half-brother to Yale. For grad school I picked Berkeley, the most scenic acceptance. My father died of complications from chain-smoking, leaving me an inheritance it seemed immoral to live on, and I resolved to become a professor of literature—but when artists I met on Cannery Row, in Monterey, suggested I drop out and move in with them, I did so. It sounded livelier. And when a newcomer to Cannery Row proposed we spend a year driving around the Mediterranean, I said, why not? Generating nothing myself, selecting among what turned up, I found that every choice swept me further afield, toward the distant, the bohemian, the romantic, the disruption I craved.

Patrick, the newcomer, was a revelation. A year older than I, full of red-haired bravado, he docked his sailboat in the weeds of the tumbledown we rented. Soon he and I and his one-year-old German shepherd, Og—the name was short for dog—were taking trips in his forty-dollar Nash to Big Sur, to the Mojave Desert and finally, for three ecstatic weeks, to New York. We threw down sleeping bags by railroad tracks and cornfields, reveled in silos, in salt flats, in eastern tunnels and western casinos, the road blossoming fore and vanishing aft in a careening demonstration of the Now. Og seemed as drunk on it as ourselves, stampeding cows, biting snow, raving at Yellowstone bears, expressing his gratitude in toothmarks all over our forearms. As asphalt sang underwheel I read aloud from *The Day on Fire*, a novelized life of Rimbaud whose cover displayed a hallucinatory, Van Gogh-like sun. That sulfurous star was the icon of our future.

If a jaunt across our own drab country could summon such splendor, what might not ensue if we raged like Rimbaud across the continent that had inspired his and so many other illuminations? I had seen Europe only with collegemates, guidebook in hand, and Patrick had ventured no farther abroad than Tijuana. And why confine ourselves to Europe? Rimbaud had ventured, if disastrously, to Africa. We could avoid his mistakes. *Why not drive around the Mediterranean?* Citroën was selling a car called the Deux Chevaux for $966, new from the factory, with a year's worth of insurance and an offer to buy it back within the year for $100 less than purchase price. In the inflated currency of 1965, yearlong use of a new car for $100 was unheard of. We couldn't afford *not* to buy it. This inspiration of Patrick's reduced itself to a handy next move and I answered with my reckless yes.

I drove Patrick to Norfolk, Virginia, where he boarded a German freighter, then sent back dazzling letters from Paris, where he found work in a hotel to replace the unemployment insurance he had been drawing ever since I met him. Og's crossing required a certificate of health and a powerful injection before take-off. I lured him into a cage and delivered him to a flight to Chicago, where he was loaded into a Lufthansa baggage compartment to Stuttgart, then transferred by the International Society for the Prevention of Cruelty to Animals to the last leg of his trip to Paris. Patrick drove to Orly Field to receive Og in the new Deux Chevaux, and as he waited for Og to clear customs, some begging children talked him out of his last francs. When Patrick was presented with the cage, a customs official demanded a fee equal to half of Og's entire fare. Patrick protested that he didn't have a single *sou*. For an awful moment it appeared that Og had flown a continent and an ocean, only to fail by a distance of five feet. Then an attendant who overheard the altercation remarked that he had seen Patrick give his last money to some children. The customs

official smiled, waived the fee, and Og was cleared into France.
Patrick opened the cage door. Og sprang out, leapt on him with
a joyful yelp, then fell back in a narcotic stupor.

As the date for my own departure loomed, the enormity of
what I was doing finally caught up with me. I was casting my
future to a new continent, a drifting companion and a dog. Was
this what I should be doing with my life? Would said life survive
it? I was particularly worried about the Mediterranean's African
side. I couldn't even name the countries in order, but I knew that
Algeria had recently won its independence from France after
one of the most savage wars in recent history, and that we pale
Anglos would be floating through it with French plates. Who
knows what went on in the countries to either side, whatever
they were? I envisioned a male population in robes, perfect for
concealing weapons. Had I said yes one time too many?

It didn't help that the date of my departure was February
1, in the depth of winter, and I was flying Icelandic. It was
hardly a day on fire. When we stopped to refuel in Keflavik, the
airline's home airport, all passengers were hustled out of the
plane, through a wintry blast and into a waiting room, where
an attendant pointed out a window to a sapling nearly bent over
double. It had recently been acquired and was, he alleged, the
town's only tree. Not only did I pity it; I identified with it, even
though I flew to my fate voluntarily. Patrick, spotting me as I
stepped from the plane toward tarmac in Luxembourg, greeted
me with a shake of the hair he hadn't cut since he'd left. Soon
he was grabbing my battered suitcase, my sleeping bag and my
typewriter, and was leading me to what appeared to be a tiny
Quonset hut on wheels. Og sprang up deliriously and planted
toothmarks on my wrist.

We settled in the car and Patrick poured cheap Bordeaux
into two ceramic cups. Sheet metal enveloped us claustropho-
bically. "Welcome to our drunken boat," he said, invoking
Rimbaud's best known poem.

"It looks more like an iron lung." I had christened it.

We clinked to adventures in the Eastern Hemisphere. As he had during bursts of highway euphoria in the States, he lit a cigarette and placed it in my mouth. I knew that cigarettes had hastened my father's death, but I also appreciated that Patrick wanted to share this dizziness with me: it seemed somehow of a piece with the wine, his disorienting hair, the new terrain.

"They're Gauloises," he said, catching my scowl of surprise. "Dark tobacco." We drove off.

"The car has four gears forward," explained Patrick, his hand on a bulb that projected from a dashboard that suggested a more elementary phase of the industrial revolution. Accelerating, braking for lights, he pushed, twisted and pulled the knob with commanding turns of the wrist. The gears growled in protest. "You have to insist," he declared. Og, braced on widely spaced paws behind us, thrust his head between us; collisions with his nose had turned the rearview mirror opaque. Whenever we dipped for potholes, Og floundered to regain his balance. "Why is this car so bouncy?" I asked.

"The front and back suspensions are attached to each other," said Patrick. "That way, there are only two coil springs instead of the usual four." Seeing my glaze, he added, "Suspension. It's a Citroën specialty."

Barely over the French border, tough veal in our bellies, I announced I needed to put my jetlag to bed. Patrick pulled onto a country lane, the car bobbed across a field like a jeep without shocks, and we stopped at a large bare tree. I watched in astonishment as he lifted out the driver and passenger seats and set them next to the car. They stood converted into rickety, low-slung lawn chairs, which he heaped with our bags. "There isn't room for our stuff and us too in the Lung," he said. "Og will let us know if anyone's coming."

Once outside, even in semi-darkness I could appreciate that our miniature delivery van had ill-matched halves, a barrel-vault hold and a smaller vehicle's two-seat snub-nosed cab; with its headlights bulging from the fenders like eyes on stalks, the effect was of a hermit crab leaving too tight a shell. The back doors swung open on the storage space, just in front of which lay the sunken rectangle where the seats had been. This odd configuration proved ideal, for Patrick and I filled the storage area side by side with our feet hanging into the pit of the seats, while Og lay crosswise from door to door, a perfect puzzle piece, his head by the accelerator. It would have been cozy if it weren't so cold.

The sheet metal appeared continuous, but as I lay shivering in my sleeping bag, comatose but awake, I became aware that large cracks gaped between pieces of metal that had been loosely riveted together. The wind gathered strength, screeching desolately through the tree, and insinuated its way into this flesh-packed interior. This car hasn't been welded together, I thought bitterly; it's been stapled.

That night set the pattern, for cold continued as we worked our way southward. We bought a blanket that reeked of the petroleum it was no doubt made of, and named it Evinrude. It turned out to be unequal to the task but we persisted in adding its weight and fumes to the stew of dog and smoke. A better investment was a little blue Camping Gaz burner so we could have instant coffee when we woke up shivering.

We had high hopes for the town of Arles, whose heat radiated from Van Gogh's sunstruck paintings of sunflowers, wheatfields and other golden objects, but winter tore across its Roman arena, which we visited like the tourists we were. We drove on to the Mediterranean, a dark and horizonless blur heaving with whitecaps. It silently occurred to me that it would have been simpler to remain in the States and drive around Lake Huron.

We stood face to face with our plan to make our way around this thing. We had deliberately avoided the summer months because of North Africa's fabled heat, but we hadn't considered the other extreme. We were in no hurry to execute our ill-informed plans. Our immediate need was to get warm and our instinct was still to head toward the sun. "Which is farther south?" I asked, "the pimple of Gibraltar or the toe of the Italian boot?"

"I haven't a clue," said Patrick. "Let's check."

He pulled out our map of Europe. I fished for an envelope and laid its edge parallel to a latitude line. "Gibraltar wins," I said.

"I don't care if we go around the Mediterranean clockwise or counterclockwise," said Patrick.

"Then counterclockwise it is."

Having driven south to reach the Mediterranean, we turned right.

I looked more seriously at the map and there leapt out a name from my childhood imagination: Carcasonne. One Christmas my grandmother had given me Richard Halliburton's *Book of Marvels*, a round-the-globe compilation of black-and-white photos with an adventure-questing text, and I had been swept away by the mere possibility of this walled citadel in southern France. In the flesh a mere two hours later, the crenellated walls and roofs like witches' hats were so faithful to the book that in the depth of February they were still in black-and-white. We dove into a café.

As soon as we had ordered coffee, my spirits revived, for I spotted an upright piano. Here was relief from piano withdrawal, as well as an opportunity to speak the French I had studied for six years. I asked the waitress whether I could play.

"Certainly. We'd love it."

I got through some Debussy. There was a bit of applause, and the man at the nearest table asked if I knew any songs. I ran through some Gershwin. "How about 'The Marseillaise'?" called a woman from across the room. I belted it out.

"Can you play 'The Communist Internationale'?" shouted another patron. I had learned the tune from a socialist college roommate and gave it equal treatment.

"Can you play 'The Star Spangled Banner'?" asked the man who had wanted popular songs. When I finished it, another customer shouted, "Play the last two songs again!" Beers arrived for me and Patrick. I felt my spirit thawing.

"What *is* the politics of those people?" wondered Patrick when we were back on the road.

"None," I replied. "They just like patriotic songs." Musical requests, a new language—this was living.

When we reached the Spanish border the next morning, I felt linguistically deprived. I'd put my French to use exactly once, and now it was behind us. Outside the car, all was Spanish. I had tried to learn that language at home during my sixteenth summer, treating a first-year grammar as a do-it-yourself manual, and all that remained were good morning, thank you and the numbers. When we reached Barcelona, I resumed my studies with a second-year grammar book, the only one for sale.

I later wondered what was in the preceding volume, for this seemed adequate for beginners with its verbs in all the tenses, its arcana about the two forms of the verb 'to be,' *ser* and *estar*. Which should I attempt to conjugate for the waiter? *"Es bueno,"* I said, pointing to that night's flan.

"Claro," he snapped back. *"Aquí la comida está buena."*

Along with the slight rebuke for stating the obvious where all the food was good, I noted the corrected grammar. Patrick, who thought anything worth saying could be communicated by gesture, suggested I cut the pedantry. Dismissing Patrick, I inflicted Spanish on all targets as we pressed southwest along the coast.

One night, just after we had gotten to sleep on a turn-off over the sea, there was a growl from under the dashboard and our tight quarters were speared by two beams of light. *"Buenas noches,"* said two loud voices. Og was up now, scrambling to stand on Evinrude, which was draped over our legs, and barking in a lathered fury. I could see the gleam of flashlights on two black patent leather hats: these were the *Guardia Civil,* Franco's feared police.

"Turistas," I yelled, authentically rolling the *r.* My heart was pounding, but even this was an opportunity.

"No se pueden quedar aqui," one of them yelled back, and I quite understood.

"Nos vamos," I yelled.

"Buenas noches," each of them pronounced again, louder this time.

"Buenas noches," I replied, pleased to complete the exchange even though it meant moving on in the night.

In Almeria, a gaunt old man who had seen our French plates asked in French where we were headed.

"Around the Mediterranean," I replied.

He grew wide-eyed with horror. "A grave error. *C'est impossible."* He drew a flattened hand along his gullet and made a clicking sound. "Arabs!"

Lit courses had pointed this figure out. In *Julius Caesar* he is the soothsayer who cries, "Beware the ides of March!" In *Moby-Dick* he is the pock-marked stranger named Elijah who warns against embarking on the *Pequod.* In "Heart of Darkness," the two women who sit knitting black wool outside the shipping office don't even need to speak to convey the folly of sailing up the Congo. I'd had persistent visions of Arabs slitting our throats or bothering us in some other fashion, and the man had spoken my fears.

Unnerved by the encounter, we reached Málaga as Lent began. Rain was unrelenting as we paraded our reeking dog through the streets. We waited ten days for a change of weather, gave up and pressed on past Torremolinos, a disco- and

beach-blast ghetto so repulsive that we didn't honor every stop
sign. The coast became wilder, the sky more overcast, the
towns sparser, and we reached the turn-off to Gibraltar, object
of our right turn in France. We pulled the other way instead,
into El Camping Motel. We had seen that word *camping* often
on triangular signs along the road, and our response had been,
why pay when we could camp free? But our most vivid human
contact since crossing the border had been two *Guardia Civil*
and an ominous old man. Perhaps better company could be
bought.

We got more than we paid for. Perched on a barren hilltop,
with rows of windswept saplings to garnish the bleakness, stood
one-room chalets, showers, johns, basins for washing clothes,
and a small café full of Peace Corps volunteers returning to
the States from Gibraltar. "Where are you guys headed?"
asked a young woman just back from Schweitzer's hospital in
Lambaréné.

"We're planning to drive around the Mediterranean," said
Patrick.

There was a charged silence. "Do you know what's going on
in North Africa?" she asked.

"I know there was a long war when the Algerians liberated
themselves from the French," I said. "It sounded nasty."

"It's *still* nasty," she replied. "You might not want to drive
into the middle of it. How about Egypt?"

"I'm sure there are tensions." I heard myself sounding lame.

"Yes, there are tensions. How about Tunisia and Libya?"

"I'm not really up on them," I said.

"I'm not up on them either," she said. "But don't you think
you should be up on them before you cross their borders?"

"If you make it intact through Egypt," said a young man
stationed in Kabul, "there's the eastern Mediterranean up
next. Had you heard that the Palestinians and Israelis don't
like each other?"

"We're going peacefully, innocently," said Patrick. Patrick believed that innocence was a contagion that could reverse disease. "People will see that about us. Maybe we can even be an example of how you can go from place to place without all that negativity."

"The Holy Fool dodge?" said a Congo volunteer. She sounded half angry. "Be careful of that one. It gets people killed."

"Whatever we do, we won't do it for a while," I said, hoping to lighten the exchange. "This miserable wind starts in North Africa. We don't want to freeze on their sizzling sands."

"That makes more sense," said the Kabul volunteer. "Spring is the best time. For tourism and for troop movements."

As these voices rang in my ear when we were back under Evinrude, I was grateful as well as spooked. It stung to come off as naïfs, but people who had engaged the world had fleshed out my own alarm. I didn't want to dampen Patrick's enthusiasm, but I'd counted on time to show us the way through, or to turn us back. Time had just been heard from.

Along with a splash of reality, the overnight revealed the merits of the *camping*. For sixty pesetas a day, one dollar, we didn't have to worry about police spearing the Lung with flashlights. We could wash our clothes and ourselves. We didn't need to buy an unwanted beverage from some establishment just because we desperately needed their bathroom. For Og, there was scampering space away from traffic and a restaurant that might have scraps. Best of all, there was company, gloriously unpredictable, which we could get away from just by returning to our vehicle. According to the map on the restaurant wall, a campground awaited us along the coast to the north, in Cádiz, and another around that city's bay. We put Africa on hold.

Cádiz turned out to be a dreamlike white city, a labyrinth of sea salt riding a sand spit that hooked into the Atlantic, and its highly anticipated campground was a walled triangle of dirt, an office, a john, a pingpong table without paddles, and no clientele but ourselves. Patrick bought a cheap guitar before we proceeded to the next campground, one El Pinar, thirty kilometers around the Bay of Cádiz. We overshot it and found ourselves funneled into a one-way street through a town so packed that it generated the kind of anxiety sprung by long tunnels. We reversed direction and were shot back through a parallel nightmare running the other way. Emerging among country fields, we pulled off on a dirt track past El Pinar's roadside restaurant, climbed through its namesake pine grove, broke into an open field and parked by a small office.

We poked inside. From the ceiling hung a ham by its leg bone, along the wall stood a waist-high wine bottle encased in wicker, and an elderly man, all dignity in a beret, accepted our sixty pesetas. *"Yo soy Bernardo,"* he said. "I'm afraid I must trouble you for your passports. You may reclaim them this afternoon. Come by and we'll chat for a bit." I immediately took to the clarity of his speech, the enunciation of every last letter, my own ease of comprehension.

We admired the insularity as we scouted for our site. The large open area, with room for several dozen campers, was hemmed by trees on three sides, and sloped upward to its fourth horizon, a row of stucco showers and a row of stucco johns separated by a raised stucco pool, which stood empty. Its connection to the outside world cut off, El Pinar was a pastoral stage set awaiting its actors. A trailer next to some strung-up canvas was the only sign of occupancy, and we positioned ourselves as far from it as possible.

As soon as he was out of the Lung, Og bounded over to the trailer. A woman with a pink face and flying hair popped out, laughed her way over to us and sang out, "Popcorn at five, loves. Come on over."

Popcorn in a trailer wasn't what I came to Spain for. I left Patrick to his guitar and headed for a chat with Bernardo.

The little office was dense with cigarette smoke. "Some wine?" offered Bernardo. He bent down and tipped the huge wicker-encrusted bottle toward two tumblers. In the semi-darkness the wine looked almost black. I took a sip and felt the juices from the back of my mouth rushing to meet it. It was dry and tasted as dark as it looked. "It's good," I said, hating my primitive vocabulary.

"It's from the north. The locals drink sherry because this is where they make it. But sherry's for having one glass, not for conversation." He pulled out a pocket knife, spun the ham overhead until he reached the part that had been sliced, and shaved me a sliver. "Try this."

The leanness was wonderful but I didn't know how to say that. "It's very good too."

"It's *jamon serrano*."

"Where's *serrano*?"

He laughed. "*Serrano* isn't a place. *Serrano* means it's from the mountains. It's an adjective that derives from *sierra*."

"I love that kind of information," I said. "I'm trying to learn the language."

"You've come to the wrong place."

I was taken aback. "Why?"

"Because what people speak here is Andalusian, not Spanish. Technically it's Spanish, not a dialect, but it's such bad Spanish that it doesn't count as Castilian."

"Where are you from?" I asked.

"Asturias, in the north, where the wine is from. Along with my Spanish. But who do I have here to speak correctly to, aside from Lola, my wife?"

"Me," I ventured.

He refilled my glass.

At five, Patrick and I dragged a couple of campground chairs to the Englishwoman's kitchen shelter, a canvas rigging between a tent for possessions and a tent for sleeping. Equally pink but rounder, more gelatinous, was her husband Teddy, clearly our compatriot.

"Looks like you two have been here awhile," I said.

"It's home number one," said Teddy. "Pine trees, peace, Bernardo treats us right. And it's only thirty kilometers from the PX."

"PX of what?" asked Patrick.

Teddy squinted through his horn-rimmed glasses. "You American? Rota. It's one of our two bases in Spain. We stable two atomic submarines there, which you should know about since your taxes are paying for them."

"Patrick doesn't pay taxes," I put in.

"Rota's where I get my cigarettes," said Flo, taking a drag on her Winston. "And where we can get you anything you want. Last year Teddy mothballed 'is uniform and got 'is pension. It's PX for life."

"We've been in every campground on the Iberian peninsula twice and this place is number one, except that it's next to Puerto Real," said Teddy. "Other campgrounds are next to hill towns, walled cities, ports, places with cathedrals and stores and restaurants, and El Pinar is next to that piss-complected dump."

"We drove through it and it was all so close I couldn't see it," I said. "It looked like there was no place to park."

"Only thing they done right," muttered Teddy. "Nothing to park for, so they didn't blow space on parking."

"What's home number two?" I asked.

"San Roque," said Flo, naming the first campground we'd stopped at. "It's six k's from Gib. I can shake money out of the Bank of England."

Teddy and Flo were gone the next morning, and when they returned late afternoon, Teddy hauled a fifty-pound bag of Gravy Train to our campsite. "Thought Og could use this," he said. "Popcorn's almost ready." Flo greeted us with a shopping bag full of peanut butter, Wonder Bread, strawberry jam and sixpacks of Budweiser. "Next time we'll ask you what you'd like, but this time we thought we'd surprise you." I tried to pay them from my traveler's checks, which were holding steady in our low-budget existence, but they waved me off. "Some other time," said Teddy.

After a day, Patrick and I felt so much at home that it was as if we had been there a week, and after a week it was simply routine. I typed it up on a table borrowed from the office while Bernardo wandered the grounds like a philosopher king, supervising the gardener, the old lady who cleaned the johns, the occasional maintenance man, extending a hand, bantering, dispensing wisdom. Every afternoon he paused by my typewriter and said, *"Hablamos un poco de español."* As we sipped two or three glasses of Asturian red, he spoke a great deal of Spanish while I answered *si* or *entiendo* and slipped in nuggets I had picked up that morning from the grammar book.

And, unbelievably, Patrick and I were still shivering. The wind persisted, rain was sporadic, time wouldn't pass; it was time to move on. Other campgrounds awaited, with significant cities attached. Sevilla to Córdoba, to Granada, and back to Málaga. There was the campground deep in olive trees like platoons of spiders; the campground where Patrick threw a clod of earth at a cry in the night, bursting a lizard like a balloonful of water; the campground where the restaurant was labeled SNACH BAR. Back to Cádiz, back to El Pinar, back to popcorn, around the circle again. Our days on fire had become a trip on ice. Said Teddy, "Don't miss Holy Week. It's not worth crap in Puerto Real. Go to Seville."

The streets were packed with worshipers in black as Lent crawled to a climax. Bearing tapers the size of rifles, figures in purple and white and black tunics filed through the night peering through the eye-slits of hoods that soared another meter over their heads. Drums and flutes made a skeletal music;

horns cried in unison; crucified Jesus and the Virgin Mary, re-
splendent in brocade and painted flesh, tilted on a high surf
of shoulders through the streets. Once when a Virgin came to
rest, an old man on a balcony broke into a hoarse, melismatic
chant that sent a chill through my nonbelieving self. As we
were waking at the Sevillian campground after our third such
evening, Patrick said, "I'm going back to Paris."

I looked at him, stunned. "What?"

"We're drifting, literally going in circles."

"I thought we were doing small circles until we did the big
one around the Mediterranean." I wanted us to keep the dream
as long as it didn't come true, and resented being wakened by
the dreamer.

"It's been clear for some time that we're not going around
the Mediterranean. Now we know better. I need to work. I'm out
of money and don't want to use yours. You'll find that people
open up much more to a single person than to a twosome. You'll
make friends more easily without me, and you're better off
without someone who doesn't want to learn the language. You'll
find your experience is just beginning and I'll catch up on it
later. I'm leaving you the guitar and the car and Og."

I wasn't impressed with Patrick's ill-matched consolations.
Bewildered, I drove him to the station. This was where saying
yes had led.

2

So narrow were the streets of Puerto Real, so claustro-phobic its intersections, that the town seemed a kind of sieve to snare the human being. Obstructing the road from Sevilla to Algeciras, artery-clogging one of Spain's major connectors, the town funneled through-traffic into one-lane, one-way parallel chutes two blocks apart, as if to speed unwanted foreign matter through its bowels. These slots were paved with the town's highest quality bricks, overlaid with strips of asphalt to ease the traveler through town, but the asphalt was so widely spaced that it was never possible to get all four tires onto the smooth part at once. Cars banged their way through as best they could, braking for cross-traffic that included bicycles, mule carts, motor scooters, Mercedes taxis, women with shopping bags and kids chasing balls, all springing in ambush from blind intersections. The handful of parking places on the half-block plaza was chronically taken, but outsiders had no motive to stop. Those who didn't have business in town simply positioned the tires of one side on the asphalt, steadied their minds and blasted through on the horn.

The side streets were even less welcoming to ve-hicles. Buildings pressed nearly flush with the street, leaving a buffer of sidewalk like the molding of a wall. Tight and straight as hospital corridors, rutty with cob-blestones and packed dirt, these clefts were rectangles receding toward the vanishing point, their walls barnacled with protruding windows that began near the ground and rose twice human-height, further cramping the token walkways. The windows' double protection of iron grilles and wooden blinds appeared to cage the houses' occupants—but most of them were neither at home nor on the sidewalk; they were out in the middle of the street, joining the burros and bicycles in choking the advance of drivers. Because it was impossible to see what was coming where such sluices crossed, some of the corners had been rigged with convex mirrors that gave a slithering impression of side traffic. Entering their warp, vehicles swelled from mites to mastodons, oozed across like sea creatures, then shriveled to mites again before winking out. In most of the industrialized world, drivers and pedestrians squared off and considered each other the enemy, mindlessly changing roles when they switched category. In Puerto Real there were no categories to switch. There was little car ownership apart from businesses, and citizens afoot considered it their mission to supplement the mirrors in getting what vehicles there were through town. Here was obstruction's bright side, for any Puertorrealeño over the age of eight became a traffic cop when he arrived at an intersection, scouting for vehicles, holding the endangered driver off with an upraised palm, then shouting *Dale!*—literally *Give it!* and meaning *Blast ahead!*

Puerto Real's dozen streets running one direction and eight the other were better explored on foot. The finite number of blocks mysteriously multiplied when one was among them. Packed into their grid were three movie theaters, an open market with meat and vegetable stalls, a functioning church, a non-functioning church, clothing and furniture stores, supplemental plazas without parking places, countless bars and tobacco stands, and enough shoe stores to suggest that Puertorrealeños were centipedes. The clamor of tires and warning horns through the twin chutes resounded as if through tunnels, and its sidewalks pinched down to catwalks, but the walker who braved them to reach the core was rewarded by a six-block pedestrian mall. It was here, rather than at the shrunken plazas, that citizens paraded, occasionally shopping, mostly gazing at merchandise through windows while encountering each other.

The waterfront relieved this density and revealed its ragged skyline, rounded by the church dome and bound on its flanks by modest new apartment buildings. A cement pier crumbled through a stubble of mud and weeds to tether a few fishing boats and a Chilean freighter awaiting demolition. Next to the pier lay a blocklong strip of sludge that comprised the town beach, and a block the other way the trim police station and the Frente de la Juventud—Franco's youth center—faced each other over a triangle of weeds and dust. The expanse of waterfront façades, peeling from salt-laden gales, was graced by a few ratty date palms like arthritic feather dusters. The collective shabbiness of all this was somehow endearing, and across the bay—thirty kilometers by road but little more than a kilometer by water—shimmered the city of Cádiz, low and unnaturally white as an imaginary reef.

In the shock of Patrick's departure from Sevilla, which I had not seen coming, I felt unmoored. I had no notion of what I would do with myself—but I knew just where I would do it. The one place that had felt like a kind of home was the campground a kilometer from Puerto Real. Teddy and Flo would invite me to popcorn and Bernardo would pour a glass of wine, or three. Og would have grass to run in. Life at El Pinar might be limited, but limitations were an antidote to emptiness.

I returned to the expected welcome and staked out my corner to camp in. I set up the typewriter and read the last of the books from Gibraltar. In sole possession of the guitar, I figured out chord positions on the frets and tried to fake some classical pieces. Behind the campground was a path by a railroad track, perfect for walks with Og. Either shaken by Patrick's sudden

absence or sensitive to my own distress, he never ventured farther than a few feet from my heels and growled if anyone approached the row of johns when I was inside, so that it took me
ten stalls to pee.

Soon the limitations of the campground were no longer an
antidote and there I was, only a short distance from an unex-
plored town. I had been repelled by that mysterium of packed
surfaces, noise and flesh, but desperation drove me along the
tracks to Puerto Real. Once initiated into its crosshatch, I
walked the streets like biological transects, poked into stores,
studied the town profile from the waterfront, followed the tides
of its inhabitants, combed its parallels and perpendiculars. As
a town that wore out shoes, it centered on the pedestrian street,
which was crossed by five side streets. The liveliest public
concern lay at one of those intersections. Like a connoisseur
of church architecture who circled a cathedral inspecting but-
tresses and gargoyles before crossing the portal and advancing
to the altar, I had sifted and probed my way through town before entering the Bar Central.

That first entrance into what became, in effect, my house
of worship, was disconcerting, for there was scarcely a place to
stand within earshot of a bartender, voices were pitched to project, and faces were serious. I was barging into something that
had its back to me. But individual backs parted and someone
barked, "This fellow wants a drink." The bartender who served
me was one of two near duplicates behind the bar. He angled a
tumbler under a spigot, drew slowly, then handed me my foam-
capped request.

"Where are you from?" asked the drinker who had spoken
in my behalf.

"The United States."

"*Un yanqui,*" he said.

"Yes," I replied, not keen to be identified as an American,
yet proud to be on the anti-slavery side of the Civil War.

"Cigarette?" asked another man, shaking his pack of dark tobacco so that the cigarette nearest me stood up.

"He probably prefers Chesterfields," said the first speaker.

"No," I said, plucking the cigarette, "I smoke these." Patrick had started me on this vice, and in the trauma of his departure I had upped my consumption.

"Do you like sherry?" asked another man.

"My mother drinks it," I said. "I haven't tried it since I had some of hers."

"It's what we drink," he said, and it was true that while a few patrons were drinking beer, most were holding glasses like miniatures of my own, bright with gold. "But I don't think what your mother drinks is what we drink. Finish your beer so you can have a sherry. Manolo!" He had turned to the bartender who served me. "A *fino* for this young man."

I don't enjoy gulping my beer but I did as commanded. I traded my empty for a shrunken glass that was full. The color was lighter, blonder than what my mother served at bridge parties. Under the gaze of several expectant pairs of eyes I ventured a sip. The man was right: it was a new taste. It was sharp and bitter, and I wasn't sure I liked it, but the men were waiting for a pronouncement. *"Está bueno,"* I said, hearing my linguistic lameness.

"Of course it's good," said the man who had invited. *"Es cojonudo."* While I knew the word *cojones*, I didn't recognize the adjective. He was saying that the wine was wonderful by way of saying that it was large in the testicles. With perfect comic timing he looked at me severely, then burst out laughing, joined by his friends. He had expected me not to understand.

"Finish that *fino*," said one of the others, "so you can try an *amontillado*."

It was the day after this initiation into the not-so-closed society of the Bar Central that four of its participants showed up at my campsite. I hadn't paced the drinking and I felt it. It would

have startled me to know that the five of us, with a thirty-year
age difference among us, would become a fixed social quintet.
The twin eighteen-year-old bartenders, never identical, were
more divergent the longer I knew them: Manolo rounder of
face, more extroverted, leaning forward and shaping words
with his hands as he talked; the more angular Luis leaning
back, speaking in measured tones, taking the longer perspective, coming to conclusions rather than erupting in dialog; the
pair always facing outward, addressing us rather than each
other. The fifteen-year-old Skinny, compact and brilliant-eyed,
was so self-possessed, so sure of every motion in the world,
that he was simply a smaller adult. The actual adult, the forty-
five-year-old Sparkplug, added a deceptively formal touch in a
frayed suit jacket he wore at all times, protective coloration for
his observing slyness, his undeceived amusement, his cracks
that undercut. The apparition of these personalities was rather
formidable on a hangover.

Once the apparition became a daily event, shock gave
way to friendship, turning me away from my own void, filling
me with their exuberant lives. The town had sent its emis-
saries. Bernardo, attracted by the first morning's commotion,
strolled up to say *buenos días*, bantering a bit while establishing himself as the man in charge, a stratagem he repeated
from time to time. "As your guests, they're welcome here,"
he told me. "They seem responsible enough, but they're like
the rest of the people here. They're ignorant. They don't even
speak properly."

I asked them, in turn, what they thought of Bernardo. "He's
all right," said Manolo, "and very correct in his manners. His
beret looks very distinguished, since nobody wears one here.
He's a snob."

After several mornings of watching me boil water one cup at
a time for instant coffee, Flo invited the lot of us for a pot that
she brewed. "Don't like coffee myself," she laughed, "but I 'ave

to make it for Teddy anyway. Takes tea to get *me* going, love."
Teddy usually stayed inside the sleeping tent and worked cross-
word puzzles, but Flo gushed that she was enchanted to have
company and encouraged us to gather the campground chairs
around the oilcloth, where she served us and followed the back-
and-forth of talk without understanding a word. "Look at 'im,"
she would say, pointing to Skinny. "Doesn't 'e 'ave the brightest
eyes you've ever seen?" Whether it was the quality of attention
or some physiological tremor, Skinny's eyes, which were nearly
black, seemed to be continually throwing off sparks.

"What's she saying about me?" pressed Skinny.

"That your eyes are brilliant," I said.

"You'd be better off with a brilliant mind," stage-muttered
Sparkplug.

Og was another strong-willed member of our group, showing
his indifference to the rest of us at closer quarters than Teddy.
When one of my guests called his name, he raised his head
and stared at the person as if to ask, *what do you want,* then
returned his bored chin to his paws when he saw there was no
message. He withstood their petting, as he tolerated all human
contact, giving no sign that he was pleased or put off. They
would throw a stick and yell, "Get it, Og! Get it!" He knew
full well what was intended, but they had to repeat their cries
before he roused himself. Eventually he would lope into the
weeds, emerge with the stick, then drop it halfway back, well
out of reach, so that anyone who wanted a repeat of this dis-
pirited performance would have to get up from coffee and fetch
the stick himself.

"Doesn't Og get bored with life in the country?" asked
Manolo.

"What's the alternative?" I replied.

"Town. We've had enough coffee for one day. I'll buy him a
glass of wine."

"I think he prefers beer."

"That's what you thought about yourself until recently," reminded Manolo.

We filed through the gap between the johns and the empty pool and reformed our knot on the cartwheel ruts in back, along the tracks into town. Og sprang to life, charging ahead, then waiting stoically as we caught up. When he raced to Puerto Real's blind intersections, my friends panicked. They yelled Og back, commanded him to stay, and grabbed his collar as we approached the terrifying chutes through town. For all his headlong bursts, he always stopped at cross streets, looked around, and waited for a second opinion before venturing across. Og's car sense, untaught, seemed as good as our own, but it played out within a brinksmanship we never got used to.

The five of us, accompanied by Og, entered the Bar Central like some contingent of the Mob. Manolo took over the bar, poured five *copas* of wine and another wine in a saucer, which I deposited at my feet. As I had expected, Og sniffed it and turned away. "Pour him a beer," I suggested.

Manolo rinsed the saucer and was about to angle it under the spigot when he recognized the spillage problem. "He'll have to drink bottled," said Manolo. He uncapped and poured, and I set it down. Og sniffed it, undecided. "Drink your beer," I commanded. He ventured a tongue, contemplated the flavor, ventured another tongueful, and another, and was off. I was already familiar with this approach, since this was not Og's first beer: he would hazard a taste, pause to make up his mind—or for the effect to kick in—and then he was launched. He was never so crude as to request another, but neither did he ever refuse one more saucer.

A dog who drank, or who even entered bars, was a novelty, but Og was never denied entrance into the many concerns we patronized, and perhaps there was no law against animals in bars because the matter had never come up. As his drinking became familiar, the topic switched to his bloodline. Arguments broke out over whether he was a *pastor alemán*, a true German shepherd, or a *mixto lobo*, a shepherd mix. The verdict was so evenly divided that I finally decided that opinions had less to do with the merits than with the fact that Puertorrealeños liked to square off and debate, and here was fresh material. I enjoyed being in the thick of these otherwise repetitive disputes, for new vocabulary was flying, and my first specialized language concerned fine distinctions between the true shepherd and the cross.

Og was, in any case, not the star of our group, for that was Skinny. Legal age for public drinking was fifteen, and Skinny had his self-imposed ration of one or two drinks a day, then wagged a finger of refusal at anyone who wanted to include him in a round. Bars, for him, had better uses, for most of them had billiard tables and at age fifteen Skinny had become champion of Puerto Real's 18,000 inhabitants. Bets were an unvarying *duro*, a heavy nickel-sized coin worth five pesetas, and in quantity they were serious money in the stricken economy of Franco's Spain. Most of Skinny's nine siblings were younger than himself, and his cue stick made a significant contribution to their support.

When billiards was in progress or a debate about Og's genealogy bored even me, I sometimes asked fellow drinkers about this place where life had unexpectedly beached me. How did Puerto Real come to exist? What sustained it? Puerto Real, went the founding legend, was the spot where Isabella first saw the sea. She ordered that a town be built on the spot, and that was why it was called Royal Port. She wanted it laid out in rectangular blocks, and in that grid it remained.

Puerto Real lay between the great sherry towns of Jerez, Puerto de Santa María and Sanlúcar de Barrameda to the north, and Chiclana de la Frontera, which produced a fine local wine, to the south, but Puerto Real produced no wine itself.

This was because it had bad water. No, another would object, it was the poverty of the soil. No, it was inhospitable weather, the incompetence of the people. It was my own suspicion that Puerto Real pulled its viticultural weight by providing much of the consumption that kept Chiclana alive. Its greatest employer was the boatyard of Matagorda, four kilometers to the west, which repaired freighters from all over the world. There was also a minor evaporative salt operation, and Puerto Real served as a market town for surrounding farms that raised sugar beets and ranches that raised sheep and goats. Cádiz, across the bay, had a true claim to fame, for it had been founded by the Phoenicians and was the oldest continuously inhabited city in Europe. Puerto Real was renowned for nothing. Unlike the surrounding sherry towns, it didn't even have rich people. It was a blue collar town, barely getting by, and without the boatyard it would not exist.

The contrast between packed, gritty, hard-playing Puerto Real and the self-enclosed little haven of the campground could not have been more stark, nor a life divided between the two more schizophrenic. I would return from several hours among scrapping dock workers at the Bar Central, and there would be Teddy, taking the sun on a blue air mattress while Flo, in their shadowy alcove, cooked the next meal, or cleaned up after the last one, or read a novel by Frank Yerby. Teddy might clamber to his feet, turn his back ostentatiously to the rest of the campground and whisper through a nearly closed mouth, "Say, I'm about to take off for the PX and I can get you some Gravy Train. What else do you need?" When I started to reply, he would hiss through lips tight as a ventriloquist's, "Shh, not so loud! I don't want *Blabbermouth* to hear. Maybe you should meet me in Puerto de Santa María and I could pass it to you there. Wait, he's standing by his trailer, sticking his nose in our business again. Quick, what else do you need?"

Teddy so exceeded the mark in looking American that he seemed a kind of parody: one could imagine him molded from butter. The near-perfect globe of his head rested on his shoulders with scant detectable neck, while his narrow eyes, puffed cheeks and compressed mouth suggested an icon from a baby food label, now nearing middle age. An eternal green sweater rode his upper torso like an overcupped bra, while an undershirt spanned the rest of his stomach to his khaki bermudas. Smudged glasses clouded his squint and a wide straw hat, tilted back farmer style, gave him a coarsely woven halo. This blur from the States was perfectly complemented by Flo, all wiriness from the Midlands, eyes dancing, mouth awestruck, dishwater hair exploding in electric shock. Deaf in one ear and hard of hearing in the other, she would lean forward and gape wide-eyed at Teddy, repeating, "Anh? Wot's 'at?" The thread lost, she would lapse into a brown study that suggested tragic meditation, only to snap back with some bright and trivial remark, eyes newly laughing. Occasionally I tried a comment of my own—that the wind had blown my typed pages away, that I missed playing the piano—but they were talkers, not listeners. Teddy mooned about getting a little cabin to retire to, maybe in Canada, and Flo would snap, "Go on! We'll be useful right 'ere. Wot this place needs is a drive-in sandwich shop. We'll open one right down the 'ill, next to the restaurant."

The only future that actually existed, however, was next Wednesday night, when they would drive their beat-up Simca forty kilometers to the naval base for bingo.

Retirement at El Pinar would have been so idyllic if it weren't for Blabbermouth. Teddy had been a master sergeant, but Blabbermouth made colonel. Teddy was forbidden alcohol and cigarettes after years of abuse, but Blabbermouth lay on his back all day drinking beer, which his wife poured. Blabbermouth's wife, a tall but mousy German woman named Daggie, had a neurotic compulsion to wash their entire wardrobe every day.

Blabbermouth had deliberately positioned his trailer as far as possible from the wash basins, so that Daggie would have to cross the entire campground to get to them. Back and forth went Daggie, her nine-year-old daughter in tow, engaging all intervening campers in hysterical conversation. After pumping them dry, she reported back to Blabbermouth, who sipped it with his Schlitz. Teddy and Flo lived in constant fear of this axis.

It obsessed their conversation: Blabbermouth sponged for months off Bernardo without even getting him the steel dog collar he asked for from the base. When Teddy and Flo went off for a week to San Roque, Blabbermouth turned Bernardo against them. Then Blabbermouth tried to beat them out of their good campsite when they returned. Blabbermouth strutted around El Pinar pretending to know everything. He didn't know beans. And Blabbermouth mistreated his daughter, who was a terrified shadow of Daggie. I too felt sorry for the daughter.

It would be just like Blabbermouth to turn Teddy in for getting me supplies from the PX. Teddy tried to play it cool. Once, returning from the base with a box containing two ten-pound bags of Gravy Train, peanut butter, jam, tooth powder and cans of soup, he staggered halfway to my campsite before his arms gave out. "Hey," he shouted, "here's that . . . empty box you wanted."

"What?" I hadn't caught the last part because his mouth was closed.

Teddy gave a panicked nod toward Blabbermouth's campsite. Blabbermouth was rooting around his trailer with a can of Schlitz in his hand. Alert to the danger, I bounded over to help Teddy, answering in a loud voice, "Thanks, I really appreciate this. If you have any more *empty boxes*, please let me know." Shortly afterward I went up to Teddy with the money. "Shh!" he greeted me, "he's only right over there," and rolled his eyes toward the trailer across the campground, where Blabbermouth lay glazed on his back, a can in his hand.

Blabbermouth, resident thorn in Teddy's side, had passing competition. When he was at the wheel of his Simca, evil was anything else on the road. "Balls! Did you see that bastard cut in? Who does he think he is, the Generalísimo?" He jammed his brakes to avoid a donkey, pulled around it and cut back in time to miss an oncoming taxi. "Son-of-a-bitch like that shouldn't have a car, so they give him a cab. Makes me so goddd dddamn maddd . . . ." His mouth in the rear-view mirror was a glued seam.

Flo turned around and grinned. "Did you 'ear 'im? Balls, 'e says." She laughed and gazed delightedly out the window.

Evil was also the *Levante*, increasingly springlike as it pelted us from a warming Sahara. Shelling and devouring bag after bag of peanuts in the shelter of their luffing canvas, Teddy held forth. "I wanted to stay in that chalet in San Rocky where we were protected and away from Blabbermouth, but *she*"— and here his voice rose in supposed imitation of Flo—"*she* has to stay here in this typhoon. You take back there on that hill outside Gib, with the *Levante* howling like forty hyenas, at least we could get inside. Makes me so pissed off I'm going to take a leak."

Flo waited for him to disappear into one of the stucco johns, then leaned forward open-mouthed, hair exploding. "Did you get a luke at 'im now? Thinks the wind's all my fault, 'e does. It's good you talkin' to 'im like 'at. Takes 'is mind off my makin' all 'at wind." She laughed and lit up a Winston.

Blabbermouth and the wind met their match the day that Teddy's passport and PX card were lifted from his back pocket in Cádiz. It was one of Teddy's sliest triumphs. The thief actually thought he was getting money! He must have been a fool to think anyone would leave his wallet sticking out of his back pocket! Flo and I were aware that there was a going market for passports and PX cards, and we agreed that if the thief was disappointed, he and Teddy deserved each other. But Teddy,

behind his façade, was seriously wounded, and I invited him
and Flo for consolation drinks in town.

They had never actually been out of the car in Puerto Real,
and I got us a table at a bar, not the Central, on the pedestrian street. I ordered wines for myself and Flo, and a Pepsi for
Teddy. I took off to look for peanuts and returned with three
bags. Teddy's eyes lit up. He tore open the first cellophaned
hundred and began shelling and eating. A group of small children gathered in hopes that a peanut might be parted with.
Between bites Teddy held forth on the ignorance of the pick-
pocket. That amateur!

He reached the end of the first bag, grabbed the second
and tore it open. Flo could stand it no longer. "Could I 'ave a
peanut?"

"Oh, sure, here." He pushed one across the table.

She handed it to a little girl who had been staring wistfully.
Teddy looked betrayed.

"May I have a couple," I asked. With a sullen glance Teddy
pushed two in my direction. I ate one and gave the other to the
little girl. Flo objected to two going to the same child while the
others stood watching, grabbed four more and passed them out
one apiece. I grabbed a handful without asking and the raid
was on.

As the children devoured his peanuts, Teddy reached the
boiling point. "Why don't those little bastards get away from
here? What do they think this is, kids' day at the zoo? That's
the trouble with this place, everywhere you go they follow you
around so you can't even . . ." He stopped short as if he'd just
seen a vision. "That's him."

"That's who?" Flo and I said it together.

"That's him, the one who picked my pocket."

We followed his gaze to a nondescript middle-aged
Puertorrealeño who had stopped to talk to some friends on the
corner. Flo and I exchanged a glance that said we were sure

this wasn't the man who had picked Teddy's pocket thirty kilometers away, and that we didn't know what Teddy was going to do about it.

Nor, it turned out, did Teddy. He stared as if enchanted. "Should I call a *guardia*?"

"Better take a luke at 'im first, up close," suggested Flo.

Teddy sat looking stunned, then rose with the poise of Sean Connery and strolled over to the group. He peered for a moment from the side, strolled back and sat down with icy calm.

"Well?"

"That wasn't him. He couldn't have grown that much hair in one day." He grabbed the remaining peanuts and stood up. "Let's get away from these little bastards."

I paid in a hurry and Teddy drove in reckless silence back to El Pinar. He pulled next to their tents and we got out as the motor idled. The car leapt forward and died in a cough. "Goddam sonofabitch. Everyone gets out before I've had a chance to stop. Balls. It's no wonder this car . . . ," and the rest was lost in the *Levante*.

The drink in town to distract Teddy was only one more failed attempt to repay them both for their endless kindness. I hardly got to eat the food they black-marketed for me at the PX, for at midday I was summoned to consume sandwiches and at dinner I would be ordered to help them with some ham hocks and beans. I hardly needed Gravy Train for Og, for they filled him with leftovers. If I tried to chip in for food, they protested that it was practically free at the base. If I started to light a Celta, Flo would shove over a pack of Winstons and remark, "'ave one of these. I can't stand those things and I can't see how anyone else can." When they saw me boiling water on my little burner, they insisted I save my gas and use their stove.

I began to feel guilty: I was sponging off the lonely, the aging, the childless. When they were off playing bingo one Wednesday night, I left a large bouquet of flowers on their

table. They seemed mildly annoyed, and Flo complained that
when she transferred them to the pitcher they really belonged
in, they drank up all the water and died. When they invited
me to the beach on a morning when I was not expecting the
Puertorrealeño, I said that I was planning to stick to the typewriter. They said that it would be no fun with just to the two of
them, and they didn't go. Feeling bad about it, I invited them to
the beach the following day, a Sunday. I scoured Puerto Real
for food but the markets were closed and all I could find was
some lettuce. When I returned, Flo remarked that she didn't
like salad, then whipped up a basket full of liverwurst sandwiches. Only two could ride comfortably in the Lung, so Teddy
drove us to a beach on the way to the base, where Flo didn't
want to eat in the car and we downed our liverwurst quickly in
the wind Flo was responsible for.

One day opportunity finally struck. Teddy roared up to my
campsite on the back of a Puertorrealeño's motorcycle and informed me that his car had broken down. It was stranded at
a garage in Puerto Real and they didn't have the parts to repair it. Would I run him to Puerto de Santa María for what it
needed?

I leapt from the typewriter and we took off in the Lung.
Puerto de Santa María didn't have the part either and we reversed our direction to Cádiz, three times as far the other way.
Teddy spent the day soliloquizing about his prowess with the
whores in Lyons, Paris and Singapore. "That girl breathed sex
so strong, if she pissed on a tree you could smell it six months
later," he observed. "A stiff prick has a hard head and no conscience." What hardboiled thriller were these lines from, I
wondered, and what was the line I was about to type when he
pulled up on the motorcycle? We located the part, then Teddy
disappeared into the garage and failed to emerge. As my frustration neared the breaking point, Teddy appeared bearing
twenty liters of gasoline for the Lung—far more than we had

used. We arrived back at El Pinar to find Flo waiting with an extravagant chicken dinner. There was no way to repay them materially, and I officially gave up.

As I beat a path back and forth from the campground to Puerto Real, and its inhabitants appeared from between the pool and the john to visit me, I was constantly aware of the disparity between the town's jam-packed, impoverished thousands and the ease and sheer space in which a few retired military loaded up at the PX as if picking mangoes from the tree. In the campground's pastoral comedy my friends were the rustic walk-ons, passing tourists were the drive-ons, Og and the gypsy dog Charlie played the requisite lowlifes, Teddy and Flo lavished their courtly generosity while Blabbermouth ever threatened evil from the wings, and Bernardo at his office door, wine in hand and beret askew, observed it all like Prospero surveying the island from his cell, menaced only by his liver.

3

A lifelong insomniac, I triggered cackles instead of sympathy when I referred to myself as an *insomniaco*. The word is *insomne*. A person who plays piano, male or female is a *pianista*, never a *pianisto*. On the other hand, a man who cooks, who makes cuisine, is a *cocinero*, and a woman chef is a *cocinera*. These words were hard to get right—and there were so many of them!—but they were not hard to *get* because they all had equivalents in English, nice crisp cognates, and the versions in each language meant exactly the same thing. What to make, on the other hand, of a word like *cachondeo*? Though not hard to pronounce, it didn't call up any word in my own language and its meaning eluded me. In its nominal, verbal and adjectival forms it salted conversations, and it seemed to spring from some philosophical stance toward life itself, some attitude that could only reveal itself through repetition in shifting situations. The enigma of *cachondeo* remained at the back of my mind, one of its many stowaways as our social quintet made the rounds, revealing new corners of the more tangible enigma that was Puerto Real.

When Bernardo admired Og's choke collar, and therefore might appreciate such an item for his own dog at the house, Manolo suggested we commission one from the forge. We funneled through a grey antechamber into a bituminous gloom heaped with baby carriages, twisted fan blades, bicycle frames, skillets, tangled fire tongs, Sevillian windows that looked on their sides like barbecue grills, motors detached from any identifying function. Men hovered like shadows around a small blast furnace, their tongs gripping iron rods that were turning ruddy and malleable as their own faces. Beside the forge, like a companion dwarf star, stood an iron pot full of bright yellow kernels ready to pop. "Que cachondeo!" exclaimed Skinny. We displayed Og's collar, a silvery chain with a ring at each end, and from this Stygian bog two days later emerged a perfect black replica.

We crossed the railroad tracks behind town and entered a street of packed ochreous dirt, wide as a boulevard, with formally spaced trees, a bar with an outdoor patio, a pair of small villas that looked as if they once represented wealth, and a long building Skinny identified as a school run by the Silesian monks. "This must be the rich neighborhood," I remarked.

"There isn't any rich neighborhood in Puerto Real," said Luis. "The villas are getaways for people from Cádiz who have forgotten they exist. This street is the fairground. Once a year it has its great moment."

We arrived at a feature that more than made up for Puerto Real's lack of distinguished architecture, an idyllic fusion of dunes and soaring pines. Nearly a kilometer long and several dunes deep, its labyrinth of ridges was held in place by a brambly understory whose shoots were restrained, in turn, by a netting of vines. The slanting and scaly trunks of the *pino piñonero* didn't break into branchwork until the crown, where they flared into a mesh of green. From a distance, the needles fused into mossy, skyborne hummocks that sealed off a world beneath them. That hidden world was mostly empty space, the great hollow between the canopy and the underbrush, a penumbra upheld by the trunks and seething with wind through the needles, flecked with birdsong and pungent with loam or dust, depending on whether or not it had rained.

The troughs between dunes were the town's recreational paths, its playground, its lovers' lanes, its getaway from itself. There was no seeing from one trough to the next, no way to predict whether the next person to emerge from a dune was creditor or missing friend. There were a few orienting features: a well, a climbing tree, a swing suspended from a branch, a clearing that filled with rainwater, stumps carved into seats with a piece left standing for the back. There was the *pino gordo*, which had been rigged with iron rungs that the tree had since engulfed. But there was no strategic high point from which to grasp the layout. From the outside, it was as if a cloud had descended over choppy waves; from inside, it was more like an enormous partitioned room, an atmosphere of raised sand and lowered light, a composting dryness, a baffling of voices, a density. Whatever self you arrived with from the compacted town loosened its belt a notch, or exhaled in relief, or changed the subject with whoever it was with. "What does *cantera* mean?" I asked Sparkplug, the target of such questions because he looked old enough to be wise.

"Rock quarry. Have you seen the oyster shells in the buildings in town? That's *ostionero*, a kind of limestone they mined here and used for construction in Puerto Real and around the bay. They say some of the stone for the cathedral in Sevilla may have come from here."

"You mean the dunes are actually the remains of a *quarry*?"

"Yes. The hills and hollows are what's left of where they excavated and where they put the dirt. Before they dug, this place was as flat as everything else around here. When they got out the last rock, they seeded it with pines and nature did the rest."

So what I had taken for dunes were actually heaps of overburden—and yet no place on the Bay of Cádiz looked more natural. Created by Puerto Real, it matched the dimension of Puerto Real itself, a labyrinth of curves to complement the linear maze of the town. Man proposed and nature disposed. A

self-contained Puerto Real of sand and trees, Las Canteras was
a kind of anti-Puerto Real, its thrown shadow, all secrecy and
rondure, a Puerto Real transformed by dream.

"Do you remember when this place was a quarry?" I asked
Sparkplug.

"No, they ran out of stone in the last century. Then they just
came here to get firewood and branches for charcoal. Even now
you never see any dead limbs. They get used."

"I come here to trap birds," said Skinny.

"Kids put this place to their own use," said Sparkplug. "And
the old-timers get water from the well to use as a laxative."

"Have you tried it?" I asked.

"It's never been my problem," said Sparkplug.

"What he needs is water to shut him up," commented
Skinny.

Neither an adolescent nor a fascist, I hadn't thought of
breaching the freshly whitened two-story waterfront building
that housed *La Frente de la Juventud*, the Youth Front, which
fronted only weeds and a clutch of ratty palms. All over Spain,
said Sparkplug, buildings had been turned into social clubs
where the properly indoctrinated young could work their way
up in Franco's party, the *Falange*. Even though my friends referred to it simply as *el hogar*, the home, it didn't sound welcoming until I heard the irresistible bop of a ping-pong ball.
"Do you think they'd let me play? I asked Manolo.

"Como no?"

Nobody objected as we entered a large bare room adorned, as
were all governmental spaces in Spain, with a crucifix, flanked
by Franco and a previous dictator, José Primo de Rivera, where
the thieves would be in a more traditional crucifixion. A dozen
teenagers yelled encouragement at two who were exchanging
short volleys. Manolo whispered that we might have to wait
to play, since the winner of each game tried to hold the table
against a new challenger in the next. Being last in line gave

me time to size up the local talent, which was unimpressive. A childhood of working off grudges at the family table had made ping-pong the single competitive sport I had mastered, and I felt confident. When my turn finally came up, the rust wore off fast and I sank into the trancelike aggression that comprises decent playing. I won the first game with ease, then the next, and the following. I made quick work of Manolo. I played until I was played out and quit, undefeated.

Immediately I became a regular. I showed up unaccompanied and played as long as I liked. When I lost a game after winning four or five, I simply got back in the challenger line and won again. My twenty-seven years didn't show any more than my politics, for I had always looked years younger than my age—a curse during the vicious school years, now a blessing whose scars didn't show. With no more ideology in evidence than the ubiquitous wall decoration, *el hogar* was becoming my home after all. The man in charge, I was told, happened to be the nephew of the second-in-command of the *Frente* for all of Spain, but he kept to his office upstairs and I knew only the glorious table, the copy machine, the training room for boxing and the gym. I conceived the ambition of becoming Puerto Real's ping-pong champion, as Skinny was its billiard shark, and I savored winning my crown by beating a bunch of teenage fascists. One afternoon as I waited in line to dispatch the current winner and take over the table, I felt a tap on the shoulder. I turned to face a man in his forties. Descended from upstairs, it was the dread nephew, and though he was not large, his sternness made him seem the puppeteer among the puppets. "Please understand that no offense is intended," he said, forcing a diplomatic smile, "but these facilities are available to members only."

Shortly after my fall-out with the *Falange*, our quintet piled into the Lung and headed a short distance north of town. "The Puerto Real cemetery isn't like other cemeteries," said Manolo as we parked, "no murky fogs, no drippy trees. It's a happy place. If anyone asks, tell them you're Catholic."

We filed through a high rust-colored wall and entered a bright quadrangle with rows of headstones, iron crosses and small statues. There were no trees and the grass was largely burned out and trampled. "Look at the sunlight. Is this not a happy place?" I was happier in the penumbra of the pines, but held my tongue. We made our way admiring the art and certain favored verses, and reached the far wall. I asked about the rows of small compartments.

"More graves," said Manolo. "These are less expensive and generally older. Look, this one's open. You can see the bones." I peered closely, squinting against the blazing wall, and made out a few powdery shapes. There were more open compartments along the way. Manolo stopped at a compartment at the far end and crossed himself.

"Who is it?" I asked.

"My grandmother."

We took another aisle, pausing to admire some lacquered Virgins and glassed-in photos of the deceased. Manolo pointed to one of the more decorated tombs. "These verses are so beautiful I know them almost by heart." He read them to me but the Castilian was too ornate and I had to read them myself, asking about some of the words: the loved one is separated for a time from her beloved on earth, but they will be reunited in Heaven. "I read these verses every time I come," said Manolo. We wound our way back to the entrance admiring a few more details. "Is this not a happy place?"

"Yes," I agreed, to put an end to the phrase. "Very happy."

"Be with you in a moment," he said, ducking into a small urinal next to the portal.

Sparkplug, who had been hanging back, strolled up. "See that happy wall over there?" he said. "During the Civil War, they lined people up against it and shot them."

Skinny, who had loitered outside the entrance, joined us as we headed back to the car. "I don't like to come here," he said. "It's too depressing."

Depression never lasted long, for all excursions circled back to the *cachondeos* of the Bar Central. In the heat of the day, sherry was too heavy unless one were headed toward a siesta; beer was the refresher. Though always available in bottles, the first draft beer had been introduced to Puerto Real by the Bar Central only the year before and already it ran a strong second to sherry. It was consumed in two daily waves, stimulated in part by the Bar Central's art in achieving the perfect ratio of air to liquid. Too many bubbles made the beer weak and foamy; too few made the brew sour and the customer drunk rather than playful. Appreciation of the perfect aeration of beer constituted initiation into the de facto club that the Bar Central had become.

By noon coffee drinking had tapered and the twins, their father and their uncle were drawing the first drafts. Reinforced by tapas of goulash or potato salad or anchovies or cod, serenaded by jeremiads about boatyard contracts, beer drinking crested until mid-afternoon, when customers headed home to the day's first full meal. Beginning around nine in the evening, halfway around the clock, beer-drinking's second, more tsunami-like comber swelled and broke at midnight's last call, when clients made their mock-insult farewells and poured out the door. Hangovers, known in Spain as the *undertow*, guaranteed that these two high tides would recur the following day.

With four family members on hand, service was quick, but so fraternal was the Central that trusted customers were allowed to pour for themselves when bartenders were busy or on errands. Against my protest that I could wait for my brews, Manolo insisted I learn the art. Obeying orders, I rinsed my *caña* under the water spigot, held it under the beer spigot and drew back the lever slowly. Foam shot to the top of the mug in

a snowy peak that avalanched into the grill beneath. "No!"
shouted Manolo. "Pour a bit straight down the drain first, turn
it off, angle the *caña* to the spout, then pull the lever *fast*.
Just before the beer hits top, let go." I tried as best I could,
achieving two thirds beer and one third foam. "Try it again!" I
did, slightly shrinking the foam. I would gladly have splashed
my way through an afternoon pouring without consuming until
I could attain a glass that was pure gold, but I would have
drained an entire barrel of the family profits. At age eighteen,
Manolo had already been doing this professionally for five
years and I could only become his foil:

Tomorrow must be a holiday.
Why
There is a good movie playing.
And so?
They only play good movies on holidays.
That's how you know you have a day off?
Obviously.

The pines and dunes of Las Canteras may have been Puerto
Real's shadow self, a municipal island repaired to now and
then by some, but its daily escape, as necessary as sherry, beer
and tobacco, was supplied by Hollywood. Because there was
nothing for a young Puertorrealeño to do after dinner but parade the streets or go to a bar and drink, movies blazed into
the gap, drawing half the citizenry every night. There was one
indoor palace, open all year, but more popular were the two
summer outdoor theaters. American outdoor theaters, while
they lasted, were drive-ins, expanses for cubicles on wheels,
confining viewers to the modules they arrived in and converting
theaters to parking lots. Puerto Real's open air houses were
simply theaters with the roof left off. Each had a main floor of
folding chairs surrounded by bare cement walls and a balcony

of wood-trimmed benches. The assigned seats of the main floor
cost ten pesetas, sixteen cents. The balcony cost only half that
and the open seats, steeply tiered, gave the better view.

Because one of the outdoor theaters was managed by
Skinny's brother's best friend, Antonio del Cine, our quintet
was in and out of the facility at all hours, privy to its inner
workings. Continual changes of movies at three theaters gave
steady employment to the painter of posters, who arrived almost daily from Puerto de Santa María to wield his brush.
One morning I watched him kindle some mystique for a Jeff
Chandler oater called *Flaming Arrows*, which had come out
during the brief craze for 3-D movies; I well remembered
peering through glasses of polarized cellophane and ducking
when a volley of arrows suddenly turned on the screaming audience. Puerto Real would be seeing it in two dimensions, but
vividly announced. A wooden frame six feet long and a foot
and a half wide lay flat on a table, its stretched canvas overlaid with white paint that revealed traces of a previous picture
underneath. The brush suddenly swept so rapidly over the surface it seemed to move without mental interference. In rapid
succession letters appeared in dark green, so thick and fast
one gasped to see them arrive perfectly spaced at the far edge.
FLECHAS INCENDARIAS. The hand dipped the brush in
ochre, capped the letters with cockeyed little tongues, and the
words caught fire. The effect was so perfect one winced to see
it improved, but a skin of tangerine flickered around the ochre
and the flames grew hotter. The brush plunged into black and
sliced some mysterious barbed parallels on the right. Suddenly
three arrows pierced the last syllable of *INCENDARIAS* from
behind and emerged mid-word. In smaller script on the bottom
the brush added *en Eastmancolor* and *martes y miercoles*,
Tuesday and Wednesday. A slapdash black scalloping framed
the whole effect. The artist called Antonio down from the projection booth. Antonio removed the frame from the table, set

up a ladder outside, and hoisted the new marquee over the door
while a handful of children gathered to watch. Before Antonio
finished folding and stowing his ladder, the artist had packed
his brushes and was headed back to El Puerto de Santa María.

Antonio's theater depended on outer darkness and the show
didn't begin until nine. Though the sun had set, there was still a
glow to the backs of buildings. Last flights of birds drifted over
an illumined strip of skyline over the screen. Viewers arrived
playfully, shoving and insulting each other, jostling for position
on the wooden benches, getting up to bop each other on the
head and losing their seats. For a half peseta they could quench
their thirst from a clay water jug they held overhead so that its
coolness jetted down the throat. All were well provisioned with
cigarettes and sunflower seeds, which were passed at length. As
usual, nobody had remembered to bring matches, and fire had
to be found. Someone was spotted smoking and his cigarette was
passed around to light everyone else's. By the time it returned it
had burned to the nub, and a mock fight ensued.

The show began with the newsreel, when there was still not
enough definition to make out certain lettering, or to carry the
features of black delegates to the United Nations. Gradually
Puerto Real slipped into silhouette and four scattered TV an-
tennas gained prominence, gathering images out of the dusk
and assembling them in bars below. There was much excitement over the sports segment of the news. With so many up-
coming changes of show, including double features, previews
were numberless. True night descended, the first stars appeared, and at last the feature began. Usually the friend next to
me had seen it three times and shared all the good scenes before they occurred, joyfully spoiling the surprise. At frequent
intervals more cigarettes were passed, with the inevitable loud
scrounge for a match. Long-time veterans of the films turned
them into cachondeos, maintaining running commentaries, and
their wisecracks went off like popguns. During fight scenes,

the true crowd pleasers, the entire audience screamed *heen!*
with the delivery of each punch. The soundtrack of brawls was
drowned out by the audience: *Heen! Heen! Heen!* At any point
a cat might amble across the top of the screen, pause to bristle
at nothing, then wander off indifferent to the shoot-out underfoot. Seldom more than half involved in the proceedings on the
screen, I was always surprised to glance up and see how far the
constellations had traveled since the projector began.

Smoke was dense, even in the outdoors, but by now I was
too addicted to care. The menace was whole sunflower seeds.
Someone invariably poured a heap into my hands in exchange
for cigarette, and there was no stopping a friend who had spent
his last pesetas on the only generosity he could afford. My
friends had the trick of popping them into their mouths and
giving them a special crack with their teeth so that the kernels
fell intact inside and the shells were poised for ejection. For
them this ordeal was over before the picture began. I never
mastered the procedure, and halfway to intermission I was still
spitting out the shell and losing the seed, spitting out the seed
and swallowing the shell, swallowing the whole thing, correctly
spitting out the shell and finding nothing large enough left to
taste. I couldn't slip them into a pocket for later disposal, for we
were packed so tight on the bench there was no way to sneak a
hand into clothing, and I certainly couldn't drop whole seeds
to the ground, later to have them discovered uneaten. With the
picture well underway and a distressing handful still to go,
I usually just crammed them into my mouth indiscriminately,
then swallowed and spit out a random mixture of seed and
shell, hoping not to get sick.

The movies themselves were the only dull part of the
evening. The majority of the pictures were non-Spanish, one
to fifteen years old, most frequently American. Since subtitles
would ill-serve a public that was largely illiterate, the pictures
were all dubbed in Madrid. George Raft rallied mobsters in

flawless Castilian; stranger still, Jerry Lewis, whose baby-voiced muggings were the grandest assaults on English in celluloid, spoke a more exquisite Castilian than was ever heard on the streets of Puerto Real. If I didn't understand a scene, it was explained to me in such detail that I missed the next several and fell even further behind, so I learned not to ask questions.

The generic film was the Spanish western, shot in Spain with a Spanish cast that included one tall blond Spanish-speaking American to play the lead. A plot-generating opening scene of gunfire, plunder and rape played itself out in a two-hour vendetta of reprisals and counter-reprisals to a quiet resolution in which, say, a grief-stricken mother watched her quarreling sons return to the ranch draped dead over their homeward-plodding horses. Along the way a villain has been punched over a balcony (*Heen!*) and freeze-framed a thrilling instant midair before landing with a delicious thud, a drunk has smashed every bottle in the bar simultaneously, the sidekick has yucked and capered his nonstop quips and cartwheels like a one-man carnival, several hundred Indians have materialized from a field of boulders and dispatched some extras, the sweet young thing has bent down to fondle her sick little sister's hair while the camera zoomed in on her surprisingly creamy breasts, the priest has delivered a sermon on the evils of violence, and the plot has deferred to a cockfight, a rodeo and one cowboy song in English. The most slickly produced of such flicks starred an American I never heard of, one Clint Eastwood. Shot in Italy, these particular films—*A Handful of Dollars; For a Few Dollars More; The Good, the Bad and the Ugly*—gave me the subversive sense of sitting through what passed for American moviemaking but was clearly more absurd than any American audience would tolerate.

The favorite, honored with an annual showing by popular demand, was also set on the American frontier. A hymn to innocence that rendered rapes and vendettas in song and dance, it was the musical *Seven Brides for Seven Brothers*. The music was left undubbed, but the sounds of the English lyrics had been learned by all and were reproduced unintelligibly at full cry whenever Howard Keel and his castmates broke into song. Fight scenes had been memorized blow by blow, and as soon as they began, audience members sprang to their feet and assumed the roles, reproducing the choreography like practiced understudies who needed no reference to the screen. Nearly the whole town attended showings of *Seven Brides*, which had passed from theater into ritual, and it was my own greatest movie-going thrill to be compared to curly-haired Russ Tamblyn, most winsome of the seven brothers.

High spirits at the movies seems the ultimate in harmless fun, but it struck terror into the *guardias* charged with keeping order. These were not the notorious *Guardia Civil*, for whom life held no terror except the death of Franco, but the *guardia municipal*, whose function was to direct traffic, silence drunks and keep the peace. They had full authority to eject anyone for the slightest disturbance, real or imagined, and to deny them re-entry for as long as they wished, but Andalusian audiences were unimpressed and treated them like substitute teachers. If a *guardia* entered during intermission just to make sure nothing erupted, every youth in attendance laughed and jeered and clapped in unison until he had completed his round. One Saturday night I watched three local *chachondos* arrive with wads of paper soaked in gasoline. They lit them one by one, let them burn to maximum effect, then put them out with the water jug. Fire and smoke rose from the bleachers, the audience hooted and clapped, and no one stopped the misbehavior—for the three *guardias* on duty had fled at the first sign of flame.

The *guardia municipal* were particularly cowed, said Manolo, because of a showing of *Aida* the year before. Whoever made the preview knew the audience, for a voice-over camouflaged the nature of the film by covering any cuts from the sound track. When the audience, primed for an exotic thriller, realized they were in for nonstop arias, they began to clap and scream and sing pop songs en masse. Three *guardias* entered and attempted to restore order. In no mood to be trifled with, the audience surrounded them, pushed them into the men's room and locked the door, and there they remained for the duration of the film, when they were let out by the equally terrified projectionist.

Talk of movies, and of audience reactions to movies, saturated Puerto Real conversation. As soon as a show let out, people flooded the bars to talk of what they had seen, even though they had seen it over and over. I had always considered movies isolating, a case of people sitting in the dark and living vicarious lives instead of communicating with each other. In Puerto Real the vicarious experience was shared, for the town traveled together wherever the feature took them, then pored over the memories of that journey. Perhaps spectator sports served that function elsewhere; Puerto Real had no spectator sports. Puerto Real had movies and movies, as much as sherry, were the social glue. They were the total audience experience, so enveloping that audiences themselves became legendary. There was the time in Sevilla when a newsreel showed Franco on vacation, grinning and surrounded by a string of man-sized barracuda he had presumably caught. Someone yelled, "Council of Ministers!" The house light flashed on. Instead of the feeble *guardia municipal*, the *Guardia Civil* stormed in. Up and down the aisles they interrogated moviegoers. The audience sat stony-faced and anonymous—and finally prevailed, for the picture resumed. Like supporting actors, those Sevillians entered movie folklore.

Movie postmortems saturated town and followed me to the campground. One night after I'd seen a particularly bad comedy, Bernardo asked me what I had seen. I paused, then took a verbal leap: "A film of *cachondeo*."

Bernardo froze. "Don't *ever* use that word." He asked me to describe the plot, then said, "We have a better Spanish word for that." His eyes were dancing as he waited for me to ask.

"What is it?"

"Americanismos."

Conversations among the social quintet, over coffee from my burner or cadged from Flo, were less elevated and mainly concerned the stars. Here my ear for Andalusian phonetics was stretched, for I had not cracked the system for converting English names to Spanish. I had no trouble identifying Dorees Die or Alfraid Heetchcoke or Baytee Dahvees, but it took me a moment to realize that Lay Hota Cobe was Lee J. Cobb, *jota* being the Spanish letter *j*. I was also briefly stumped by Barner Bross, then deduced that Bros. was an abbreviation for *hermanos*. My favorite transliteration was Shah-kess-pay-YAH-ray, for Shakespeare. But when it came to the simpler Hone Bie-nay, I drew a blank. My friends couldn't believe it. He was the hero of dozens of Westerns. He made more money than anyone else in Hollywood. It was impossible not to know him.

"Write his name down," I said.

Manolo lettered a scrap of paper and pushed it across the table. John Wayne.

The obsession with Westerns in particular revealed a further astonishment: these Andalusians knew far more American history than I did. I felt chagrined that I had gotten through high school and college and into graduate school without a single course in American history, and I was profoundly ignorant of my own country. Knowing the birth places and dates, career trajectories and circumstances of death of Billy the Kid or Doc Holliday or Marshall Dillon may not have added much to the filmgoing experience, but Manolo and Luis were capable of such feats. More significantly, they also knew the history of the Louisiana Purchase; the date, concerned parties and politics of the Missouri Compromise; the causes and consequences

of the massacres at Little Big Horn and Wounded Knee; and
the date of the official closing of the American frontier. If it
was possible to have a deep experience of shallow entertainment, the twins had it. Aware of the gap in my otherwise decent
education, I was stunned to be picking up American history,
particularly the history of the American West, from eighteen-
year-old bartenders in a Spanish campground.

Not that a saturation in movies was always well-informed.
One morning Skinny excitedly described to me an Italian
thriller he had seen the night before. It was called *The Valley
of the Men of Stone* and it concerned the leader of a Roman
regiment who was burned to death by a fire-breathing dragon
and a king's son who had been turned to stone by a monster
with a head full of snakes. "But a hero comes," said Skinny,
"and kills the monster in the end."

"Perseus?"

"Perseo."

"Stabbing him while looking in the mirror?"

"Then you've seen the picture?"

"No," I said. "It's a very old story."

"Then it must be true."

The reason why Puertorrealeños poured out of their living
quarters to congregate in streets and bars and movies became clear when Skinny invited me home. We filed through
an entryway in one of the claustrophobic streets and entered a
courtyard surrounded by doors. Along a second-story balcony
ran more doors. Skinny greeted neighbors standing around,
some of them keeping an eye on a wooden privy, waiting their
turn. We continued to a far corner and Skinny opened a door.
There was Skinny's older brother, the great friend of Antonio
del Cine, whose eyes had given him the nickname *el japonés*.
There were other brothers and sisters, nine in all, along with
Skinny's mother dicing an onion, Skinny's father laid off from

the boatyard, and several others, hands to be shook, faces toward which to say *con mucho gusto* or *encantado*, a bewilderment of humanity, too many to absorb or sort out, simply a lot of people in a small space. The apartment was merely a pair of rooms with a curtain between them, and more curtains to screen the beds. Skinny disappeared into the second room, briefly leaving me with the gaping strangers. He returned with money for the movies. I told his relatives, now collectively, that I was glad to meet them and we recrossed the courtyard, saying *adios* to the neighbors eyeing the john. On the way out, in a now-revealed front corner, I noted an oven and two women cooking.

Soon we were back in the street as if released from a packed cell. "How many people live in the courtyard?" I asked Skinny.

"I've never counted. Lots. There are three families downstairs and another four off the balcony. My own family has a dozen people, the rest of them less. The smallest family has six."

I did a mental calculation. "Sounds like sixty or seventy people."

"Could be. I've no idea."

"Is there just one place to cook?"

"There are two more upstairs. Basically, there's a stove for every two families."

"And there's just one bathroom for all of them?"

"There's just one well and there's just one bathroom. I didn't point it out, but the shit runs into the street in a little canal. We keep a board over it but that doesn't stop the smell."

"Doesn't the wait to pee get uncomfortable?"

"The worst is not being able to dance around with all those people watching. No, the worst is just the damp, from rain and the constant humidity from the well. The walls sweat. Winter or summer, I feel like I'm always half soaked."

I visited Skinny's apartment a few more times on such errands, saw the more sparsely inhabited quarters where the twins lived with their parents, and now and then I was asked into some other crowded habitation, but no one ever invited me home to socialize or take a meal. I knew vaguely where Sparkplug lived with a wife and son, but never crossed the door. It was obvious that to converse with an individual in his home, one had to take on the whole family. There was, ironically, more privacy in the press of a bar, in the street, or between the dunes of Las Canteras, for there you could communicate with the individuals of your choice, with no need to appease the extraneous. People who grew up enmeshed mostly thrived on it, eagerly trading the congestion of the home for the crush of the movies, functioning at ease en masse. Still, public socializing offered a degree of choice, a liberation from the family tangle, and Puertorrealeños fled to it.

From a kilometer's distance, in the privacy of the campground, I thought about Puerto Real. It faced a wide and almost perfectly round shallow bay that was set with a few other towns, larger than Puerto Real, with stretches of marsh and beach and dunes to keep them in isolation. On land, the town was surrounded by vaguely undulating fields with grazing goats and mules and burros and cows, interrupted by tiny habitations, hovels of country people that sometimes gathered into hamlets, crossroads. And there was Puerto Real, eighteen thousand people living in a knot that measured less than a square kilometer, crammed into apartments, packed into courtyards, portioned onto a grid of tight streets, eager to get away from each other, impatient to recongregate in some other configuration. The single large employer was chronically laying people off, no one had money to spend, and life was lived with a determination that it should be enjoyed despite all. How had Puerto Real come about? I brought it up over coffee, directing the question to Sparkplug.

"Puerto Real was screwed from the beginning. I suppose you've heard that it was founded by Ferdinand and Isabella."

"It's literally the royal port."

"The sentimental story is that Isabella wanted to found a town where she first saw the sea. The real reason is that the monarchy wanted a port in the Bay of Cádiz for strategic reasons. That was in 1483, nine years before they sent Columbus on his way.

"It was royal property until Phillip the Fourth sold it off to pay his debts in 1646. An admiral bought it whole and sold it piecemeal. The town lived by building boats. At the end of the eighteenth century, yellow fever arrived from Cádiz and wiped out a lot of the population. Then England bombarded Cádiz and the Gaditanos fled to Puerto Real. Then Napoleon invaded. Cádiz was a fort at the end of a sand spit and it was the only place in Spain that didn't fall. All the important people from the government were garrisoned there. The obvious place to attack it from was Puerto Real. After Napoleon's troops sacked and pillaged the town, they tore most of it down to build their fortifications. You've noticed that Puerto Real has no splendid old buildings like the other towns?"

"I was afraid to ask."

"That's why. Puertorrealeños took off for San Fernando and Chiclana and El Puerto de Santa María, which Napoleon left alone. After Napoleon they came back and rebuilt. Building boats was no longer such good business because there was less overseas trade after the colonies became independent, less need for boats. Then a cholera epidemic hit. A civil war, Franco, what you see. Spain is screwed and Puerto Real is doubly screwed."

Was Sparkplug the pessimist among us by nature, or had he simply lived the longest and learned the most? I did know that Puertorrealeños met their condition with an attitude called *cachondeo*. The only way to learn such a word was to begin using it, sometimes wrongly, until it was shaped and internalized. Bernardo's disapproval did not at all disrecommend it. If the

word was impolite, then so was life. The most difficult words
to master are the ones that become indispensable, that have
no substitutes, that reveal a hole in your own language, and
eventually I would feel the lack of *cachondeo* in English. Its
irreverent meanings included joking, drinking, playing tricks,
affronting the proper, song, dance, making love, avoiding un-
pleasantness in general and work in particular. All this might
evoke an English phrase like *fuck all*, but *cachondeo* was far
more resonant. A good time was a *cachondeo*. So were a false
promise, a swindle, a dull knife, overpriced fish. A *día de cachondeo* was a holiday. *Cachondearse* is to make sport of. If
one is *cachondo*, expressed with *ser*, one is a wise guy; if one
is *cachondo*, expressed with *estar*, one is horny. If a dog is *cachonda*, she is in heat. If the moon is *cachonda*, the night will
be a wild ride.

As a stance, *cachondeo* regarded life with cynical detachment, treating it as a plaything, an object of ridicule, an absurdity that couldn't hurt the knower who could see through it.
Cachondeo was in everyone's heart, but not at the bottom of it.

4

Puerto Real, even from the slight remove of the campground, so consumed me that I cared for little more than my immediate surroundings. A war building up in Vietnam and the proposed damming of the Grand Canyon both struck with a pang, then blew away in the *Levante*. There was no news of Spain itself to follow, for the dictatorship of Franco, now in its twenty-ninth year, had settled vast and static over a numbed population. If anything was actually happening in the country, word of it never escaped.

For news I set my own words down every day. Something nearby was always happening, and if I lacked a piano keyboard, I did have the keys of the portable Smith-Corona I was given at eighth-grade graduation, the one hefty article I had brought across the Atlantic. When I ditched Berkeley for Cannery Row, I told myself it was to become a writer, even if I had nothing to say. Fiction was considered the great literary form and I took a stab at it. On one occasion I had the experience of two invented characters actually talking to each other while I took down dictation, and I thought, this must be what real fiction writers experience. I shipped it to *The Atlantic Monthly* and got back a hand-written note from the editor-in-chief, saying, "Well written but rather slight for us—may we see more of your work?" I knew I should send something else immediately, but I

had already offered my best, and I mailed something longer,
denser, more contrived—and got back the form reject I deserved. Fiction was not my forte.

I had, however, been entranced by literature of travel and
place ever since I had devoured that gift from my grandmother,
Richard Halliburton's *Book of Marvels*, and was further stunned
when a bottom shelf one day beckoned to me with an earlier
Halliburton title, *New Worlds to Conquer*, a first edition actually signed by to my grandmother by Halliburton—whom, she
confessed, she had once interviewed for *The Chicago Tribune*. I
went through a teenage bout of reading about Tibet, then seized
the volumes of Lawrence Durrell's *Alexandria Quartet* as they
came out, fiction that rendered place in prose that raced my
pulse. I next discovered that Durrell had written a trilogy about
Greek islands, acquiring a house and immersing himself a year
or more on each island, labeling the results "residence books"
rather than travel books. In this kind of book one didn't need to
invent characters and put them through their paces; you simply
soaked up what was around you, then extruded it in prose.

Into this reading fell an invitation to float for two weeks
through Glen Canyon, a stretch of the Colorado River nearly
two hundred miles long that was about to be dammed—
a journey that may have been the last before the floodgates
closed. Material at last! I kept a journal that turned into a no-
vella-length piece of prose deliberately written in the voice of
Durrell, aware that I was not being derivative because I was,
after all, a far different person writing about a place Durrell
had never seen, and that to internalize someone I admired
would only reinforce who I was. I put it through five drafts, then
stuck it in a drawer, confident that I had a piece of literature
behind me—but what market was there for an item too long for
a magazine, too short for a book, and whose genre was the lowly
river journal?

As I typed away at El Pinar, always outdoors, rocks on papers to fend them from the *Levante*, I merely recorded details of a life I didn't understand the way a musician works on his chops. I was too directionless to pretend that I was writing a "residence book" in the manner of Durrell. My only readers would be the recipients of letters that plundered my notes. That was audience enough, for since the early grades I was obsessed with correspondence, and life still held no greater marvel than the arrival of a letter. On settling in Puerto Real, I dashed off notes to all contacts, instructing them to send their dispatches to American Express's thin branch in Cádiz. Every couple of weeks, accompanied by Manolo or Skinny, I drove around the bay to harvest the meager results. Or were the results missing rather than meager? Back in Málaga, when Patrick and I still pretended we were going to drive around the Mediterranean, we instructed American Express to forward our mail to their office in Tangiers. Perhaps in Tangiers lay the missing cache of hand-addressed envelopes and canceled stamps that raced my heart whenever a functionary handed them over.

As the currency of this mail receded, my anxiety grew that it had to be rescued before it was too late. It was simple enough to take the ferry across the Strait of Gibraltar, stay overnight after hitting American Express, then return on the ferry the next day, but what to do with Og? The way he crowded my heels after Patrick's departure made me realize that his world had been shaken. Teddy and Flo would gladly have fed and cared for him, but if I suddenly disappeared in the Lung, he might leave the campground in a frantic search. The Lung was his home. Someone had to come with me to Algeciras and stay with Og in the Lung overnight while I went to Tangiers. But who? Manolo and Luis couldn't leave the bar, Sparkplug was obligated to his family and Skinny was too young to drive. Then Frank arrived at the campground.

Frank had been given ten days leave from the naval base at
Rota, site of Teddy and Flo's beloved PX, and was already on
his fifteenth day of freedom when someone who gave him a ride
deposited him at El Pinar. After he shaved off his two-week
stubble he looked like El Cordobés, Spain's favorite bullfighter
and male pin-up, and he was so ingratiating that Teddy and
Flo served him ham hocks, the social quintet invited him on a
town tour, and I allowed him to use Patrick's sleeping bag and
to dress in Patrick's clothes. One night in town Frank drank a
liter of anis and tried to throw himself off the dock. He invited
us to help him rob melons. He broke the door of a W.C. with his
fist. Even without knowing of Frank's capers in town, Bernardo
was not charmed, and growled, "He's just one more fleck of
American riffraff pullulating around Europe."

Frank had arrived merely AWOL and I tried to convince
him that he should return to the base, serve his ten days in jail,
not turn into a citizen of nowhere, not become a deserter. When
we were out in the Lung, I even considered doing him the favor
of driving him to Rota and turning him in. But I needed to
remember my own status with the draft. Summoned terrified to
a recruiting station in Oakland three years back, I had nursed
a plan to get into language school and see myself through service translating and decoding, perhaps on a ship anchored in
some scenic locale. I aced the written exam, only to be pulled
naked out of a medical inspection line and seated in an office.
The doctor looked me in the eye. "Does the acne on your back
bother you much?"

"Sometimes it bleeds a little," I replied in a voice so flat it
sounded melodramatic.

He turned grave and said, gently as he could, "I'm afraid I
must find you unfit for military service. But you must report for
another exam next year. If your back clears up, you may yet be
allowed to serve."

In the months preceding the next exam I stayed out of the sun, ate fatty foods and scratched every eruption until it bled. I failed the next exam with ease, then received no more draft notices. If one caught up to me in Spain, I intended to ignore it, claiming that it had been lost in, say, Tangiers. I thought that Frank, for the sake of his own future, should not become a deserter, but when he turned into one on his thirtieth day away from the base, I duly toasted him in the bars of Puerto Real, then saw that he was safely cocooned in the sleeping bag when he passed out. I liked to imagine that by harboring a deserter I was making my own small protest against an unpopular war—that I was somehow brother to protesters being clubbed in American streets—but it was clear that Frank was innocent of the least political concern and had merely dropped out of the service to party.

Frank, then, was free to stay with Og in the Lung while I went to Tangiers for the mail, and now my question was whether I could trust my car and my dog to someone with a panther tattoo crawling up his arm. We drove to Algeciras, spent the night camped in a field outside town, and I woke with what felt like the flu. I needed to get the mail as well as the fever out of my system, and pressed ahead. I bought a round trip ticket; Frank would pick me up at noon the next day. Addressing Og like a rational creature, I asked him to remain with Frank. Aware that Naval authorities might be dragnetting for their deserter and that there would be consequences for me as well if they found him in possession of my car, I boarded the ferry.

Europe retreated, the Rock of Gibraltar shrank to a pale bungalow, the peaks of Morocco loomed imposing and blue, my head throbbed, under my arms I began to sweat, and I could no longer watch scenery from the rail. I collapsed into a chair. How could I have considered circling the Mediterranean when I dreaded the thought of the Arabs waiting at the dock? It was said that they yelled at passengers to hire them, grabbed their bags, seized their arms. I had wedged a comb teeth-up and crosswise in my wallet, and even on the ferry I maintained a territorial foot on the typewriter case that served as my overnight bag. The boat slowed for the Dark Continent.

As I stood in customs line braced to be grabbed by an aggressive Muslim, I felt a tap on my shoulder. Doubling my grip on the typewriter case, I turned. A girl with a peach-colored face, blond hair to her waist and an adolescent smile began stammering at me: "You speak English?"

"Yes."

"I feel so embarrassed. I've never done this before. A bunch of us kids are starting a pension for young travelers. We were sitting around bullshitting this morning, trying to figure out how to get customers, and I suddenly said, 'Why don't we go down to the ferry and hustle like the Arabs?'" She brushed her hair aside like a contestant for Miss Indiana. "So our boss said, 'Sure, why not? *You* do it.'" She handed me a card that said The Sundowners. "We're most of us Canadians. If you're looking for a place tonight, we have room." My toothbrush and sweater cleared customs and the blonde ushered me to a waiting car and introduced me to a middle-aged Canadian entrepreneur. She smiled at him. "Here's the result of our first hustle."

I was soon seated in the pension's salon. "Cup of tea?" asked the owner. Dying for a cup of coffee, I accepted. I asked how long he had lived in Tangiers.

"Eight years. But I may not stay much longer."

"Why not?"

"Drugs and homosexuality."

I was stuck by the immediacy of this plunge into topics one does not usually field with the first sip of tea. "What about them?"

"They're everywhere. They saturate society here. It's terrible." And with that he was launched. Pressure built in my head and my nose began to drip. The man was a Jeremiah of sin and vice. A clock on the desk marked a half hour, an hour, and the blonde refreshed the tea. Under no obligation to respond to this monologue, I let my mind pursue its own track. If this man wanted to leave, why had he just opened a new business? Why had he stayed eight years if he objected to the social climate? He could be living an uncontaminated and blinkered life in Toronto, but here he was amid evils he professed to abhor. My inner pop psychologist was roused, and I began to theorize: It must be that the man didn't abhor these activities at all; in fact, he was drawn to them. It was only here, amid the practices that most threatened him, that he could feel moral and clean. And conflicted. He should let go, enjoy the local pleasures, maybe take up with a drug dealer. I drew a moistened finger under my nose and the blonde served another cup. "I need to get to American Express," I repeated every time the renewal of tea allowed me to get a word in.

"Irma will be going soon."

I had been pinned to the sermon for nearly two hours by the time Irma, another blonde, this one cropped, came into the salon. She agreed take me to American Express if I accompanied her on her own errand first.

"If there's time," I said.

"American Express doesn't close for hours. I need to go to the Kasbah."

To a head boiling over, all places were the same. "Sure."

It was a relief to leave the pension, walk several blocks to a wall and pass through a gate. Low nondescript buildings, hard to make out behind the wares they sold, squeezed a street full of people in jeans, in robes and fezzes, in Oxfords and sneakers and sandals, most women in cloth to the eyeballs, the men with lean parchment faces, their hair shaved into pelts. The only wheeled vehicles were bicycles. Vending tables and doorways rioted with urns and trays of brass, carpets on racks, tarnished rifles, sacks of grain, brocaded purses, pillows, slippers, chess sets, ceramic plates and earthen pots, bolts of color interrupted by barber stalls. Stacks of cloth rode by, poised on

heads. Pedestrians didn't talk; they shouted: the human voice
was bedlam. Couples speaking German hovered over jewelry.
In all this mercenary clutter, not one hand detained us with
a touch and no one tried to sell us so much as a postcard.
Passages as narrow as hallways broke off at random angles; we
were on a main axis. After several blocks we reached the hub
of this wheel of walkways. There sat the Kasbah's largest business, a drift of wire-backed chairs around little round tables:
the Café Central. As we settled at an outside table, I noticed
that numerous customers were as blond as Irma, some of them
groggy. Fellow Canadians, I suspected, publicly zonked.

We ordered mint tea. Irma tried to hold my attention with
an exhaustive account of a year she spent at an Austrian ski
resort while I studied the foliage in the hot sweet tumbler, then
ogled the passing fauna, various as marine life. A dark and
pockmarked young man plunked himself down without intro-
duction. He greeted Irma familiarly, then leaned forward and
asked in a breathless and intangibly accented English whether
I would like to exchange some money. I was about to ask him
to move on, remembered I had no dirhams and didn't know
the price of tea, and replied that I might. On passing through
customs I had been required to declare the amount of cash I
carried and was warned that I would have to produce receipts
for all conversions and expenditures, but I figured that transactions like this must be common. I suggested an amount, tried to
calculate how many dirhams I was due for my pesetas, became
snarled, and Irma said, "Wait a sec."

She emptied the contents of a generous handbag onto the
table: books, mascara, hankies, a pocket screwdriver, a guide
to Nîmes, a tube of Ipana, and the sought-for sliding monetary
conversion table. We agreed on an exchange two decimals over
the going rate. The Moroccan smiled winningly and asked if
I would like to keep my pesetas until the arrival of the dirhams. I agreed. Irma extracted a Winston from our littered

table, lit up, and resumed her memories of last March in Bavaria. The young man returned with the agreed number of dirhams, and just when I thought the deal consummated, Irma reopened the debate over the advantageous decimals. Piles of pesetas and dirhams, ready for pocketing, sat side by side beneath our rising voices and began to attract interested glances from passers-by. While my knowledge of the black market was slight, this transaction seemed overtly uncool. Suddenly the Moroccan snapped, "For god's sake, hide the money!" Irma squashed it with a paperback of Jung's *Psyche and Symbol*. We agreed to the previous amount and retrieved the cash from under the book. I thought we were finished with the Moroccan, but he leaned forward and revealed the real reason for his visit. He could lead us to Hans.

"Hans?" I said to Irma.

"The Austrian ski instructor I just told you about. He's been missing since October."

We left some dirhams for the waiter and followed the Moroccan down one of the passages that radiated from the Bar Central. The walls pressed tight and we walked single file to allow others past us. Irma and I were the only blondes on this street. Daylight dimmed. Women peered at us like spies through their veils. The shouts disappeared; suddenly it was so quiet we could hear the crunch of our shoes. My sense now was of surfaces pressing in too close and quick to focus, of uneven brick or tile underfoot, of charred stucco and jaundiced plaster, of an ankle nearly twisted in a drainage runnel. Perhaps it was only my flu, but I felt we were turning phosphorescent. Then there was a building overhead: we were in a tunnel. I was anxious to emerge, but instead we followed the Moroccan through a door and felt our way up two flights of stairs. We regained the light, which fell blindingly into a shabby courtyard. We made our way along a balcony to a door, and the Moroccan knocked. After an interval a voice croaked, in English, "Come in."

At first I saw nothing at all through the smoke. The first object to clarify was a small dog propped against the wall on its back with all four paws in the air. My mucus was penetrated by the alfalfa-and-molasses smolder of weed. Burlap tacked over the window allowed just enough daylight to make out a square of mattresses around a coffee table that held a bouquet of iron spikes, an *objet d'art*. Across one wall sprawled an abstract mural in glued bamboo, and penciled onto the facing wall were caricatures from a greeting card series known as the Nebbishes, labeled with cute nicknames. On one mattress lounged a young man whose hair flowed in saffron curls over the shoulder of his Mexican poncho. On an adjacent mattress, cross-legged, sat his contemporary, with a several-day stubble and blond hair cropped like Irma's. Irma addressed him: "Hi, Hans."

Hans laid a hash pipe on the table, marshaled his limbs with concentration, stood and asked us to sit. "Yeah," he said, "I got sent away for six weeks. Stupid focking dope charge. I'm back in business. The guards chopped my focking hair, but it will grow back by the time I leave this focking room. Will you please focking *sit*."

We settled on the unclaimed mattresses. "This is Bruce," said Irma. "He's cool." My nose was dripping and I sniffled grandly.

Hans reminisced about life in prison as he refilled the pipe, making the carnal word *focking* sound strangely disembodied. He passed me the pipe. I had no idea how the dope would affect my cold or what further disease I might pick up, though I was aware of what I was passing on. Did anyone here care? I took a shallow drag and handed the pipe to the Moroccan, who passed it without interest to the odalisque in the poncho. He and Irma both took deep hits. I was aware of a deadline approaching. "The mail," I murmured to Irma.

"We need to be going," said Irma to the room in general, and without further ado we left, following the Moroccan around the balcony, down the stairs, out the tunnel, down the passageway and to the Bar Central. We shook hands with the Moroccan and continued. "I don't think I'll have Hans back in my life for a while," said Irma, making her one comment on her errand.

We issued from the Kasbah into traffic and continued a few blocks to American Express. It was five minutes until closing. The man on duty looked blank when I gave my name. "It doesn't sound familiar but I'll check." He disappeared into another room and returned a moment later with a single envelope. I knew with a glance that it was a letter from Mom.

When I was in the street, I read Irma a sample sentence: "Since you insist on going to Morocco, don't drink any water or eat any raw vegetables."

Irma laughed. "She's absolutely right. Let's buy some wine."

"Can you drink in Morocco?"

"I do."

The hit of hash had made no dent in my misery but I was willing to try alcohol. When we entered a liquor store, there was no one on duty. "Nobody's here," I said. Irma put a finger to her lips and pointed over the counter. I inched forward and peered down. A man was crouching on a small rug, his head to the ground. After a few minutes he stood up casually and asked, "How can I help you?"

"A bottle of rosé," said Irma.

Out in the street, she said, "I don't want to go back to the pension. I can't take one more of Jack's sermons. Let's watch the sunset."

We walked a mile and found a park bench where we could look north across the water to the mountains of Spain. "Damn," she said, "we didn't bring anything to open this with."

Urchins, ranging in apparent age from eight to eleven, began to gather. "Dreenk! Dreenk!" they shrieked.

"Knife? Knife?" she answered.

One of them produced a small pocket knife and Irma began to dig. Bits of cork fell to the wine and the rest slid out clean. She handed me a swig, then took one herself. "Dreenk! Dreenk!" continued the kids. Irma handed the bottle to the child with the knife, who gulped and handed the bottle to the others. More germs were being spread but I didn't stop them.

The wine was half gone by the time we got it back. "The rest for us," said Irma. The warmth began to curl in my stomach and I started feeling decent for the first time that day.

The next morning, postal fever gone and the grippe much abated, I watched Gibraltar grow from a pale bungalow back into a rock as Africa receded like a misfired drug trip. Would my car and my dog be at the dock to greet me? I was relieved to find that, unlike the U. S. Navy, I had not been deserted by Frank. Full of his own adventures since I left, he led me to the Lung, where Og yelped, then planted expressive and well-deserved toothmarks on my right hand.

Frank had found the perfect place where we could hide out. We? The only thing I needed to hide from was association with Frank. As I took the wheel, he directed me north of town through a narrow river valley over gutted pavement, then onto a gravel road that cut through a field and stopped under a cluster of oaks. Beside the grove lay a small reservoir and a building full of machinery that Frank identified as the Algeciras waterworks. A trail led out of the trees to a spit of tall grass that became the final place I had been led by quixotic pursuit of a letter from Mom.

Here we floated so languidly that I lost count of the days. The waterworks was manned by an extended and raucous crew that left it in the hands of alternating night guardians, one a local peasant who kept screaming *joé*, an Andalusian corruption of *joder*, or *fuck*, and the other a Frenchman who had come to defend the Republic during the Civil War and had gotten caught. Sentenced to sixteen years of forced labor, the Frenchman was living out his life at the waterworks while he tried to figure some way to turn himself back into a legal resident of France. Emerging from the cave of cement that yawned like a carcass in the light of its hanging bare bulbs, the Frenchman would summon us to keep him company, regaling us all night with accounts of his life while serving us pots of lethal black coffee. When we finally got to sleep, the day crew would arrive, find us in our sleeping bags and yell at us for being *señoritos*.

Twice a day our watery hideout was the focus of intense activity. The removal of a board increased the flow over the mossed cement to either side of our shelf of grass, encouraging fish to commute between the swift stream and the slack deeps of the reservoir. Fish headed downstream swept by almost too fast to follow, but the first to brave its way upstream was always a shock. Too large to immerse itself, its frenzied splatter seemed a heroic struggle merely to keep wet as it lingered in a meaty shimmer. The waterworks seemed far from any human community, but during the hours just after dawn and before dusk, when the mountains were emerging from shadows or sinking back into them, children appeared as if by combustion. They lifted the board, tensed in the grass until the crucial moment, then sprang forward flat-footed but fast over the spillway's slick moss and thwacked the fish on their heads with sticks. Teams that worked with clubs and nets were unbeatable, and the most agile children of all simply grabbed the fish with their bare hands.

Prize catches were a foot and a half long, and fish even half that size were considered a full meal. After the children and the day workers went home, the night guardians built a fire and roasted fish, which we ate with heavy bread brought by the local who said *joé*. Sweet and filling, the fish were also threaded with bones like microscopic rebar, enabling them to muscle their way up the spillway with more grace than they slid down our throats. While we lived at the reservoir, Frank, Og and I lived exclusively on this fish, and on the bread provided to retain our company.

Frank was particularly anxious to retain my company, and when he sensed me growing bored by a life of coffee and naps and straining bones out of fish, he sprang his surprise: three *kif* cigarettes he had bought in Algeciras while waiting for the ferry to dock. The temptation was slight, for drugs held little interest for me, and even less in Franco's Spain while accompanied by a military deserter for whom a search was likely under way. My habit of saying yes to more adventurous people's suggestions, having gotten me to this continent and then to this reservoir, guaranteed that I would light up, even as jitters prompted me to suggest that we get stoned somewhere less public than the waterworks, preferably in the car. And ruin good weed through acting chicken? objected Frank. No, we should mellow out with an afternoon of fishing.

Perched on the far bank of the spillway in a shaft of sun Frank seemed to choose for the entertainment of the water-works, we touched fire to doobie. Frank insisted we trap the exhaled smoke in our cupped palms for maximum satura-tion. The first cigarette produced no effect and Frank lit the second. It too accomplished nothing. Then everything began to inflate, swelling perceptibly like a time-lapse movie, while a harsh staccato chord hammered repeatedly as if it touched and recoiled from something hot. Was it produced by my pulse, quickening against my temples? I felt overtaken by dizziness while an untouched part of my brain looked on in fascination.

A grey Mercedes with plates from Madrid pulled up to the waterworks and a hulking, self-possessed figure emerged and talked with the French guardian. As we sat on the bank, the two men strolled toward us. The Frenchman wished us a good day, then chatted to the stranger about the heat and the kids' fishing technique. The stranger's Spanish seemed overcareful, textbook, as if he were foreign, and an intricate plot took place in my mind: Frank had been observed buying *kif* at the waterfront, had collected me from my suspicious overnight in Tangiers, we had been followed to our hideout at the waterworks, and now the agent was ready to draw the net. Behind his studied casualness, the man appeared to observe us with hidden urgency. He exchanged knowing glances with the Frenchman as the chords in my brain struck more insistently. "Time to fish," announced Frank, lifting the board of the spillway.

I tried to look intent on the stream, and when the first fish swam by I grabbed a stick, charged over the slick moss, slipped, slid downstream as if seated in a bobsled, and grabbed the cement bank just before being hurled into the reservoir. Feigning nonchalance, I ambled back up the bank, aware that the Frenchman and the stranger were still within view. I tried to rally with a display of agility when the next fish swam by, slipped and slid toward the reservoir again. Frank was laughing unmercifully. We were doomed.

When the two men finally disappeared through the trees, the effect of the drug left with them, leaving only raw nerves. I explained my anxiety to Frank, who was still laughing and replied that I'd truly gone over the bend. "If you're so worried," he managed at last, "ask the Frenchman who the guy was."

When the grey Mercedes pulled away an hour later, I strolled up to the waterworks to ask who had spoken such flawless Castilian. "That was the veterinarian from Madrid, here to inspect the cows. Most people from Madrid speak that way. At least the educated ones."

After the afternoon's bout of paranoia, I was relaxed enough to share the last *kif* cigarette with Frank in the sleeping bags, and was asleep within ten minutes. In the morning I woke up aware of how far I had strayed from my element. Where had I wound up in pursuit of a letter from Mom? I missed Puerto Real, missed my friends. Frank was a survivor, but if he wasn't, there was no reason he should take me with him. By nightfall I was back at the campground.

5

One morning Flo leaned forward breathlessly over tea and announced that she and Teddy had been out night-clubbing in El Puerto de Santa María the night before. The spot was smashing, with lit-up palm trees and a romantic garden plus a band that was really mod. And guess what was standing empty next the band? Flo took a dramatic drag on her Winston and exhaled, fixing me in the eye.

I set down my Nescafé. "What?"

"A piano, love. A piano. 'Ow long are you going to let the poor thing sit there, waitin'?"

I could see there would be no peace over morning coffee until I checked it out.

When I had mentioned to Flo that what I lacked in Puerto Real was a piano, I had meant that I missed my daily practice time alone, which gave me the kind of peace that others seemed to get from religion or yoga. I enjoyed drilling Bach, Chopin and Hindemith, fantasizing that I might some day play these composers in public, even as I recognized that in reality I never would. I was proud of my memory and the ability to fake almost any music by ear—but these gifts also served to point out my block against sight reading and the unreliability that came from shoddy technique. Still, I had jammed for beers on Cannery Row and in Aspen I had been paid to knock out background for parties, melodrama and

silent films. Headed toward El Puerto de Santa María in the
Lung, with Og in the passenger seat, I felt I was merely appeasing Flo.

Beyond El Puerto de Santa María, on the road that paral-
leled the westward curve of the Bay of Cádiz, a bare arc of neon
sprang out of the darkness. EL OASIS. I left Og in the Lung and
entered a well-appointed small building, a pseudo-clubhouse
complete with fireplace, armchairs, compact bar and dance floor.
The building was empty, so I passed through its side door into a
luxuriant garden. The air was soft, underlit palms splayed their
fronds against the constellations, and an oval dance floor floated
like a lagoon amid winding foliage. Along one side stretched a
bar of slatted bamboo, with two bartenders on duty and a wall
of bottles in seemingly every color from infrared to ultraviolet.
A breath of wind loosened the fronds, groups chatted at their tables, couples stood in the dance lagoon waiting the next number.
Suddenly all hell broke loose.

From a loudspeaker came the strains of "Wipeout." Backing
the dance floor, knee-high and framed like a proscenium, stood
a bandstand with three guitarists and drums. I ordered a cuba
libre from the bar and stood to watch. The lead guitar, small,
fair-skinned and sandy-haired, played with an assertion that
declared that he was the lead in all senses. To one side of
him, equally small and seated on a stool, with a pair of braces
leaning on another stool behind him, was the bass guitarist;
to the other side, flicking *Wipeout*'s three chords in rhythm,
stood a larger figure whose wire-rimmed glasses gave him the
owlishness of a university student. At one end the drummer
slashed across his torso at the snare and the timbale and the
cymbals and boomed the base with an unseen foot on a pedal
while maintaining a sphinxlike remove behind glasses that
looked as dark as his black hair. As "Wipeout" gave way to
"La Historia de un Amor," the instrumentalists were joined by
a singer, lean and angular and wild of gesture, who whipped

the weeping lyric into drama. These five musicians, in their late teens, were suited in unmatching dark jackets, white shirts and ties, which gave them the air of a junior chamber of commerce running amok. On the opposite end from the drummer, as advertised by Flo, stood an upright piano.

Draining my rum and coke, I intercepted the intellectual guitarist and pronounced a few phrases I had strung together. "*Soy un pianista. Quizás puedo tocar con Ustedes.*"

He looked baffled. "*Momento*," he said, then called, "Diego!"

The sandy-haired lead guitarist ambled over. "Yeah, what's up?"

Simultaneously relieved and disappointed at the English, I explained that I was a pianist, that they had an unplayed piano on stage, and what would they think of my joining them?

"A piano with a rock band?" said Diego in gum-chewing G. I. "Jesus, that's new. Just a minute." He called the others over. Five voices exploded at once. After no detectable conclusion, Diego turned and said, "Sure, as long as it's OK with the boss." He disappeared and came back. "He says we can't get a mike into the piano tonight."

"Good," I said. "Let me learn the songs without the mike." Without time for a second thought I found myself on stage, playing along with the next set.

Learning conditions couldn't have been more ideal. No sound I made could spoil anything there was to ruin, for even I seldom heard a note I played. Only a few Spanish ballads needed a bit of familiarity, for the rock numbers, most of which I didn't know because I avoided that category as a listener, consisted of the same three or four repeated chords, and it was a case of identifying pattern rather than learning music. One of the non-rock songs was "Blue Moon," a Richard Rodgers tune I had played since I was nine, whose chord pattern—C major, A minor, D minor, G7 in a repetition as circular as the moon itself—gave rise to the sequence's very nickname, the

Blue Moon progression. Rodgers, sabotaging his own cliché, threw a phrase of the bridge into surprise flats, which I played. The band sailed right over them as it continued the Blue Moon progression, and the mix, could it have been heard, would have been mud. Flats were an unneeded complication. The Blue Moon progression, I saw, would get me through this gig.

When we stepped off stage for a break, the drummer offered me a cigarette. "We get free drinks," he said in slow, difficult English. "You probably not. You drink what?"

"Cuba libre," I said. "*Con todo gusto.*"

He seemed relieved at the change of language. "*Me llamo Ramón,*" he said, extending a hand.

"*Soy Bruce,*" I said as we shook.

He told me that Starfis had been together for a year, that they had been playing for two months in El Oasis, that El Oasis was considered the best club in the province of Cádiz, that they were lucky to be playing here. I couldn't see Ramón's eyes, hidden behind prescription sunglasses, but I could study his straight nose, his full mouth, his smooth olive skin and the glints in his black hair, and while I knew that tastes in appearance varied, this seemed to me the most perfectly formed human being I had ever laid eyes on. The owner of El Oasis was French, Ramón was saying, a man named Monsieur Baron who had been kicked out of Morocco when that country gained its independence.

"A *pied-noir,*" I said, a black foot. From French novels I had learned that this was an expression used for colonials who had been kicked out of North Africa.

"You don't have to be French to be a *pied-noir.* I'm a *pied-noir* too. I'm from Casablanca. I've only been in Spain for four years."

"You're a Moroccan?"

"Not a *moro!*" said Ramón, flaring up. "I'm a Spaniard, born in Morocco. My parents are both Spanish."

Something suddenly clicked. *"Tu parles français?"*
"C'est ma première langue."

It was time to bang away at the piano unheard. A half hour later, at the next break, Ramón bought me another drink and I said, *"J'ai un chien dans la voiture et il faut le laisser courir. Viens."* Come meet my dog, who needs to be let out of the car. After Og sniffed Ramón and bounded off, Ramón continued his talk of the club and the band, now in French. They played six nights a week, from nine-thirty until two in the morning, and were paid 180 pesetas a night, the equivalent of three dollars, three times the Spanish minimum wage, plus all they could drink. They had their days free, spent their nights shuttling between the bandstand and the bar, had money to spend, even money to save. It was worth appeasing M. Baron to keep it going.

Having driven to El Puerto de Santa María to placate Flo, I drove home resolved that I had to play in the band because Ramón was in it.

On the second night the amplification for the piano was still not ready, giving me another long evening to polish my contribution to this mayhem. I already had a sneaking suspicion about this piano, and a peek under the lid confirmed that it was made in Chicago, as was I. On the third night the lid was flipped all the way open and a mike dropped into its bowels. Musically exposed for the first time, I racketed my way through the set. Now that they were audible, my sounds seemed all wrong, even misconceived. Even though I couldn't tell whether the piano was too loud or too soft, I was sure it was out of balance with the guitars and voice. The hammered chords sounded phony. Was it *La Bamba* or merely a bomb? M. Baron was standing in the middle of the dance floor, listening to find out. By the end of the set I lost hope. M. Baron nodded, then Diego flung an arm around my shoulder. I was the newest member of Starfis.

As the nights wailed into weeks, and eventually months, the setting turned familiar. The Oasis clientele consisted of wealthy sherry-producing families of El Puerto de Santa María and especially of Jerez, the next town to the north, whose very name had been corrupted into the English word *sherry*. The few foreign visitors and the occasional stray from the American naval base could be distinguished from the locals by superior dancing, for whether we ground out rock, slow ballads or pulsing mutilations of Andalusian folk tunes, inhabitants of the province performed a slow and unrhythmic box step. Foreigners and naval officers were too sporadic to show attendance patterns, but the locals who were our dependable trade arrived in a steady crescendo from Tuesday, after our night off, until Sunday, the week's climax. "Why don't more people show up on Friday or Saturday and take advantage of the weekend?" I asked one of the waiters.

"Because people who come here like to drink, and they'd rather have their hangover on the boss's time than their own."

I apologized that I had no dark jacket, white shirt and tie, and offered to buy them if I were told where. M. Baron made them dress like that, Diego replied, but maybe I wouldn't have to; didn't I have some alternative? I next showed up in an article of clothing that shamed me, for it was a grossly oversized sports jacket I had brought from the States simply because it had been instilled in me that I should carry such an item for social emergencies, despite my contempt for formal clothing. M. Baron didn't flinch, and seated at the piano in that pale and spacious blazer like wings on the wrong angel, blond hair spiraling from my skull like beer poured too fast, I must have been an exotic sight among those dark and trim-suited Andalusians.

As the repertoire became familiar, then comfortable, then stale, I gradually realized that as long as my arms remained in motion and sounds from the piano reported over the speakers on the correct three chords, what I actually played didn't matter. There was no needed to stick to the hammered chords that had struck me as phony, for no one knew what a piano in a rock band was supposed to sound like. Tentatively, then flagrantly when nothing happened, I turned the bashing of rock harmonies into scales, arpeggios and octave practice. I spliced in riffs from Chopin, contrived counterthemes. I did all I could to remain musically awake, for it seemed unprofessional as well as embarrassing to let boredom show, and the lateness of the hour had its own hazards. A few of the ballads, such as *"María Elena"* and *"Las tres caravelas,"* not to mention the notorious "Blue Moon," were so slow and wandering that I occasionally felt my head drop forward, then jerk back upward with a snap, even as my fingers plowed dutifully onward. The player of an upright piano does not face an audience, and the fact that I could show no more than my profile or back may have been my salvation.

I discovered new musical opportunities when we were asked for "Lara's Theme," from *Dr. Zhivago,* and Diego replied that we didn't play classical music. I could have played the tune, and I began to listen to customers' requests. When Diego told another customer that we didn't play *"Besame mucho,"* I replied that I did, and proceeded to do so. Ramón joined me on drums. "D minor!" I called to Paco, the bass guitarist, and thus a trio within the Starfis sextet was born. Finally, a dividend from my half-sister's disastrous marriage to Eduardo, the kook from Caracas! Eduardo had been a philanderer and an abuser, but he had also deposited albums of the Spanish standards at the house as I was growing up, so that *"Solamente una vez," "Sabor a mí," "Noche de ronda," "Malagueña salerosa"* and many more were in my repertoire. Now they were added to the repertoire of Starfis, bringing to El Oasis music that comported far better with its palm trees and its bamboo bar than "Hard Day's Night." It was a neat paradox that I learned the contemporary pop music of Great Britain and the United States from an Andalusian band while supplying the core songs of their own tradition.

The trio, meanwhile, led to further possibilities when I was asked, as an American, to play jazz. It never seemed to me that my pop renditions counted as jazz because jazz was spontaneous invention, the recreation of a tune from inside the player, a transformation through assimilated style and technique. Jazz could not be faked, and therefore I did not play jazz. I settled for upbeat versions of the Gershwin tunes I knew well. But as I played those tunes night after night, relaxed, well lubricated with cuba libres, wholly involuntarily jazz began to happen. As if on missions of their own, my fingers took off. The sensation was exhilarating and the sense of finding a sudden new way through a tune reminded me of a satisfying ski through powder snow. There was no danger that these musical diversions and discoveries would run away with the band—"Wipeout," after all, was "Wipeout"—but I was glad to have found some alternatives, some dodges to keep from nodding off.

Being a member of Starfis was not just a matter of showing up to play at nine-thirty at night and leaving at two; it was a way of life. As we migrated from one home to another, listening to new releases, trying things out, I discovered that the stark difference between Puerto Real and El Puerto de Santa María was the difference between the lower and the middle class. In Puerto Real, the packing of large families into tiny spaces prevented home socializing, whereas in El Puerto de Santa María the decently furnished apartments of families half that size obliged our floating band.

By day the personalities that merged in performance separated into their social selves. I soon learned that on the first night I had heard almost all of Diego's G. I. English, which I had taken for fluent, and yet he seemed an American born in the wrong country. What English he had, learned during a job at the American naval base, was almost an act of self-discovery, for as a child he had sounded his *r*'s in the American way, a speech impediment in Andalucía, and he had to learn laboriously to roll them correctly. His older brother Paco walked with braces because of being struck by polio while small, and seemed the most serious of the group. Flavio, the wild-gestured romantic singer, postured and came out the buffoon, yet was working at El Oasis to provide for his widowed mother while preparing to join the Church, as monk or priest. His pomp was nicely countered by the bespectacled second guitarist, gentle-mannered, intelligent, light-hearted Pepe.

And then there was Ramón, gazing impassively amid the whirlwind of his drumming, self-possessed and aloof, who didn't see Spain until he was fifteen, who had spoken Spanish at home and French at school and had learned the sophisticated defenses of a European growing up among Arabs. While the others had been nursed by the narrower if deeper roots of Andalucía, Ramón had been compounded in a crossroads of race, religion, language and culture. In a Spain where *sencillo*, literally simple, actually meant straightforward, trustworthy, direct, Ramón was considered *complicado*—as was I.

This unlikely pack of personalities drifted from one family residence to another, from livingroom to livingroom, from kitchen to kitchen, like wandering scholastics. The needle was set over and over on one of Ringo's riffs: how did that off-beat go, and were those four fast or six superfast beats just before it? Were the paired voices on that song John and Paul, or John and George, or George and Paul? Did they know, I put in, that "Till There Was You," a Beatles favorite we played nightly, was not by Lennon and McCartney? They might profess to hate musical comedy, but "Till There Was You" was from *The Music Man*, a musical comedy by one Meredith Wilson. They looked blank, but in their new American pianist they had acquired an arranger, translator and scholastic in his own right. My days of wrestling with Patrick's guitar paid off, for now I could show the position of a D flat minor or the seventh chord of a blues ending, and I tried to harness that knowledge in service of the Starfis repertoire. The middle part of "Blue Moon," for instance. Did they know that in the original the phase doesn't just repeat three times? The third time, the melody drops and the chords change into flats—and here I took the guitar and demonstrated. Why do that? they objected. That was extra effort for nothing and the song worked perfectly well the way they played it. Meanwhile, what did these words mean?—and suddenly I would be required to make Spanish out of *In that jingle jangle morning I'll come following you* or *Then her face at first just ghostly turned a whiter shade of pale* or *'Scuse me while I kiss the sky.* Or was it *piss the sky?*

With their pianist and arranger and translator they also acquired a car and a dog. A friend of the band who delivered beer also delivered band members to El Oasis when they didn't take a taxi or walk, but that business van could not be modified to promote the band, nor could Starfis project its charisma through personal appearance, straightjacketed as we were by M. Baron's dress code. Resorting to more inventive means, we unrolled the pharmacy's widest adhesive tape into large angular letters that proclaimed STARFIS on both sides of the Lung. Curious to know what we were going to such lengths to publicize, I asked Diego, "What does Starfis mean?"

"Starfis?" he repeated, savoring the sound. "I made it up myself. It's the English word *starfish*, without the *h*."

Piling into the car, the disabled Paco in front and the rest in back, they ignored my protests that they were unraveling Og's training and goaded him into paroxysms of attention-getting hysteria as we slowly toured the streets of El Puerto de Santa María. The din was tolerable only to ears already debauched by electric guitars, and far preferable to me were the times we rolled silently through town with Og in the passenger seat, his bowl overturned on his head. What surely put the band on the map, more than anything we ever played, were the times I drove with my nose to the dashboard, peering through the sub-windshield vent with Og's paws braced on my shoulders, which afforded El Puerto's citizenry the spectacle of the Starfis van cruising through town chauffeured by a bored German shepherd wearing his dish. "Now there's a dog with car sense," remarked a pedestrian in a voice pitched to carry.

At times it seemed that rock studies and publicity tours by day and our four and a half hours on the job were only a prelude, or an excuse, to get to the celebration after work. Festivities couldn't begin immediately, for mikes and drums had to be dismantled, cables unsnarled and instruments stashed in the back room. It was useless for me to take advantage of that time to run through a few classical pieces, for as soon as I started on a bit of Schumann, a waiter would come up and say, "Don't play that. Play *Extraños en la noche.*" As I started "Strangers in the Night," another would say, "No, play *Volver a comenzar.*" I would play a few bars of "Begin the Beguine" and another waiter would shout, "Not that! Play 'Light My Fire.'" Even a waiter who got his request never listened to it through, and I wondered whether they only wanted to show that they knew some song titles. There being no recreation time on the El Oasis piano, I closed the lid and helped carry out speakers. We nursed the last cuba libre on the house to get through Paco's nightly communion with the pinball machine, and bought a bottle of sherry or two at cost, to go. It was usually after three in the morning by the time we piled with Og into the Lung.

We roared off through town taking all the one-way streets the wrong way as if running rapids while the crowd in back rocked the chassis, yelling *suspensión*, soo-spenss-YONE! Only cats and dogs still prowled. Having asked how to say *Get the cat!* and *Get the rabbit!* in English, phrases until then unknown to Og himself, the band screamed *Geddecá!* and *Geddawabba!*

as Og lathered himself into a fury. By request we let Diego and
Paco off at their house and proceeded past the sherry distill-
eries and down the waterfront to our nightly picnic spot.

We parked under a ghastly blue arc lamp, removed the two
seats from the front of the car and set them on the sidewalk.
Bread and potato omelets or sausages or fish were pulled out of
bags, having been prepared during the afternoon by compliant
mothers. The four of us crowded onto the seats, the singer and the
second guitar on one, Ramón and I on the other, with Evinrude
and another blanket over our knees. We uncorked the sherry
and passed it, drinking from the bottle, toasting the darkness.
Sometimes someone brought a flamenco guitar and strummed
some new release of the Beatles. A pair of *guardias* usually happened by. We smiled and said *buenas noches*, or *buenos días* if
the sun were already rising, and they would depart as if they
couldn't decide what to book us for. One night we were discovered by the three song-requesting waiters, and too often from
then on we were forced to part with a blanket and ration our four
portions seven ways. Under the blue pallor of the street light our
little tableau rioted until dawn, when it was my duty to drop the
others home and continue to Puerto Real. I would crawl numb
into my sleeping bag for any rest I could snag before the children of campers screamed me back awake. During the months
at El Oasis, my sleep was mostly sweat and bad dreams.

There was one serious flaw in our El Oasis contract: only Diego
and Paco were members of *el sindicato*. The syndicate was
a vast network of state-controlled labor unions, and it began
applying pressure to have Starfis turned out of El Oasis for
deficient membership. It began with rumors, then two grey-
faced and dark-suited representatives of the music syndicate
appeared one night to ask questions of M. Baron. The following
day came a phone call from El Puerto's chief of police.

The chief explained that El Oasis could no longer hire musicians without papers while others in good standing were out of work. But there were no other competent musicians in El Puerto, replied M. Baron. A band was available in Jerez, said the chief. They played badly and he didn't want them, answered M. Baron. Fine, said the chief, there is a pianist in Jerez, a guitarist in Cádiz, a sax in Chiclana . . . . "*Maravilloso*," said M. Baron, "they may all be formidable virtuosi. But if they can't play together . . . ."

That night M. Baron stormed up and down in front of the bar, the veins bulging from his forehead, his French *r*'s growling from his impassioned uvula. The owner of a business establishment had the right to hire whom he pleased, in Spain or Morocco or any place else. They could pull what they liked on him, it was all *merde*. Starfis would play exactly as long as he wanted them to play.

Meanwhile, just to be safe, band members began to get their papers in order. Keeping the job meant joining the syndicate, and the syndicate required birth certificates, diplomas, photos, letters of recommendation. Each musician's case was different: Ramón, lately of Morocco, found that most of the material he needed was in Casablanca; Pepe's status as a singer made him an Attraction rather than a Musician; I, the American, had neither nine months' residency in Spain nor an American union card to transfer. All band members accompanied each on his errands as our days of rock scholasticism turned into an obstacle course of schools, offices, churches, police stations and bureaucratic egos that got compared to male genitalia. The quest led farther and farther afield, to Cádiz, to Jerez, even to Sevilla, some hundred kilometers distant, myself relentlessly at the wheel. Nonstop beers were required to wash it all down, so that I often drove back nearly insensate through a nightfall of donkeys, bicycles, carts and pedestrians, to face an evening at the keys until 2:00 a.m. We lived on our nerves and felt the authorities draw in.

One day after we had been to the Puerto de Santa María
police station three times, to be given three different reasons
why we couldn't play, we arrived at El Oasis to hear someone
fumbling at the piano. I charged to the bandstand, to discover
the piano was missing. I turned to face a grinning M. Baron.
Tonight we would fix the syndicate.

M. Baron had spent the day devising his coup. The piano
was concealed in a bamboo cage behind the backdrop. The
singer's mike had been rigged in the employee washroom.
The second guitar was installed in the liquor pantry. Ramón's
drums were set up in the utility room.

"It won't be easy to play together," said Diego.

"Who cares?" replied M. Baron.

That night, the usual ashen twosome appeared at El Oasis
to complain about the usual barrage of illegitimate music, and
found it all being picked calmly on two guitars by Diego and
Paco, our two legal members.

"Muy bien," said one of them to M. Baron, "where's the
piano? Where's the singer? Where's the drums?"

M. Baron shrugged and smiled. What singer? What piano?
What drums?

The pair departed without comment.

But M. Baron's little *cachondeo* solved nothing and the
band swiftly lost faith. Remarks turned bitter. "I'm a Spaniard
and I love Spain," the second guitarist told me, "and I have
nothing but contempt for this. Life in this country doesn't need
to be as hard as it is. Come the revolution, we will enlist Og as
a guerrilla."

We assaulted Sevilla once more, this time to present our
case to an agent known as El Pulpón, the Octopus. A florid-
gestured institution in Andalusian music, El Pulpón was an
old hand at hacking through syndicate tape. Our situation was,
he sighed, fairly hopeless. Nothing could be done for Ramón
with his papers in Morocco, nor for the second guitarist. For the

singer, perhaps. Ironically, the pianist's case was the simplest. Didn't I belong to the American union?

I didn't.

Ah, a great pity. The American union was a beautiful thing, a *maravilla*. It actually labored on the musician's behalf. It saw to his employment and guaranteed him an honorable wage. The Spanish syndicate could do no better than to pattern itself on such a model. Yes, it's a pity you don't belong . . .

We returned sourly to work, where M. Baron told us we were to play as usual unless the lights were suddenly doused. In that case we were to scram. But lights were never doused. It was at the moment of giving up that the problem was solved in the simplest manner possible. M. Baron uncovered a friend of a friend who happened to be president of the music syndicate in Madrid. Word was passed down the line. To clinch the resolution, M. Baron arranged an appointment with the chief of police in Cádiz and came away with a promise of desistance. After weeks of nonsense, the whole problem vanished.

The bass, it is said, is the instrument you don't hear until it quits, and the Starfis bass quit when Paco got the flu. Diego informed me that the band was canceling until he was better.

"You don't need to do that," I replied. "I'll play."

"You don't play bass," said Diego.

I wasn't so sure. The bass was merely an amplified version of the bottom four strings of my own cheap flamenco guitar, on which it was simple enough to reproduce Paco's repeated patterns. I had already demonstrated those patterns as the instant arranger. "Let me try it," I said. "It's the piano that you don't need. You proved that before I showed up."

Playing bass was so literally basic that I was adding countermelodies by the second set. Nobody noticed the polyphony and I was pleased that at last I could look out over the dance floor, ogle the box steppers, let my eyes rest on the garden as we played. I was almost sorry when Paco was over the flu after a mere week.

The greatest job hazard at El Oasis was not the monotony of the repertoire, which I fended off with tampering, but the blare of speakers that emptied their havoc nonstop into my ear. I was thus thrilled the night that the lights went out quite aptly in the middle of *"El Somnámbulo"*—"The Sleepwalker"—and voice and guitars were guillotined into silence. Someone yelled, *"Bru, te toca a tí!"* I groped for keys in the dark, sustained a few bars, then struck an ear-wrenching clamor as if the sleepwalker had tumbled downstairs. There was a burst of laughter, candles appeared, and I contentedly spun out two hours of dance tunes to Ramón's drumming. A husky middle-aged woman hovered around the piano, and a waiter whispered in my ear that she was an opera and television star from Madrid. I ventured the opening bars of *"O Mio Babbino Caro,"* from *Gianni Schicchi.* The woman grinned and began to sing. We made it through to a shaky cadence and she forgave me effusively for playing it several keys too high for her, asking if I knew any more opera. We blundered through *"Un Bel Di,"* from *Madame Butterfly*, and a few selections from *La Bohème.* It was magic to the performers, if not the listeners, that El Oasis, visual domain of Cole Porter, aural turf of The Animals and Mick Jagger, for a short spell had Puccini by candlelight.

Starfis experienced a bleaker atmosphere when we were invited to play a volunteer concert at the maximum security prison on the edge of town. There was no question of hauling a piano into its depths and I attended as an awestruck stagehand.

The prison was surrounded by a trench that suggested the moat of a stripped-down castle, and it felt queasy to be carrying drums, guitars, amplifiers and mikes across it while being stared at by machine gun-bearing *guardias* in flanking towers. The band threaded a small antechamber with a crucifix and a memorial plaque to the heroes who died for Franco and the Falange. We gave our names at a small desk so we could be signed out later. I gave the full version but the guard wrote only Bruce. I felt fragile as we passed through an iron door, then another, and emerged in a courtyard where several hundred prisoners strolled quietly, alone and in small groups. All were in khaki, no two of them, curiously, in the same shade. A few greeted us pleasantly as we passed and there was a general murmur, casual, quiet for such a large group. We entered a covered archway and crossed a second courtyard that was carpeted with a lawn bright as pool felt, a shock in burnt Andalucía. We proceeded through another archway, carried our burdens up a stairwell of dirty plaster and turned down a long hall. I caught a glimpse of a washroom crammed with two dozen mirrorless stone wash basins, each no more than a man's width. Through a last antechamber, a waiting room for oblivion, we reached the entertainment room. It felt like the end of creation.

The prisoners were already filing in. We hooked up our machines as best we could on an improvised boxlike stage while the other performers hovered behind brief hangings of burlap that served as wings. The folding chairs filled quickly and the rest of the prisoners sprawled in front on rows of canvas pillows. They chatted and passed cigarettes, waiting patiently for us to bully rebellious gear into shape. As I angled a speaker, the second guitar whispered in my ear, "There's nothing like a captive audience."

The show opened with a set by Starfis, followed by a flamenco singer, a young guitarist, a declaimer of Andalusian poetry and a flamenco parody. As the men watched I scanned their faces for any sign of the savage, but found a selection as random as any on the street. A small tangle of bars was set up for an acrobat. As Diego, from behind the burlap, unfolded a single melody line on his electric guitar, a dark young man put his limbs through a bizarre unraveling of balances, extensions and handstands. The electronic melody, freed from its harmonic context, floated eerily between the stone walls. As the faces of the prisoners rose from a sea of drab green with the absorption of enchanted children, the acrobat hoisted himself to the topmost pole. Poised on one hand, with three large rubber balls clasped between his legs and a yellow ring whirling around his free hand, he hung motionless over their upturned incarcerated faces, graceful and meaningless, with no sound between the bare walls but the bodiless wail of the one guitar. At such moments I can't help but marvel at the strange tangents life has taken since it crawled from the sea.

If the afternoon in prison was our most memorable performance, the most memorable fan of Starfis was unquestionably *El Rey de Jazz*, the King of Jazz. A small man in his fifties who appeared at El Oasis every night in an elegantly tapered suit, he had the thin hips, pinched waist and grossly exploding shoulders and biceps of a fanatic weightlifter. The flinty eyes, eagle-beaked nose and drooping mouth of his small head glinted with mischief from beneath the gangster-like brim of his wide straw hat. He is the only human being I have met in the round who seemed to have been drawn by a cartoonist.

His conversation was reduced to the word *conoces*, which means "do you know." *Conoces Frank Seenatra? Conoces Beellee Holidie? Conoces Duke Ellingtone? Gene Krupa, Fats Wallair? Conoces Baynny Goodman? Lee-onel Hamptone? Harry Jahmays? Conoces Johnny Desmoned. Al Heert? Conoces Layna Horne?* His mind seemed to resemble a giant catalogue.

Jazz musicians were his great passion, but one night it might be songs from films. *Conoces* "Az Time Goes By," *por Hoagy Carmichael, de la película Casablanca, con Hoomphray Bogart y Lauren Bacall, hecho por Barnair Bross? Conoces* "Smoke Gets een Joor Eyes," *por Hairomay Kairn, de la película Roberta?* Another night it would be *Conoces filosofía?* Drawing his jacket tight to further swell his chest and shrivel his waist, he would fix us with a beady stare and demand, *Conoces*

Emanuel Kant? Feetche? Neeyaytzchay? Weelliam James? Conoces literatura? Conoces Dostoyaivski? Conoces Melville? Shakespair? Tolstoi? Victor Hugo? Emile Zola? Emile Zola, heh? Emile Zola. El naturalismo. Emile Zola. In the middle of an inventory, with no warning he would shake his head and go *brrr!* like someone throwing off a bad chill. One of the waiters told us he ran into him once on the beach doing push-ups and chanting *Chass Atlas, Johnny Weismullair . . .*

His conversation, however unusual, was merely a warm-up for his dancing. Standing impatiently by the piano waiting for us to get through the rock and Latin tunes, he would mutter, "'Lazybones.' 'Lazybones,' eh? 'Lazybones.'" At last the lead and second guitars and singer would break, leaving the piano, drums and bass to improvise a bit of jazz. To humor El Rey it would be "Lazybones," slow and easy. With a sense of the momentous he waited at the edge of the dance floor and like a serpent called from the jar began to emerge. Hands against his flank, his torso started to writhe. A growl emerged from his throat. Uncoiling from a pantherlike crouch, his limbs grew loose and sinewy. He straightened, stretched, tilted into a backbend. Holding an imaginary trumpet to his half-parted lips, he muttered, "Deet-dat-DEET-dada-da-da!" With a profound sigh he threw his trumpet to the second table, and extending his arms like wings eased into the eagle rock. Customers began to shout. *Alza! Anda!* The music cadenced to one lingering blue note and he crept back to the piano. "*Conoces* 'Sain Looees Blues'?"

One night he asked us to drive him home. Securely installed in the Lung, however, he refused to divulge where he lived. The second guitarist remarked on having seen him several times in a certain stretch of the riverfront, so we drove him there and parked. My fellow musicians piled out the back with Og, and one of them opened the passenger door for El Rey. He ignored the hint. *Conoces* "Ze Moon Eez Jellow"? *Conoces* "Sopheesteecated Lady"? "Mood Eendeego?"

No, I said, *no los conoco.*
Conoces Alfraid Heetchcoke?
No.

Suddenly the second guitarist pushed Og into the back of
the Lung and screamed, *"Geddacá!"* Og, crazed to give chase
to the phantom, vaulted over El Rey's shoulders, sprung from
his lap and flung himself out the passenger door.

El Rey didn't flicker an eyelash. *Conoces Fred Astaire?*
Conoces Eleanor Powell?

"Og! Og! Here! *Geddacá!"* Other band members joined the
hysteria as Og leapt back into the car, over El Rey's shoulders
and out the door.

*Conoces Jeenjair Rojairs? Cyd Charisse? Conoces Eerveen
Bairleen?* Over and over Og cycled through the car over the
oblivious Rey de Jazz as he reeled off names in a trance of
incantation. *Seedney Greenstreet? Veencent Price? Jorge Raft?*
I tried to look bored and desperate but couldn't help breaking
into a smile. El Rey's eyes lit up like sly little marbles. Ah!
Conoces Baseel Rathbone! Maurice Chevalier! Ma Pairkeens!
His voice found new fervor as he leaned imperceptibly forward to provide more commodious passage for Og. In an act
of desperation, two guitarists and Ramón grabbed El Rey by
the arm, pulled him bodily from the car and screamed, *"Hasta
mañana!"* They piled in with Og and I gunned to a getaway.

El Rey's brain seemed nothing more than a guest list of the
living and the dead, but one night after an attack of twenty phi-
losophers I asked him what he thought about life himself. "It is
impossible to know whether there is a god," he replied, "but the
existence of the traditional Christian god seems unlikely. The
mind is isolated by what it receives through the five senses, and
life therefore means, if anything, only what one chooses for it
to mean. In the core of himself, each man is after all alone."

I was taken aback by this little speech of El Rey's, thought
out, polished, even cribbed as it may have been, and perhaps

I only found it profound because it was what I thought myself. I even felt bad about our running Og over and over across his lap, even though El Rey gave no indication he felt bad about it himself. But El Rey's vision of loneliness didn't resonate for long, for loneliness was an emotion I had never felt less of.

The very photographs with El Rey de Jazz, taken by El Puerto's roving photographer, showed it. There we were, grouped around El Rey, who crouched on the dance floor with his arms out, grinning beadily at the camera, while band members individually mugged their awe and Ramón and I, arms around each other's shoulders, grinned like the two-headed boy. There we were with the band, the guitarists with their instruments, Ramón and I behind them in another clinch, an inverted drink tray over our heads like a shared halo. And there we were, the twosome, posing with guests, who always gave us copies of their shots: every spare moment at El Oasis, I was with Ramón. As soon as a break began, we were guzzling cuba libres and sharing our lives in French. Ramón had nearly a dozen half-siblings in Morocco, products of his father's first marriage, but that marriage had broken up, his father had married one of the forty employees of his shoe factory in Casablanca, and Ramón was the only son of that marriage, so that he had grown up essentially as an only child. My father had three children by his first wife, half-siblings who functioned as two aunts and an uncle, but that marriage had broken up, my father later married a woman half his age, and as the only product of that second marriage, I too grew up as essentially an only child. Then what were we two only sons? Close friends? A couple? A unit?

The very neutrality of that Saxonism captured it: we were a unit. The life of rock-and-rollers in El Puerto de Santa María gave us little time to enjoy that unity, so when Bernardo finally filled El Pinar's gaping cattle watering tank, converting it to the campground's advertised pool, I invited Ramón for a swim. I picked him up in El Puerto de Santa María and we splashed

through the afternoon, then dined on ham hocks with Teddy
and Flo, toasting Flo for having directed me to El Oasis. Then
work summoned us back to El Puerto.

The next day I said to Ramón, "You left your briefs when
you were changing in the tent."

"I didn't forget them," he replied. "I left them because I
want you to wear them."

After that dropped handkerchief, it was a short step to invite Ramón for the night.

Two weeks after Starfis reached its victorious stalemate with
the syndicate, we told M. Baron we were taking a month off,
starting the middle of August. Our alleged reason was that the
microphone which produced the echo effect needed repair, and
Starfis did not wish to compromise its sound, nor risk some
interfering buzz by making do.

It was true that some piece of equipment was always breaking
down. I learned that a rock band, like any confederation of
machines, was a monster into which life had to be breathed
against its will. With proper wheedling and murderous intent
it could be made to do its tricks, but the relationship was that
of oppressor to captive and needed to be sustained by fear; and
like the subdued, the battery of rock instruments was always
watching from the corner of its eye for a small subversion, any
little malfunction that would bring the whole towering indig-
nity to collapse. Our excuse for quitting was nonetheless a lie.

The real reason was that we would no longer be humiliated by M. Baron. From the beginning, his name among band
members had been converted to M. Cabrón, or big goat, a reference to the cuckold's horns and the most serious insult in the
Spanish language. At first he had been all smiles and trilin-
gual charm, then the complaints began. The microphones were
chronically set too loud for people to talk. The piano was out
of balance with the guitars. Then there was the matter of the

drinks, and here M. Cabrón had a legitimate complaint. Much as we liked cuba libres, that wall of bottled color behind the bar represented an opportunity, a challenge. The only way to make sure we sampled it all was to start at one end and work methodically to the other, break by break. We expected the bartenders to balk at this ambition, but they conspired, helping us keep track. A purple syrup whose label appeared to say *passion* in Hungarian proved undrinkable and got spit into the nasturtiums. A series of bottles as alike in their contrasting colors as croquet balls, all labeled BOLS, seemed to deserve my eye's dyslexic SLOB. The Courvoisier, on the other hand, was quite palatable. Our musicianship on these mixes was inspired, particularly the new freedom of my jazz, and I felt that our starting sober and adding liquor as we warmed up musically spiraled our talents into musical heights that the same alcohol, ingested before we began, would have unhinged.

But M. Cabrón did not understand this. One night we were handed three tickets for the evening and informed that they were good for soft drinks, beer and cuba libres. Grumbling that the new system was *poco caballero*, we acquiesced. After a second evening when I carried the last two sets because of an electrical breakdown, I asked how many tickets I would need for a whisky to relax with. Word came through a busboy that whisky could not be bought for three tickets nor twenty tickets nor any number of tickets. Tickets *could not buy whisky.* Furthermore, I was not to set drinks on the piano. The reference was to the second guitarist having spilled a soft drink on the piano the night before the arrival of the tuner, who complained that the keys were a bit gummy. As steward of the piano, I would be responsible for its continuing condition. This was overkill, and as flawless curator of the family Steinway, I felt insulted.

Finally, there was the disagreement over the breaks. One night M. Cabrón announced that he wished us to play continuously for four hours. We informed him it was impossible. They did it for him in Morocco, he said. We are Andalusians, we replied, not Moors. He dropped it, then a week later ordered us to play for forty-five minutes, then break. No, we countered, we will continue to play the sets agreed upon.

When we announced we were taking a month off to repair a microphone, then M. Cabrón didn't know whether to explode or to laugh. It was unheard of. Everyone was so delighted with Starfis. He and Madame and the regulars all agreed it was the best band El Oasis ever had, and business was swelling nightly. August was the peak month. All that energy invested in straightening our papers! Nobody took a month off to repair a mike you could buy new for two nights' pooled wages. He had been in the nightclub business all his life, but not even in Morocco . . . .

The debate raged for several nights, then we relented and agreed to play out the summer. A week later came a rumor from a busboy: *el patrón* had been overheard on the telephone arranging for a band to come from Madrid to finish off the month of August. The next day the news was confirmed by M. Cabrón himself. Starfis was a superb band and we would be welcome back for the winter season. But it was boring for employee and guest alike to hear the same music every night. He liked to change. Yet it was true that Starfis had never played better than this very evening. Come, have a round at the bar, what would you like? Whisky on the rocks, I ordered calmly.

The following night we returned long enough to size up our replacement. We found five seasoned troupers in red shirts: piano, guitar, drums, sax and lady accordionist, smoothly professional, totally lifeless, bureaucrats in three-quarter time. M. Cabrón observed rather too frequently that the clientele liked slow music. A waiter informed us that their contract was up in fifteen days. Secretly pleased, we left after three numbers, plotting to secure a used piano in Seville. M. Cabrón, counting his losses to bad combos, would see how the future had passed him by . . . .

Even though we were out of a job, there was no let-up for rock-and-rollers. From house to house we went, disrupting mothers and siblings, parsing The Beachboys and Procol Harum, copying riffs onto the flamenco guitars with which the unplugged had to make do. Members of Starfis mingled freely with the members of other groups and exuberant hangers-on, extended clans of rockers, and it soon became apparent that our band, recently of the province's top club, was merely the crest of a whole subculture that had exploded in El Puerto de Santa María—as it had in the rest of Europe—during the early sixties.

In that ancient sherrymaking town of 60,000 people jammed into a few square kilometers, a ship-building community where Columbus had supervised the construction of his Santa María before sailing it off the edge of the known, were several professional and a dozen amateur groups all playing music from beyond that edge. The wailing static of cheap speakers shrieked from El Puerto's unused schoolrooms, abandoned buildings and formerly peaceful patios. Radios and juke boxes burst with last month's and next month's groups, most of them shamelessly plagiarizing the Beatles and the Stones. Scholiasts held forth on superiority of Fender guitars over their rivals, or the comparative intonations of *ye-ye*. The movie theaters of Puerto Real might be showing *Seven Brides for Seven Brothers*, but films in Puerto de Santa María, Jerez and Cádiz were often suspended for traveling congeries of rock groups with a pop singer thrown in for variety, line-ups that toured theaters and sports fields like Chautauquas. One Starfis sidekick told me he didn't know much about music, but wasn't the electric guitar, even in appearance, far more beautiful than the old wooden one?

The cultural impact of rock culture came clear to me when I was invited to hear some flamenco by the quiet Domingo, who

sold pots in the market under Ramón's balcony and who was
my favorite new friend after Ramón himself. I knew better than
to include the others, and I even implored Ramón in vain: when
I listened to the wrong music, we were not a unit. "Let's go to a
tasca," Domingo would say with an emphasis that implied we
were about to do something low.

A *tasca* had no glittering zinc bar, no doors thrown wide to
the street; it was typically a small and dingy room or two with
barrels of sherry in the wall, a few small tables with stools
and creaking chairs, and a clientele of old men, most of them
drunk. Their music boasted no technology, for the instruments
consisted of one or at most two guitars, usually battered. The
men welcomed us and bought us drinks because we were young,
an audience. They were hoarse, they slapped the guitars as if
they were percussions or horses, and they splayed their hands
across strings so loose that they perennially buzzed, in defi-
ance of all technique. The lyrics, typically about hopeless love
for a woman too many stations above them, or the agonizing
purity of the Virgin, were Spanish at its most Andalusian, so
that *amado*, beloved, came out *amao*, diphthongs wailed as if
through the nose in soaring and falling trajectories that no more
needed to be on pitch than Ramón did when he screamed that
he couldn't get no satisfaction. This, of all the world's popular
music I had heard, was the most stirring, and here, even more
than in the idyllic gardens of El Oasis, I felt in my element.

How I longed to fold Domingo's musical passions into
Ramón! Our racket, seductive to youth for reasons I couldn't
fathom, was swamping the deep and the genuine, and music
that had aged like sherry for generations in these streets was
being lost. I had Ramón, I had an exciting new life, and our
role in this cultural leveling shamed me. In my now prolifer-
ating Spanish I held forth. The flamenco they affected to de-
spise for being obsolete was at that very moment enjoying an
enormous vogue in England and the United States, exciting

the very generation that had created and popularized the rock-and-roll that was music's highest destiny. In Ramón's case I could understand that the wailing *melismas* of El Puerto de Santa María's ancient drunks might recall, consciously or otherwise, the call-to-prayer of the muezzins in the minarets of Casablanca, childhood city to which he could not return, and of the Arabs with whom his fellow Spaniards sometimes confused him, to his immense disgust. For young Andalusians, flamenco summed up the oppressive past, the unevolved technology, the indulgent flaunting of sentiment, the repressive politics, the narrow lapels of all that separated them from the dazzling new brotherhood of freedom dawning in the Western capitals.

It would have undermined their musical prejudice to have been able to hear in the blues of Jimi Hendrix or John Mayall the same modal shifts and sliding semitones that shadowed their uncle's *soleares*; that charged the *cante jondo*, the deep song, at the neighborhood *tasca*; or that infused the *saeta* some old wino launched during Holy Week to La Macarena. For Africa, musically, had come full circle. The sliding chants and muted wails that crossed the Atlantic on slave ships, that bred with European music in Savannah and New Orleans and spread through Chicago and Detroit and San Francisco and then spiraled with fresh fuel from London and Liverpool to obscure corners like El Puerto de Santa María—were the same cries and laments left behind by the Moors when Isabella drove them back to their point of origin. In Andalucía in the mid-sixties, Africa met musical Africa like points of an omega, and the space between them was the gap between generations that failed to recognize, each in the other, its own face.

One dusk in El Puerto I gazed up at a balcony over the market and saw two seated old women in black. Their faces bore a family resemblance. From a radio beside them came the blare of a pop song. There was a message from the announcer, then a guitar began a soft flamenco. A male voice entered, quiet but tense. One woman's feet began to move. The music gathered momentum and the voice became charged with feeling. The woman's hands moved with her feet and a smile spread over her features. As the voice grew taut, the woman's lips began to murmur against each other. Forming the words of the singer, she no longer bore resemblance to the woman seated motionless beside her. A young man appeared from an open doorway, casually switched stations and left. The lips stopped, the hands were still. A voice crooned to the beat of lost love in English. The women—who were Ramón's grandmother and aunt—sat solemnly as before, faintly reflecting each other over the dimming market.

6

What, I asked myself in rare moments of introspection, was I doing with my life? Thanks to my not looking remotely my age, I could appear with Ramón in photos like his contemporary, a matching scoop of a different flavor, but in fact he was nineteen to my twenty-seven. Bilingual and then some, with intelligence coded in his genes, Ramón had no more schooling than the high school withstood by the other members of Starfis, while I had my unmentioned Ivy League degree and half of a Masters from Berkeley. Not so far back I had been studying to become a professor of English in some American college, and now I was running with an Andalusian teenage pack. As an actual teenager I had run with no pack at all; inward and terrified of my contemporaries, I had spent my adolescence in class, at the family Steinway, nose in a book, alone in the woods. The relief from that self was exhilarating, and as I sped toward the rockers of El Puerto, it struck me that it was better to live life out-of-sequence than to miss getting it all in.

But even for a pseudo-teenager between jobs, the awkwardness of life in a car and a tent was getting old. Autumn rains struck and penetrated the canvas, soaking the typewriter I didn't have the good sense to sequester in the car. On an alley in Cádiz I found a cave the size of a broom closet reeking with oils and rancid metals, where I handed over the grade school graduation present to a man in a green eyeshade. He squinted at it. "Are you a sailor?" he growled.

"No," I blurted. "Why?"

"This is a beautiful machine and it's been mistreated. Objects get battered this badly only at sea."

"It was the rain."

"The rain. Sure, the rain. There's always rain. Also, there's shelter."

"Can you repair it?"

"It will set you back one-hundred-eighty pesetas."

"When can you finish it?"

"Come back tomorrow at the same time."

The typewriter was returned to me in mint condition twenty-four hours later at a cost of three dollars, but still I was stung by the abuse. I was relieved when Bernardo, needing to go north for a few days, installed me in the office. He showed me how to sign campers in and out and where to put the money; I would be de facto campground manager. But after the departure of the French, who had filled the clearing with their screaming children and blue tents all of August, business had shrunk to the handful of regulars, and no one came to camp in the rain. I set my dazzlingly restored typewriter on Bernardo's desk and caught up on my notes, then slept on a floor without one drop of moisture. I dreaded Bernardo's return.

I should have welcomed it, for Bernardo had a saving surprise. The campground restaurant out by the highway was being closed. Did I want to become its guardian? I would be given a small room on the side, free for as long as I wanted it, and all I would have to do was to occupy it, to keep an eye on the building and to run the occasional errand for Bernardo. Aware that I was merely the feeder of the real guardian, I accepted. I was ecstatic.

The closing of Restaurante El Pinar was inevitable and I only wondered what miscalculation had brought it into being.

Long and low on the brow of a hill, it commanded a sweeping
view of the Bay of Cádiz. I had eaten there a couple of times
with Patrick and we had marveled that two doddering waiters,
with no other customers to distract them, were unable to convey
to our table in a timely manner the indifferent food it had already taken an age to cook. The only public food in Puerto
Real to declare itself with a sign, it priced itself beyond reach
of locals while campers, a notoriously cheap crowd, ate in their
tents. That left motoring tourists, of whom there were few, and
the occasional traveling businessman who no doubt found it an
outpost of progress. Euthanasia was overdue.

For me it was pure windfall. My room was a mere swept-out
storeroom that made Bernardo's office seem palatial by comparison. Its dense, leak-proof walls, secure against the wind
and the rain, were breached once by a window whose iron grille
made it impossible to clean. Nearby stood a pair of bathrooms
marked WC, alike and both left open. There was no electricity
or hot water.

I was ecstatic because of the outdoors that surrounded it.
The restaurant itself counted as outdoors, since all but my
room was locked. Mine were the dance floor and the choice of
terraces, with views of Cádiz and no less than four lesser towns
ringing the bay, four subsidiary diamonds and the twenty-four-
karat capital, all gleaming beyond the salt marshes. Across
the highway stood an evaporative salt operation with an occasional employee, no ongoing activity and a large cone of salt
whose missing chunk I imagined bitten off by a passing camel.
Most gloriously, the restaurant was backed by a full acre of
pine trees that plunged down the slope between the highway
and the campground into permanent weedy shadow. These
were the trees of Las Canteras, *pino piñonero*, with straight
boles that branched near their tops into a heaving canopy that
stuck in the wind's throat. Here Og would labor at his guard
duty. My own terrain was reached by a set of stairs that angled

up the restaurant's side, past the smudged window to a flat roof
surrounded by a low wall: an elevated patio, an *azotea*. Here,
weather permitting, I would actually live.

The room wouldn't accommodate much furniture, but there
was none at all. A table and chair could be rustled from the
campground and I asked my friends if they could locate a bed.
Skinny knew of one for sale. We sized it up in one of Puerto
Real's teeming warrens. It was a narrow wooden frame with a
webbing of fine chains for springs, a mere cot with a sag in the
middle, shorter than I was. The seller's younger brother sidled
up to me. "He's selling it because the last person who slept in
it died of tuberculosis."

Recognizing the *cachondeo*, I replied, "Then I'll rest in peace."

Puerto Real's only bed for sale, it would elevate me over
the cold cement. Also, it would provide guest seating for two,
rounding out the single chair and the table where the typewriter and the butane burner ruled in rotation.

I was concerned about Og's proximity to the highway, where
traffic barreled toward Sevilla or Algeciras, but he never went
near it: after all, this dog was himself a driver. The other four
members of the social quintet enjoyed the new setting for
morning coffee. We hauled campground chairs onto the terraces, under the pines, up to the roof, and crammed ourselves
into my chairless room when the weather was foul. Here also
was a place to receive Ramón. I would pick him up in El Puerto,
or he would catch a ride with one of the numerous Portuenses
who went back and forth to Cádiz on business.

I took Ramón by the Bar Central to introduce him to my
friends, who later sometimes encountered him at the campground. Superficially both sides were polite, but Ramón took
no interest in them, while the well-dressed aloofness that got
him labeled *complicado* in middle-class Puerto de Santa María
played even less well in ship-building Puerto Real. The fact
that he communicated with me in French didn't help. What

do you think of him? I asked my friends. *Es muy chulo,* they replied. He puts on airs. That was fine with me, for I had no ambition to integrate Ramón with my underclass social life. Ramón responded to something deep in my interior and I was happy to have him to myself.

Ramón became another fixture of El Pinar, overnight or for days at a time, enjoying the long light, the last sun burning hotter and redder as it sank through the pines, the hospitality of the ever generous Teddy and Flo. "I can understand most of what you guys are saying," chattered Teddy when we rudely spoke French in front of him. "When I was stationed in France, I spoke French so good the locals thought I was one of 'em. Did you get a look at all those Frenchies in their blue tents last summer, walking around like they dyed their underwear blue?" After socializing, Ramón and I would climb the little stair and arrange the air mattresses and sleeping bags on the *azotea,* then float the night embraced by the wall of our private basin, stars wavering through the pines as if it were they, not the canopy of needles, that were stirred by the heaving branches and the wind seething around us.

As I settled into my new estate, I was summoned to play piano three nights a week for a jump in salary at El Candil Verde, a night spot on the near side of El Puerto. Flavio, the Starfis singer, was the only familiar face, nor did familiarity ever extend beyond the mastering of each other's names. Braying to little purpose was a hulking one-legged Sidney Greenstreet of a bad sax player whom the *sindicato* had once tried to foist on Starfis during their nightly raids on El Oasis. The beat was clocked by a young drummer whose head, sleeked by a fifties duck's-ass haircut, swiveled in a frozen grin over a bop that never varied once he had selected from his array of five, and who spent his leisure hours on the fringe of the naval base learning with more conviction than Diego how to be an American. The

melodies were shaped by a surprisingly mellow trumpet player
whose musicianship was never harnessed to any communal effect. At another American upright, this one a toothless despair,
I floundered for any harmonic compromise that might keep
our five independently crooning, squealing and caterwauling
voices from complete disintegration. Since we never actually
rehearsed but merely showed up when it was time to play, we
never pretended to a group name, but the lettering on the bass
drum proclaimed us LOS IMPERIALES.

Our incoherence was apt for The Green Candle. The outdoor dance floor suggested a parking lot, due to being permanently ringed by parked cars, but the inference of clientele was
deceptive and the source of the cars remained mysterious. A
hovering suspicion of old seafood was explained by a nearby
fertilizer plant fed by the residue from El Puerto's fish market.
Our three-night schedule was more like a weekly one-night
stand, for at least once a week the *Levante* blew with such
ferocity that the club was closed, presumably to protect the
imaginary dancers from being swept into the mysterious cars,
and on another night one of our numbers would be called to
play a fair in some other town: the owner would mournfully announce that we could not play without him, while I stifled the
observation that neither could we play with him. The Imperial
Ones were unregal even in death, and merely scattered. Flavio
found a job singing in some spot no one had ever heard of near
Jerez, the trumpet player found more reliable work in Cádiz,
the drummer moved to Rota to be with the Americans, and finally only the sax player could still be seen in El Puerto, drag-
ging his great hulk on one leg back and forth across the street
between the tobacco stand where he worked and slept and the
bar where he played dominoes, heaving and sinking as he drew
breath like a beached sea mammal.

Despite our outrage at mistreatment by the demeaning M.
Cabrón, Starfis eagerly returned to El Oasis when invited to

play the month of October. The clientele had drastically fallen off since the thick of summer, the wind that had blasted the parking lot of El Candil Verde now screamed through the palms, and the indoor bar, sealed off from our bandstand in the pseudo clubhouse, saw all the action. Our own number was reduced by Flavio having defected to that spot near Jerez, and I was suffering a musical setback. Almost nightly M. Cabrón—speaking, as usual, through a busboy—asked me to play jazz, and the busboy reported his mystification that I didn't comply. In fact I wanted ardently to comply, for my own sake if not for M. Cabrón's, but jazz wouldn't happen. I tried to induce it with upbeat versions of Gershwin tunes, as before, but jazz didn't want me. Part of the problem, I knew, was that M. Cabrón's ration of three cuba libres a night, spread over four and a half hours' playing time, kept us sober, and I needed to break through inhibitions. But jazz was also a kind of grace, a descent of the god, and the god didn't brave the *Levante*. The busboy kept returning. "M. Baron doesn't understand why you won't play jazz."

"I'm doing my best."

"He says, if you played it before, you can play it now."

To ask for the scotch on the rocks that might have helped sounded like blackmail, and I couldn't ask for special treatment. "I'll keep trying," I said, lamely enough.

Into these frustrations fell a night of redemption. We were invited near closing by two drunks to an after-hours spot called La Venta Flamenca, on the road north. The Lung was the designated conveyance, and we were already jammed in and rocketing out of town when I noticed we were nearly out of gas. When we arrived at the one station still open, I discovered that I had neglected to carry the key to the lockable gas cap I had bought to replace the original, which had been stolen the week before. No matter, said one of the drunks, we could go to his place. It was across the street.

Across the street I saw nothing but dark rows of government buildings. "How's that?"

He smiled. "I'm chief of the military barracks."

As we pulled through an iron gate a block away, armed guards converged on the Lung, conferred briefly with our friend, then waved us through. We parked and followed him into an office, where he produced glasses and a bottle of sherry. Toasts were made, glasses refilled, then our host slipped outside. After a suspicious interval we stepped out to investigate.

Standing by the Lung in the moonlight was our host, flanked by the armed guard, while an unidentifiable figure crouched with his ear to the gas tank and his hands next to his ear. Our host turned casually and explained that the man was in the brig for theft, a true master, a windfall, and had been summoned from sleep to pick the gas cap. After one more round of sherry we sailed triumphantly back to the gas station.

Ourselves and the car well fueled, we headed north. Suddenly the barracks chief directed me to veer onto a dark road I recognized as the old road to Jerez. As we meandered a dozen kilometers through the dark, I lost faith that La Venta Flamenca existed, even as I hoped that it would prove an enclave of true flamenco. A small burst of lights appeared off the road and we pulled in.

There was music and dancing in abundance. Buxom middle-aged women with mascara-on-plaster faces were clutching and fending off men slightly senior to themselves. The band was appalling. But the import of this spectacle didn't jell until Ramón pointed to the singer. Behind the mike, hair slicked back and trim figure squeezed into a sleek red suit, belting it to the drunks and the whores, was our missing Flavio.

The song closed with a great reunion of embracing and backslapping in which Flavio's disappearance from El Oasis and El Candil Verde, if not forgotten, was passed over. So how did he like his new job?

Flavio beamed with enthusiasm. He was making three hundred pesetas a night, more than ever before, and he could sing anything he liked. With no transition he reversed himself. It was terrible, humiliating. To sing in a whorehouse was the bottom. He hated it, as he hated all singing jobs, no matter how much he pretended to enjoy them. All he cared about was God. But he couldn't begin his studies for the priesthood in Sevilla before he saved enough money to supplement the meager state pension of his widowed mother. It was a trial, but he would have to endure.

As October drew to a close at El Oasis, the busboy stopped relaying requests for jazz, the clientele shriveled still further and our boss himself seemed to be closing down. On the final night, the busboy laid the blame at my fingertips. Starfis had been asked back because M. Baron had wanted to hear jazz, I had unaccountably and perversely refused to play it, and the Starfis contract would not be renewed.

I was just resettling into indigence at Restaurante El Pinar when Ramón arrived one morning, unexpectedly, with a new summons to play. The American naval base had contacted El Pulpón, the musical agent from Sevilla, asking whether he had a pianist who could play appropriate music for Americans. He did indeed. I was expected at the base that very afternoon.

Despite my notion of turning Frank in before his AWOL status turned to desertion, I had never actually been to Rota, and it made me nervous to follow its long grey wall up to the grey guard house flanked by an American flag in my grey tin French car. An enormous pink-skinned uniformed American made a phone call, then explained how to get to a small office building. I was greeted by a well-spoken man in a Hawaiian shirt, who seated me in his office and offered coffee. He was, he said, a nightclub trouble-shooter. He traveled from base to base, routinely found its entertainment to be a mess, shaped it up and moved on. The Officer's Club wanted cocktail piano, something with class. I would play daily from five to eight for three dollars an hour, a nice hike from the three a day I had received at El Oasis. I agreed, was photographed in an adjacent building, and was promptly issued a laminated pass, along with instructions to report for piano duty the following afternoon.

Each day's twenty-five kilometer commute over roads clogged with bicycles and mules and carts consumed an hour, and ended when I flashed my pass and entered a stage-set world of emerald lawns and white buildings. An airstrip surrounded by a cyclone fence separated the officers' miniature suburbia from the barracks and administration buildings. The houses were ranch, the cars were from Detroit, there were tennis courts and barbecue grills. The Officers' Club was a small restaurant and cocktail lounge, with males in civilian clothes accompanied by wives and sometimes children. I could drink what I wanted, and nursed my highballs at the baby grand. Officers chatted; a couple of them were interested in Spain and one had even befriended gypsies. There were requests for "Misty" and "My Funny Valentine," standards from the pop and musical comedy repertoire I drifted through. After three pleasant weeks I was summoned to see the boss in the Hawaiian shirt.

I was such a success at the Officers' Club, he said, that he wanted to move me up, to the Enlisted Men's Club. True, an enlisted man was lower in rank than an officer, but this was one of the four or five best clubs in the system, up there with Oahu and Indonesia, and many more people would hear me. The hours were the same, but I would precede a variety show that began nightly at eight. Tonight's show, he continued, featured a new dancer. "I talked to her on the phone this morning. Do you know what she wanted to dance? 'The Dying Swan.' These guys want flesh, not feathers! Why is it that every dancer I contract wants to kill the swan?"

The piano, too, was of a lower rank, a mere spinet, angled rakishly under a revolving ball of mirrors on the dance floor of a salon hung with red drapes. I was the core of empty space— first the dance floor, then a sea of little round tables with accompanying chairs, most of them unoccupied—for cocktail piano did not draw enlisted men away from the pool tables, pinball machines and juke boxes elsewhere in the building until the last set, when groups wandered in to grab seats for the show. I was able to count on a small but steady following who found in my repertoire some contact with what passed for sophistication, and I was pleased that one of them was my boss. I could also count on the petty officer from Scottsdale who wanted, daily, the score from *The Sound of Music,* and who told me he kept a picture of Julie Andrews taped inside the door of his locker. I played and loved most of Rodgers and Hammerstein, whose shows came out as I was growing up, but not even professional pride in fulfilling requests could redeem "Climb Every Mountain," "Edelweiss" and the rest, syrup that curdled beneath my touch.

One night the Richard Rodgers fans were overwhelmed by a deluge of raucous and hard-drinking strangers. By the end of the first hour all the tables were taken and more customers were jammed behind them on their feet. The Spanish waiters spun through a frenzy of shouted orders, and voices thickened until I scarcely heard what I played. Without stopping for a break, I banged the keys for all they were worth, flailing on with a sense of futility for the duration of the cocktail hour. From the corner of my eye I caught some heavy object headed slowly in my direction. It was a bulging overturned hat, it hit the lid of the spinet with a great metallic crash, and coins scattered across the floor. Bodies leapt from the tables, replaced the coins, and the hat was laid cautiously on the piano with a leafy swelling of bills. Though the bedlam never relented, there was a sustained ovation when I finished, I was forced to

take several bows, and a group followed me as I left with the
sagging hat.

"Will you drink with us for the evening?"

"Of course. But who *are* you?"

Their voices competed. "We're from an atomic submarine.
We've been underwater for weeks. We just got here this afternoon. This isn't even the kind of music most of us like, but we
could see you were really trying. It means a lot to us. You're the
first live music we've heard for months."

That evening, for the first time, I saw the floor show.

The burst of American generosity came none too soon, for
I didn't warm to this military view of my countrymen. Usually
I rushed back to Spain when I finished work, but occasionally
I stopped for coffee or a beer in the cafeteria by the PX, where
Teddy secured Og's kibble through shopping privileges that
didn't come with my job. The juke box chased "Edelweiss" and
"Climb Every Mountain" out of my system with "Your Cheatin'
Heart" and "King of the Road," and the giants around me who
fed the machine with quarters fed themselves with cheese-
burgers and jumbo bags of potato chips. Loud, broad of gesture, these were my fellow Americans, and their overstated
style seemed the expression of their very bulk. I had always
been considered small, and in grade school I was often the
shortest male in class, the shrimp—and yet the Puerto Real
social quintet was my size or smaller, Ramón was precisely the
size I was, and only one member of Starfis was taller. Country
people around Puerto Real were smaller still, miniatures even
to me, and only people from Madrid, whom I knew as occasional customers of El Oasis, were as a category consistently
larger. From viewing myself as short, I had come to see my
height as average, and now at the base I had shrunk to my
smallest size yet. But beyond mere stature, there was something puffy, boneless and unfocused about these mutations; in
this basement cafeteria they reminded me of mushrooms that

kept swelling by constant injection because nothing stopped them. This, I told myself with the innocence of someone young enough to believe it, was something I would not let happen to myself. Bodily processes could be curbed by an exertion of will. Whether my future lay in the United States, in Spain or elsewhere, I would not become a puffy American. If I could not be a sinewy Spaniard, at least I would not blow up.

My immediate future was with another set of puffy Americans, for I was summoned again to the office of the boss. Expecting my fan in the Hawaiian shirt, I opened the door on a compressed, beady-eyed man in a suit. "I'm looking for Mr. Nuane," I said.

"Mr. Nuane has been posted to another base. You'll be reporting to me. I'm Mr. Spontini." He didn't offer to shake hands. "Sit."

I sat.

"I've been to the club the last two days and I see that no one shows up to listen to you," he said without preamble, almost angrily. "I'm transferring you to the Seabees' Club. Begin tomorrow." He told me how to get there and dismissed me. I had a vague impression that Seabees were the peons of the Navy but didn't know the details.

The Seabees' Club was an overlit Quonset hut with a beer-only bar, a tangle of tables, a small dance floor and a jukebox. It was an unpromising venue for cocktail music, but I greeted the Spanish bartenders, then sat down to play so that I would be doing so when the first customers arrived. They came in wearing jeans and tee shirts. "King of the Road" didn't sound like much on the piano, but I could knock out "Your Cheatin' Heart" and didn't hesitate. A Seabee came up to me. "That's real nice. Schlitz?"

I was surprised by the specificity because I had seen several brands of beer. "Sure."

When he returned with it, another Seabee glared at both of us, then dropped a coin in the juke box. I waited for it to end, was going to play again, and another song came on. I sat at the piano bench through a half hour of songs from the jukebox, finishing my beer. The inviter asked me if I'd like another, and I accepted. "Come sit with us," he said, and I was glad to get off the piano bench, since I couldn't play.

"What do Seabees do?" I asked when I was seated at a table of five of them. At Rota they lived on two nuclear submarines that were permanently stationed at the base and seldom moved. They maintained the subs in perpetual readiness, and the subs' proximity to the Strait of Gibraltar discouraged potential threats. A war was building up in Vietnam but these submarines had no serious enemies but each other. After I had talked with them for nearly an hour, I remarked, "I feel bad about not playing."

"We'll take care of that," said a fellow Schlitz drinker. He crossed to the side of the room where all were drinking Budweiser and stood over a table. "We want to hear Bruce play the piano."

"There's money in the jukebox," said a Budweiser drinker.

"Let it run out," said the Schlitz drinker. "There's a live musician here who's being paid to play for us. We want to hear him."

We sat through five more songs, then there was silence. I got up and ran through the Beatles tunes I played with Starfis. "That's fantastic," said the Seabee who had bought me the first beer. Then it was time to close.

Over the next two weeks I sat at the bench and at the tables drinking Schlitz bought by the submarine that adopted me, while the submarine that drank Bud seldom let me play. The Seabee who had treated me first told me his name was Roger and that he had been a tool and die worker before he enlisted. "Feel my fingertips," he said.

I did.

"I can tell if something's off by a millimeter. But I can't play the piano. Would you visit me on my submarine?"

"Would they let me on?"

"I'll arrange it."

A tour of the underworld! "I'd love to."

"When you step on that ship," he beamed, "I'll be the proudest guy in the whole U. S. Navy."

Roger and his friends eyed the jukebox with increasing belligerence as the Budweiser drinkers, without threatening me personally, made increasingly rude remarks about my defenders' musical tastes. I knew that it was only a question of time before the Seabees' Club erupted, but in the meantime I was content to show up and be paid by American taxpayers to drink Schlitz with Roger. I was also a professional musician and I remained ever poised to play.

One night the jukebox stopped. I began "Your Cheatin' Heart" and a Budweiser bottle flew, not at me but at my table of defenders. Roger grabbed me and pulled me under the table, and several tables on my side grabbed their Schlitz bottles and hurled them across the room. They were answered by a volley of Budweiser bottles. When the ammunition was exhausted, Seabees began grabbing each other and pulling each other to the ground, then blows were exchanged. Within minutes there was a wail of sirens and a wedge of shore patrol burst through the door. Their mere appearance restored order and they demanded an explanation. After each side rendered its account, an officer announced that the musician hired by the base was the official entertainment of the Seabees' club, and the ship which had violated that policy would be required to leave for the evening. In the triumph of that decision, the piano-defending ship held a victory dance—to the jukebox.

When I appeared at work the next day, a bartender told me I was to report to the boss. I knocked, a voice growled, "Come in," and Mr. Spontini glared up from his desk. "Mr. Berger, you are a disruptive element. You're fired. You are to collect the money from the bursar, turn in your pass, and leave. *Now.*"

I never got my tour of the submarine, nor even the chance to say goodbye to Roger. Dollars in my pocket, I drove home from Rota knowing that at risk to personal security I had served my country.

7

One rainy afternoon just after my ejection from the base, Chano popped out of a bar and asked if I'd like to join him for a quick sherry.

A wiry little man who had been called in for a few odd jobs around El Pinar, he was clearly in a foul mood. His tight sly face looked even darker, more chiseled than usual. We belted a glass of sherry and I asked what was the matter. "Annnh!" He gave the air the back of his hand and we downed another wine.

It was still raining. "I just had a fight with my boss at the base," he said.

"Serious?"

"Serious enough."

"Can you go back to work Monday?"

He considered a moment. "Up the ass with them."

"So what happened?"

"They wanted me to work in the rain and I refused. I had a fight with the boss and . . . and that's it."

The conversation apparently ended. Then he resumed. "I was stringing cables on top of a tower when the downpour came. I told them I'd finish when it stopped raining so hard. Three years I worked at the base, to my disgrace. Not making any more there than I do outside the base. Getting up every morning before dawn, making the twenty-five kilometer trip back and forth on the motorcycle if the weather was good enough, waiting for the bus if it wasn't, all for nothing. Three years of my life thrown away."

"I just lost my job at the base too."

"Then we're in the same boat. Was your boss Spanish or American?"

"Italian."

"They're all the same."

"What will you do now?"

"Maybe go back to work at the dock or the boat factory, or sell fish or something."

Then his wiliness burned through his anger and lit him puckishly. In Puerto Real the fish at the market was very expensive, in El Puerto de Santa María very cheap. In El Puerto he had a friend at the market who would sell him the best fish at a decent price. We could transport it to the Puerto Real market and sell it at a profit, beating the price of the local vendors. We could continue it if it went well, drop it if it didn't. Was I interested?

Monday afternoon I drove Chano to the Puerto de Santa María market. In an open-walled cement building by the Rio Guadalete were reeking bins of marine life—fish that ranged in size from marrow spoons to fire hydrants, glistening tangles of squid, swellings and taperings I only recognized when they were cross-sectioned and served on a plate. Chano stormed up and down the aisles peering at them all beadily, then counted out five hundred pesetas to his friend for a box each of two varieties. We drove them back to Puerto Real, parked outside his apartment and arranged the fish in the back of the Lung for display to the neighbors. There was a box of *sardinas*, fat and gleaming oblongs of silver six to seven inches long, with a rich taste that even I knew and loved, and a box of *rubios*, nasty looking fish with pink backs, white bellies, brutish faces and, admitted Chano, an appeal more to the pocketbook than the palate. We nabbed a passing woman and asked what she thought.

"The *sardinas* are all right but the *rubios* aren't too fresh. You can tell the freshness of fish by the brilliance of the eyes, and these are getting a little misty."

I glanced at Chano, but he didn't look back.

We invited Chano's wife out to the car for a second opinion. She didn't know much about fish but wanted to know how he was going to price them.

"I don't know yet."

"Well what did you pay for them by the kilo?"

"I don't know how much they weigh."

An argument broke out among Chano's family and neighbors concerning his knowledge of the fish business. We cut it short by taking off for his father's house in the country to weigh our stock. I helped him string a mechanism of rope and rusted iron over a beam in the barn, and Chano heaped rounds of fish in the hanging scoop while I read the number where the needle settled. Then we proceeded to the Puerto Real market, where we deposited the fish amid shaved ice so it would be ready for the morning's auction.

By unhappy coincidence my musical career erupted and I was summoned to El Puerto to play a one-night stand—on the electric organ rather than the piano—after which Ramón invited me home for a late supper, and I didn't get to bed until three-thirty. It was black when I got up again at six, and still black when I arrived at the market at seven. Paco, the town buffoon, ambled up with the collar of his trenchcoat pulled over his ears and asked what I was doing up at this hellish hour.

"I'm going to sell fish."

"You mean you're going to buy fish."

"No, to sell it. You'll see."

I strolled off to find Chano but he hadn't arrived. Manolo poked into the market on his way to opening the Bar Central; we kidded for a moment about my new profession but lack of sleep had rendered me incoherent. It started to rain. At seven-thirty Chano showed up. We waited another hour for the seven o'clock auction to begin. Paco wandered back, his face looking quite sober for the first time. "You *are* going to sell fish. Be careful. There's a bad man in charge and they're all thieves here. You have no idea what goes on in this market."

The auction began and we entered our fish. The buyers were the sellers of the retail stalls and the owners of a few bars. Our fish was easily the best in attendance. Our box fell under the auctioneer's hands. "Eleven pesetas. Ten seventy-five. Ten fifty. Ten twenty-five. Ten. Nine seventy-five . . . Six twenty-five . . . Five . . ." Deathly silence. At four pesetas a kilo Chano withdrew it. The other box went through the same process, then we loaded the fish in the car.

"What happened?"

"It's the Rubio."

"But they didn't bid on the *sardinas* either."

Chano laughed feebly. "No, the Rubio is the blond little fat man standing there, the one Paco warned us about. He has no official position but he controls all the buying and selling that goes on here. The people who sell don't want any new competition and the buyers are afraid of offending them. We can enter the fish in the market because it's our right, but we can't actually sell it."

"So what do we do with it now?"

"Try my aunt's store."

Chano's aunt's store turned out to be my usual source of candles. The jammed cubbyhole also offered sewing supplies, moccasins, cleansers, wallets, knives, toilet paper, candy and a few articles of underwear, and though it eluded any namable category, fish seemed a little out of its line. We parked by the front door, opened the back of the car for display and Chano announced to the customers that we had fresh *sardinas* and *rubios* for sale.

The women went wild. Almost every housewife who entered the store bought a kilo or two, and for an hour we carried fish through the rain from the car to Chano's aunt's brass scales. We lost track of who owed for what fish and could only hope the women were dealing with us squarely. School was about to begin across the street and suddenly we were mobbed by small children jostling around the car and pushing their way into the store to keep dry. Our fish market was bedlam. Then as quickly, for no apparent reason, business stopped. I looked in the boxes to see how much remained after an hour's brisk business and discovered we had made hardly a dent. For the first time I realized the immensity of our stock.

It was only nine o'clock. "Where do we go now?" I asked Chano.

"To the country."

We stopped first at the barrio of Jarana, a handful of houses south of Puerto Real that hardly qualified as a roadstop but which I knew to be the home of several *Guardian Civil*. "You knock on the doors and do the asking," said Chano, "and I'll handle the business end." I had suspected that our activities were vaguely irregular—that we should have a permit or something—but felt reassured by the fact that Chano was taking the same risk I was while being less capable of paying any resultant fine. Still, Jarana made me nervous as a place to begin. I looked back at Chano to allay my fears as I knocked on the first door. He was hiding behind the car.

As it turned out, the women of Jarana were not interested in fish. Chano thought that business would be better farther from the highway, and the idea of remoteness suddenly appealed to me as well. "Shouldn't we have a permit to be doing this?" I asked as we pulled away.

Chano shrugged. "We'll be careful."

We made our way over dirt roads through the fields, stopping house to house. "We have fresh fish, *sardinas* and *rubios*,

ten pesetas a kilo." Fat women in black missing half their
teeth chattered in shrill voices as we set up our scales in the
rain. Small children gathered close, pushing and staring as
the women sized up the fish. There were no men, all of them
having gone to the fields. Business was brisk. A few women
were flatly not interested; others insisted we put them on our
regular route. We were making visible inroads into our supply.

We came to a collection of small round houses like whitewashed beehives. I was discovering the salesman's delight in
peering into strangers' homes, and these were too good to pass
up.

"I don't think anyone lives there," said Chano.

"I'm going to try anyway."

I walked all the way around one and couldn't find the door,
though I was sure I heard movement inside. The likeliest can-
didate for an entrance was a tall window, where I knocked.
There was no response.

"Come on," said Chano, "you're wasting time."

"No, there's someone in here," I said. I knocked again and
presently a dumpy little woman appeared from the other side
of the building and bought a kilo of *rubios*. I never did discover
how she got out.

Roads became worse, then were no longer roads. We found
ourselves wobbling down a mule path hardly the width of the car,
bouncing over rocks and tipping into ruts and pitfalls. I insisted
we go no farther. Chano insisted with equal fervor that we push
on, for the path would lead to a better path that would emerge
on the highway. We stopped the car to debate. Suddenly a figure
appeared from nowhere. "Bru! What are you doing here?"

It was Blas, a friend from the Bar Gallego, who I knew lived
vaguely in this direction. I explained my predicament.

He accepted my new career as a logical choice and sympathized with the plight of the car. He seconded Chano's reading
of the terrain and led us forward on foot, pointing to each

obstacle, untangling a mule that had tautened its tether across the path while snarling it on a tree, and indicating our route back to town. By magic, we hit two solid ruts of dirt.

We tried every remaining hovel. At another seeming dead end we crossed some railroad tracks to find a place to turn around, and I spotted a large house that had been hidden from view. We made our way up a long drive, passed what looked like servants' quarters, and stopped in front of the house. A small woman in black, a fountain of stringy hair, emerged smiling and asked what we were about.

"We're selling fish."

"And you decided to try *here?*" she shrieked in astonishment.

"We were turning around, saw the house and thought we'd give it a try."

"It's marvelous! You're a gift from heaven! I'm here alone without food in the house and would have had to walk five kilometers in the rain to market. I'll buy enough for today *and* tomorrow. You must stop here every time you pass!" Her transport continued some five minutes while we stood in the rain and grinned. Alone in her mansion, she was the maddest country wife of all.

At two-thirty we headed to Chano's father's house to relax for a bit and plan our next move. Chano's father worked the land of people who lived in back, and we sold the lady of the house a kilo of *sardinas*. "Just a minute, don't go yet," she said, and she and her husband roasted the fish on an open grill and served them to us with bread and wine. It was the greatest gift they could have offered, for we hadn't eaten all day and I'd been curious to taste our own medicine. Our product was magnificent, and during the course of our conversation about the fish trade they offered me a room to stay in free as long as I liked, should I ever decide to leave El Pinar.

Full of good food, wine and fellowship, we retreated to Chano's house, concluding it was too late to sell more fish. A third of it remained. We counted the money: it came to just enough to cover the fish, ice and gas, with twenty-five pesetas—forty cents—of clear profit. It felt like no small triumph to break even on the first day of a business we both now admitted we knew nothing about, and we speculated that once we had learned the varieties of fish, how to price, where to sell, nuances of marketing, we would have the foundation of a solid operation.

We headed to the fish market at El Puerto de Santa María, returned the empty crates and Chano bought the next day's supply—three boxes this time, but of cheaper varieties amounting to an outlay of only four hundred pesetas. We brought it back, packed it in ice we had bought, stacked the boxes in Chano's livingroom-bedroom, and agreed to begin the rounds at seven-thirty the next morning.

I had reached that point of exhaustion beyond sleepiness in which the body accomplishes was has to be done while the mind looks on dumbfounded. My duties for the day were not over, for I had promised to round up a hundred kilos of planting potatoes for Bernardo, an errand I had been engaged in now for some time. One variety or another was expected or had just been sold out in Puerto Real, in El Puerto de Santa María, in Jerez, while Bernardo kept changing his mind about what kind to buy and planting season was drawing to a close. Having confirmed during our brief stop in Jarana a rumor that potatoes were available there, I knew I should not let the opportunity slip, and braved once more that bastion of the *Guardia Civil*.

I purchased the potatoes nervously but without incident and delivered them to Bernardo's door along with a brief account of my first day in the fish trade. He went inside to deposit his change, then returned with the news that his son-in-law Julio declared I must sell no more fish.

"Why?"

"Because the license on your car is French and touristic. If they find you are doing business they might even take the car away from you."

"We've already bought three boxes of fish for tomorrow."

"So what? You cannot afford the risk."

Suddenly all my reservations and hidden fears and exhaustion and the rain gathered to cynosure in a moment of silence. "Agreed."

I returned to Chano's house with the bad news. The sky was darkening to a major outbreak. Chano was out visiting a cousin, so I sat down with his wife and children to wait. Water was rising in the public passageway off which Chano and his family lived with thirty or forty other people. Their apartment actually straddled the passageway, marooning the kitchen from the two bedrooms. Earlier in the day a series of stones had been placed in the water so that residents could get from the street to their doors, and Chano's family to their kitchen, but the stones too were now submerged. A few men went back and forth in hip boots while the women remained inside. Chano's wife wedged rags under the door to keep the water from seeping in. Suddenly the lights went out. There was a grope for a candle while the children shrieked and played in the dark. After an hour Chano returned.

Aware of his desperate situation I was prepared for him to be angry, but he took the news quietly. He assured me we could continue with no danger, and I refused to collaborate further. We sat in a quiet stupor. What should we do with the three boxes we had bought for tomorrow?

We could sell them at the morning auction in Chiclana, offered Chano, and not run into the problems we had faced in Puerto Real. If we made a dash before daybreak there would be few if any *guardia* on the road, and if we were stopped for any reason, we could just say I was doing a favor and had no business interest. They couldn't prove anything. I agreed to the plan and we arranged to meet at six-thirty the next morning.

It was dark by the time I arrived at the Bar Gallego to eat, still clammy and reeking of fish. The rain seemed to have stopped. Blas, who had directed us through the ruts and disentangled the mule from our path earlier in the day, was informing the regulars of my new career. Suddenly the rain burst back, and with a crack like gunshot the lights went out. Juan, the son of the owner, lit his cigarette lighter while I looked outside and noticed an unaccountable lurid glow in the sky. "Open the side door for me!" yelled Blas, dashing out into the rain. Juan lunged too late for the side door, for there was a scream of machinery, and in a spray of glass Blas on his motorcycle burst through the side door and into the alcove for dining. Juan swept up the broken pane by candlelight, Blas dried his motorcycle with the bar towel, and we resumed eating and drinking in the penumbra.

Back in the street I realized the lights were out all over town. The effect was hypnotic: the rain had stopped, low clouds lidded the sky, the walls of buildings pressed close, and wet pavement glistened in the streets like the beds of remote canyons. Two men with a flashlight approached and stopped to chat. Earlier in the evening they had seen two great columns of green light emerging from the fields. We joked about Martians arriving and I got into the car. A strange blue glow shimmered on the floor in front of the passenger seat. Keyed up by exhaustion and the night's accumulated strangeness, I experienced a moment of genuine terror—then realized the light came from a handful of *rubios* Chano had given me to boil for Og. I knew those fish were ugly, cheap and foul tasting, but hadn't realized they also glowed in the dark.

The alarm blasted me back awake at quarter to six. I staggered to the butane, made coffee in the dark and was in the Lung by six twenty-five. I turned the ignition: no response. The battery was dead. I gave the car a push backward down the hill to jump-start it. That didn't work either. I tried pushing it down the highway. It was no use. At seven-ten I arrived at Chano's apartment on foot. He shrugged as if this were our normal luck, then we climbed on his motorcycle and returned to the car to give it a better push than I could with one hand on the steering wheel. We pushed it halfway to Puerto Real. It still wouldn't start.

Chano went back to his house to sell as much fish as he could to his neighbors, while I went about getting the battery to a garage to see if it could be recharged fast enough for us to reach the Chiclana market before it closed. By the time I rounded up tools, removed the battery, found a friend to haul it to town and arrived back at Chano's house, it was already eleven-thirty. To my shock, he had sold nearly all the fish!

He counted the take: after expenses there was 144 pesetas—nearly two dollars and fifty cents—of clear profit. He grabbed a handful of change and we headed out for a bottle of wine. With a smile of regret for the business that could have been, we dissolved the partnership.

There was one last errand to dispose of: the three empty boxes from the last purchase needed to be returned to the market in El Puerto de Santa María. The next morning, after a restoring night's sleep, I had my friend with wheels pick up the battery, which had been left overnight on a slow charge. We hauled it back to the Lung, installed it, and I drove it back to El Pinar. The stench was overpowering, with pools of fish-steeped ice water brewing under the seats. Manolo, Luis and Skinny made the mistake of showing up for coffee. We pulled out the seats and purged every fish-soaked inch of metal with soap and brush for an hour.

Early afternoon I drove to Chano's house to pick up the empty boxes. His wife informed me he had already left for the market by motorcycle. Mystified, I loaded the boxes and continued to El Puerto de Santa María. I spotted Chano standing next to another surprise: two boxes of *rubios* he had just bought.

"What are you going to do with those?" I asked.

"Sell them in my house."

There was a silence of hard eyes.

"Let's get the boxes out of the car," he suggested, "and load in the fish."

"*Ai!* I spent the entire morning cleaning out the car. With three friends who will never do it again."

"I'll clean it this time myself when we get back."

"Look," I said, "I'm out of the fish business."

"I know. After this I'll take it on the motorcycle. One box a day."

When we got back the cleaning proved unnecessary, for the fish had not yet been packed with ice. We headed to a bar to toast the new one-man operation, and with a last gulp of sherry my career as a fishmonger was over.

8

Hoping not to be disturbed as I settled once more into indigence by the restaurant, I received another summons from El Pulpón. This time it was a Christmas cruise in the Mediterranean. At triple of the pay on the base, I would play the cocktail hour and dinner in the salon, debarking at ports of call: Alexandria, Piraeus, Naples, Barcelona . . . But what to do with Og? If I left him with Teddy and Flo, he might take off in pursuit of me, and no one else was in a position to take charge. I said no to El Pulpón and he issued no further summons.

I didn't mind that my compass was Puerto Real rather than the Mediterranean, for its very constriction penetrated me with new flavors. As I went back and forth to town on the trail along the railroad track, I exchanged greetings with men from the country who commuted on mules and burros, shrunken figures in visored caps who had pared *buenos días* and *buenas tardes* to a nasal *buená*, the last syllable drawn out as if on the oboe. Uninterested in cooking, I lived on thick bread I pried apart with my hands for the insertion of cheese or canned tuna, and most days I took a meal at the Bar Gallego, in the little room Blas had burst into on his motorcycle. The fish, occasionally nasty but usually just bland, frayed into a broth lumpy with garbanzos, but there was ample sherry to wash it down and I could always pacify my stomach with more bread. The family that ran the Gallego became close friends and their clientele didn't overlap with the Bar Central, giving me a second opinion on the gossip.

The wife and daughter who worked at the Bar Gallego were exceptions and I lived in an almost exclusively male environment. Women were in the streets, but in the company of each other, shopping or on the way to each others' apartment, and their presence nearly vanished after nightfall. Men filled the bars where my own social life took place, their voices dervishing through the smoke. In ratty black suit jackets over grey shirts, the rips discreetly stitched in black thread, they stood at the chest-high bars with their waists thrust slightly forward, leaving a little hollow at the small of the back—the endemic stance that bullfighters and flamenco dancers stylized into parody. Buying a round or settling up before leaving, these men without resources flung the heavy coins on the zinc bar with a clatter and barked to the bartender, *aqui, toma!*—here, take it!—as if in scorn of mere money.

As sherry went down and voices rose, the air rang with the word *maricón. Maricón,* one would yell, pointing. *No, maricón tu!* the other would yell, pointing back. They were calling each other queer amid much macho hilarity, often then to lob arms over each other's shoulders. Adolescent friends routinely walked the streets with their arms around each other, boys with boys, girls with girls, the boys sometimes reaching across with their outside arms so that they could also hold hands in front. The constant search for a light in a country where all men smoked was the occasion for intimate mock encounters, often with strangers. An older stopped a younger for a light, a tiny match was struck against a tiny box, and in its flare a stranger's face burst into bloom. As the older one muttered *gracia,* the younger invariably gave the faintest multiple flick of the eyebrows in a gesture of flirtation. Had the striker of the match just offered another kind of fire? Was that flicker of the eyebrow a way of putting the asker down? These exchanges were really clownery, of no consequence, and only showed a kind of self-confidence that could sport with ambiguity. As the product of an America that didn't know the difference between affection and foreplay, and that found a dark agenda in the freest same-sex gesture because it saw every spontaneity through the neo-Freudian prism of pop psych, I found the lightness liberating. This public affection, I knew, coexisted with a different kind of unnaturalness, a social separation of the sexes, and I was free to enjoy it because I too was male, not a woman cloistered in the house, or a foreign one hassled in the streets.

I relished, in fact, my insider-outsider status, reflected in the physical circumstance of becoming a social figure in Puerto Real while living alone in the pines a kilometer out of town. I enjoyed being, as far as I knew, the only American in this nondescript town of eighteen thousand souls—indeed, the only foreigner I was aware of. I was not interested in a community of outsiders, had no interest in expats running amok under volcanoes and sheltering skies, and was glad to have Puerto Real to myself. I even rejoiced that Puerto Real had no redeeming attractions, that outsiders found it ugly, that my friends in El Puerto de Santa María scorned my unaccountable attachment to the town. They only thought that nothing happened there. In reality, the tedium of Puerto Real led to one adventure after another.

On Sundays the social quintet cooked a prolonged meal—from mid-morning to late afternoon—in my quarters by the restaurant. I had replaced my little blue Camping Gaz burner, bought in a French department store, with a larger blue burner, also from France. Camping Gaz in assorted exchangeable sizes turned out to be what all of Puerto Real cooked on. Our standard entrée was the tortilla, a potato omelet, and I eagerly grabbed the knife and began peeling for our first creation.

Skinny exploded. "You're cutting away half the potato! Potatoes are expensive! All food is expensive! People don't have enough to eat!" Abashed, I learned to peel potatoes as if I were trimming fingernails. Skinny's outburst hardly reflected our own spreads, for we had usually amassed bread, ham, cheese, sardines, olives, sherry and beer to flavor the long afternoon—when it wasn't sabotaged by the French burner. There was no way to know how much fuel remained in the tank, and with stunning regularity we ran out of gas when the tortilla was runny, half cooked, and had to be abandoned.

Because my friends lacked wheels to see the countryside and our operation was highly portable, we converted Sunday meals into picnics outside towns within striking distance. Into the Lung we piled, one passenger in front, the other three with Og, the burner, the food and beverage crammed into the hold. No one ever objected when we settled in a field or streamside, and we cooked and consumed while gazing at Medina-Sidonia's white houses covering its hill like a snow cone, or at the stream outside of Benaocaz. Staring into the water, Sparkplug reached into his repertoire: "These two gypsies stole a pair of chickens and took them to a streambank, where they strangled and plucked them. When two *Guardia Civil* appeared, they threw the birds into the water. 'What are you two up to?' asked one of the *guardias*. 'Us?' replied a gypsy. 'Nothing at all. Just sitting here enjoying the fine weather.' 'Nothing, eh?' said the *guardia*. 'Then what is that pile of feathers doing beside you?' 'Oh, that,' said the other gypsy. 'There's a couple of guys in swimming and we're guarding their clothes.'"

My punishment for these idylls was to drive us all home after a day of sun and food and wine. While the rest gave in to their stupors, dozing as spent systems demanded, it was my chore to see us safely home, and more than once I trailed into irrational thought until my head snapped back, my eyes refocused in a stab of fear and my hand corrected the wheel before my cargo noticed.

We pored over the map and found a crossroad no one had heard of, one Nevero. We would throw our next picnic outside Nevero. Its five houses and tiny café were like a hidden discovery, and a strong, good-looking young man came by on a burro and asked if he could play my guitar. As soon as we heard his gravelly stammer we realized he was mentally defective. We invited him to join us and I handed him the guitar. He held it in reverse, his right hand lurching in random positions on the frets while his left swept in spasms across the strings in a mirror imitation of guitar playing. His voice fired off syllables with each fusillade of strums, speech that flew too fast for us to tell whether it carried meaning, his singing a volley of shouts peppered with silence. He happily shared our cigarettes and allowed us to take turns riding his burro, and I snapped a series of late afternoon photographs in which all of us, including Og and the Lung, appeared to have been painted by Velazquez.

Manolo took a close-up of our friend and we returned with it several weeks later. We found him in the tiny café, sitting propped against the wall and smoking. The men of Nevero glared suspiciously as we entered, strangers, warmly greeted the village idiot and handed him a picture of himself. He smiled familiarly, took the picture and held it upside down, sideways, inspected the blank side as carefully as the front, then started to hand it back. "No, no," said Manolo, turning it right and pointing to the face. *"Eres tu, eres tu, mira, eres tu!"* He stared again without comprehension, then a light entered his eyes, he rolled it into a tube and blew smoke through it, and grinned at us in delight.

When the road between Puerto Real and El Puerto de Santa María became my known beat, riders magically offered themselves, dislodging Og from the passenger seat. One such was Rodolfo, personable and well spoken, in his early twenties. His lively conversation soon turned him into my favorite hitchhiker.

Sparkplug, having occasionally spotted him getting in or out of my car, once said, "Don't ever give Rodolfo a ride without Og with you."

"Why not?"

"Because he's a gypsy."

I was mystified on several counts. "He doesn't look like a gypsy. He's taller than I am and paler than you. All the gypsies I've known have been short and dark."

"You mean, all the gypsies you've recognized."

"I didn't even know there *were* gypsies in Puerto Real. Don't they just come and go with the fairs?"

"There are two gypsy families in Puerto Real but Rodolfo is on his own."

"And why do I need Og in the car?"

"Gypsies are afraid of large dogs. They behave themselves. You don't want to pick up a gypsy without Og with you. Believe me."

When Teddy and Flo invited me and Og to the beach a few days later, I declined because Ramón was expecting me in El Puerto. "Og already told us 'e'd rather go with us, love," declared Flo. "You'll coop 'im up in the car and we'll let 'im run on the beach." Flo had penetrated Og's mind and I told him to go off with her.

As I was about to return from El Puerto late that afternoon, Rodolfo materialized in the plaza and asked if I would give him a lift. "Gladly," I replied. "Hop in." I was pleased that Og was not with me, ready to put Sparkplug's absurd prejudice to the test.

We left town chatting brightly of potholes and blind pedestrians, Rodolfo a model of decorum in the passenger seat. Road hazards thinned, the last curves dropped away and I accelerated into the straightaway between towns. With no warning or transition, Rodolfo suddenly engulfed me. His left arm was around my shoulder, his right hand was on the steering wheel, his left foot was on top of mine on the accelerator, the car was rocketing ahead out of control and I felt like I was being raped, murdered and supplanted by Rodolfo in the same convulsion. Adrenaline fought back, my own two hands tightened on the wheel, my right foot tried to kick off his while jamming the brake and I shrieked, "Stop! You'll kill us both!" My terror must have shot through his contiguous flesh, for after a quick final squeeze on my shoulder and jab on the accelerator he was back in the passenger seat, staring out the windshield as if nothing had happened. We continued in stony silence. I fixed on my driving with my heart still racing and let him out at the edge of Puerto Real, before sight of the citizenry. I never confessed this eruption to Sparkplug or anyone who knew him, and Rodolfo apparently read my sentiments, for I never laid eyes on him again.

Abel, the fine-featured Galician in his thirties who owned El Bar Gallego, had a strange growth between his nose and right eye. Raw pink darkening to dusky red at the tip, it had been swelling for three years until it had nearly attained the size of an eye itself, disfiguring his looks and cutting off the vision of his right eye looking left. The doctors in Cádiz had offered no more than ineffective salves, the threat of a painful operation that might not work, and hefty fees. Abel's last hope was a *curandero*—a healer, or herb doctor—who operated out of his home forty kilometers away, outside the hill town of Los Arcos. Would I drive him there in exchange for gasoline and free meals at the bar?

The *curandero's* house was hidden where the road curved to ascend Jews' Hill—named, Abel explained simply, for the people who murdered Christ. A squat lime-washed building shagged with vines and guarded by chickens, it lacked the antiseptic terrors of the doctor's office. As we entered, sunlight from the door picked out a few chairs facing each other.

A woman asked us to be seated. She withdrew and we stared at the unvarying fixtures of a house in the country: wooden table, chairs with wicker seats, a set of maroon iron pots on the wall, a Madonna, the foot of an iron bed protruding from a movable screen, a curtained doorway leading to another room. The *curandero* appeared.

He apologized for keeping us waiting. A small plump man in his fifties, unremarkable in an old coat, vest and frayed white collar, he gazed with kind but discerning eyes from beneath a broad-brimmed hat. Asking Abel to sit, he pulled up a chair in front of him and peered at the growth. Yes, he thought it could be treated, with a bit of bravery on Abel's part. It would have to be lanced, and a patch of herbs applied to draw out the bad stuff. At the word *lance* Abel turned white, but he gave the signal to proceed.

The lancing took place immediately, behind the *curandero's* quick hands. Abel maintained a nervous smile, exploding in an occasional *ay!* The doctor applied a cotton patch containing a poultice of herbs, offered Abel a cigarette, then dismissed him with instructions to return in ten days. We proceeded the last four kilometers to Arcos itself, where his wife's cousin, a *Guardia Civil*, lived in a cluttered apartment. The *guardia* was due at work and unable to find his gun, but he offered Abel a most welcome stiff shot of *coñac*.

We returned every ten days for the next two months, always proceeding afterward to the *guardia's* for *coñac*. After the lancing, the area of the growth swelled until it surrounded Abel's right eye. The *curandero* refreshed the poultice. After the third visit, Abel's entire face bloated and turned red, his lids puffed out and reduced both eyes to slits, and he was sleepless for three nights straight. The *curandero* listened calmly to these developments, then reminded Abel he had been warned that some discomfort might be involved.

The *curandero's* house looked like any other hovel in the country, but the yard was full of cars and taxis with plates from Sevilla, Cádiz, Jerez and many of the smaller towns. Most of the patients complained of ailments similar to Abel's: swellings, warts, tumors, inflammations, skin afflictions. One old woman had a lump on her wrist that was continually surrounded by flies, and she was convinced she would be cured if she could only keep them away. Once we entered just as a robust country woman was leaving with a pale-looking daughter on the verge of collapse.

"What's the matter with the girl?" I asked the *curandero's* wife.

"Nothing," she replied. "It's the mother who's sick. The girl is only frightened for her mother's sake."

The *curandero's* practice seemed open and straightforward, but its clandestine side emerged from conversations with patients. He had no license to practice medicine and his activities were highly illegal. His remedies were compounded wholly from ingredients he found in the countryside, recipes he learned from his father and was passing on to his son, secrets closely kept. The doctors would love to have run him out of business. He could cure many ills that stumped conventional medicine, charged far less, and only his local popularity kept the authorities from closing him down.

Bit by bit Abel's growth shriveled and by the last visit there was no trace of swelling. Within a year, predicted the *curandero*, the scar itself would disappear. For one hundred pesetas a visit—one dollar sixty cents, far less than he had already spent on doctors—Abel was cured. The *curandero* wasn't doing badly either, for just before our final visit he opened up a new bar in Arcos.

It was the topic on every tongue: a mysterious man had been hiding near Puerto Real for three days. For four days. Five. The lady who sold milk said his person hadn't been seen, only his footprints. The tobacconist said the mailman had caught a glimpse of him in the pines of Las Canteras, but he fled as soon as he realized he had been spotted. Manolo said everyone who claimed to have seen him or stumbled onto some clue was using it as a platform for the usual invention. But one could begin a conversation that week with anyone by the mere mention of "him," no further identification necessary, and the town was reduced to a single topic.

A picture—baroque, redundant, self-contradictory—took shape. He was twenty-seven years old. Blue-eyed. Overweight. He had been a professional soccer player. He was now working as an electrician at the dock. He was engaged to be married. He was under psychiatric care and couldn't stand the company of other people. He had gone out of his head after taking a reducing pill. Before he left the house he had placed his watch, money and identity card on the diningroom table. Bloodhounds were being sent from Sevilla. No, Madrid.

Variations crescendoed and peaked. Dogs never appeared. One had to identify him to talk about him. Then he slipped from the public tongue. Suddenly remembering two weeks later, I asked several people what happened. The answers were all the same: he had been found black and bloated at the bottom of a well, nine days dead.

At El Chato, the bar by Las Canteras, I had often seen the old drunk who danced and never paid for anything. Ordering a beer, he would toss it off, spread his arms and begin his famous dance, which looked like a vulture airing its wings. When the music stopped for more money, the old man would order another beer. Someone else who wanted music always primed the juke box and some Samaritan always picked up the old man's tab. One Saturday I watched the old man dance all afternoon in front of the gaudy chrome and plastic machine as, one by one, the groups left. At last there was only one table immersed in conversation: ours. The music stopped, the beer was gone, and the waiter asked the old man to pay up. He glanced anxiously toward us. My friends interrupted their conversation long enough to mumble something about the old man having pulled this once too often. Now it was time to teach him a lesson. We signaled the waiter, paid for our own drinks and left. Later that night, as we poured out of the movies, I spotted the old man across from the theater, weeping.

Manolo, Luis, Skinny and I were settled into the Lung and about to head to the movies in El Puerto de Santa María when there was a rap on the car door. It was Juan in his black suit with the monogrammed V on the pocket, with four others similarly dressed. The nightly taxi that took Los Vampiros, Puerto Real's single rock group, to their job at El Cangrejo Rojo on the other side of El Puerto had failed to show up and they would be held responsible for breaking contract, their fault or not.

I replied that we were headed to El Puerto anyway, so pile in. Some of them were carrying instruments, and by the time all nine of us were jammed in with the guitars, the driving was more like swimming fully dressed. The chassis nearly smacked bottom as we bounced out of Puerto Real's last pothole and it was a relief to reach the open highway.

I was easing off at sixty kilometers per hour, a reasonable cross between speed and safety, when the blackness coalesced into a horse and carriage. There was not a brushstroke of color, not a light, and the usual yellow spokes of this gypsy cab on its way to some fair were hidden by the rim of the wheels. One way or another, the gypsies on this stretch were going to do me in. I blasted the horn, slammed the brakes, and felt the momentum of our massed humanity hurtle onward barely diminished. I veered left, the car listed like a sloop catching wind, and I had no choice but to careen farther in the hope of staying upright. The horse and carriage fell past like a ghost ship, almost as if we had passed through it.

The held breath in the car broke loose. There were cheers, congratulations, praises to God, the cramped thumps of back-slappers, loud avowals of gratitude for my having saved lives that wouldn't have been endangered if they hadn't rapped on my door—and if I hadn't agreed to take them. Suddenly I broke into a cold sweat, my hands began to shake, and calm didn't return until the second icy beer had been directed into my hand at El Cangrejo Rojo.

Despite nodding off half drunk with a carful of passengers, a quasi-assault from a hitchhiker, and a near smash with a black carriage—any twist of which might have ended in tragedy, and not just for me—only rumor took the worst seriously. Rumor was an odd medium to deliver valid warning, for the spoken word was so freely adapted for entertainment, and conversation was so tailored to amuse, that invention often gathered sufficient zeal to challenge truth in open terrain. The day that El Bar Gallego closed because I took the family to visit relatives in the obscure town of Espera, for instance, it was reported that Abel's mother was dying and the whole family had rushed to her bedside in Galicia—despite the fact that the sister-in-law and the boy who worked in the bar remained home all day dispensing accurate information.

As a foreigner who had settled in town for no very clear reason, even to myself, I was clay ripe for this transforming touch. In the Bar Central, Manolo heard me variously unmasked as an artist, a spy, a seminary student and a crack young lawyer in town on an important case. I was in the pay of the CIA. I was researching a book on Andalucía, which put a utilitarian spin on my loud typing at the campground. I thought no version of myself could surprise me, but I was unprepared for the news of my demise from a house painter I was having lunch with at El Bar Gallego. We were talking about *salas de fiesta* and I asked him if he had happened to hear Starfis play at El Oasis last summer.

"Yes," he said, "they played very well. A sad conclusion."

"How do you mean?"

"Their all being killed."

"Killed! How could they have been killed?"

"In a car. They were on their way to a job, tried to pass another car, and were hit by an oncoming truck."

"But I'm a Starfis myself, and *I'm* alive. So are the rest. I've seen all within the last week in El Puerto. The drummer stayed with me last night at El Pinar. I'm on my way to pick him up again tomorrow morning."

No," he said, shaking his head and chewing sadly, "that is impossible. They've all been dead since October."

9

So spontaneous, so free to be eccentric was life in Puerto Real that for long periods I forgot I was living in a police state, under a notorious dictator. Without fear of consequence Starfis threw its picnics from the wee hours until dawn under the streetlight of its choice, and police merely showed up to banter as they checked us out and wandered on. The social quintet threw its own alcoholic picnics under the trees and by irrigation canals whose owners, identity unknown, never materialized to summon the law. Moviegoers gleefully locked the municipal cops into the lavatory as a *cachondeo* and the unlicensed *curandero* wielded his herbs with impunity.

The *Guardia Civil* visually commanded awe, striding in stern pairs in their heavy olive uniforms and their trademark three-cornered hats of black leather, but Abel and I went to the apartment of his wife's *guardia* cousin in Arcos after each change of poultice and found him forever addled and running late, in search of his gun or wrestling with his boots while maintaining a generous hand with the coñac. In the Bar Gallego I befriended and shared meals with a young man who was so gentle, considerate and even fundamentally shy that I was stupefied when Abel told me he was a *Guardia Civil* out of uniform. This mingling with Europe's most feared police, taming them and turning them to human beings, left me in doubt—was Spain a dangerous country or wasn't it?

When I remembered Spain's reputation for brutality, the very demystification heightened my anxiety. What was this casualness hiding? What should I be watching for? Where did risk lie?

These qualms, no doubt misplaced, arose a few days after the collapse of the fish venture, with the pungency of *rubios* and *sardinas* still rich in the car. The *guardia* I had befriended in El Bar Gallego invited me to attend the wedding of his cousin in Jarana, the little collection of houses where I had made my first fishmonger's pitch, where I had looked to Chano for courage because I knew it to be the home of several *Guardia Civil*, only to find him hiding behind the car. Not wishing to intrude on the ceremony of people I barely knew, I stationed myself at the back of the tiny chapel near the open door, where the shortness of the country people gave me a clear view.

As all craned to watch in silence, I saw three police cars pull up outside the door. This was, after all, a *guardia* hometown, but if they were friends and family of the betrothed, why didn't they come in? Suddenly the fear I had so recently experienced with Chano reasserted itself. These *guardia* were not here to attend the wedding; they knew that I had been illegally engaged in trade, had seen the Lung parked outside the chapel, and were ready to detain me at the conclusion of the ceremony. The service was brief but my alarm filmed it in slow motion.

At the conclusion, just as the guests turned to leave, my friend, in his usual civilian clothes, took firm hold of my arm, walked me out the door, greeted his uniformed colleagues politely but with authority as we passed between them, escorted me to the Lung and gave me instructions on how to reach the reception over several kilometers of back roads. Was this scene wholly innocent, with the *guardia* remaining outside because they arrived late, or couldn't observe a civilian ceremony in uniform, or simply found the chapel too crowded? Or was it possible that my friend was steering me swiftly through danger, assuring his colleagues that I was friends with one of their own?

In the absence of basic reporting, let alone the kind of shared overview reached elsewhere by analysts, commentators and news media even during the Cold War, views on such matters as the *Guardia Civil* were patched together from personal experience, anecdote and hearsay. "A cousin of mine," said a friend in the Bar Central, tossing off another *copa*, "was out hunting rabbits, several years ago now. He had a hunting permit, but a pair of *guardia*, perhaps saving the spot for themselves, told him he couldn't hunt. My cousin didn't see why not. He went home for the day but returned a few days later. He was caught by the same two *guardia*, who found him headed home with his rifle and a dead rabbit. For punishment the *guardia* made him eat it raw on the spot. The rabbit, as it turned out, was infected. My cousin became violently ill and died the next day. Several days later my cousin's brother returned to the spot. He hid in the foliage until the *guardia* showed up, and shot them both on the spot. He then removed his boots as a sign he was dying naturally as if in his own bed, and put a bullet through his brain." One didn't need to swallow the whole plot of a tale like this to believe in its atmosphere.

Guardia, I noticed, drank at will without paying, and though I never saw one drunk in uniform, it seemed a normal part of their rounds to pop into a bar for a beer or a *copa* of wine. I finally saw the owner of a bar tell departing *guardia* how much they owed, and I asked him about it. "Sure," he said, "I always tell them, 'That will be so many pesetas.'"

"How come they don't go to other bars instead?"

He shrugged. "Mine has the best wine. They come here even if it costs them."

"Don't they get back at you in some other way?"

"Of course. They know that in public they have to pay when asked, but the other day they fined me for throwing shrimp shells on the sidewalk."

"Don't the fines add up to more than the profit from wine?"

"Of course they do."

"Pride?"

He smiled a little contemptuously. "You might call it that."

Teddy had his own *guardia* story, not necessarily more reliable than anyone else's. He had visited a police station on a documental mix-up and was invited on a tour of the cells. "Those suckers were five feet square, so there was no way you could stand up or lie down unless you were puny enough to stretch out crosswise. You should have seen the slop they passed out for food once a day in a pail. And not even a toilet in that piss-complected place. Every two days they just hosed it down so all the treats washed to one end down the drain."

Og too logged in. A born cop hater, he unconditionally detested anything in uniform and whipped himself into a fury over mere *guardia municipal* directing traffic. But he saved his deadliest vitriol for the nightly rounds of the *Guardia Civil* through the campground, and Bernardo informed me gruffly that they would think nothing of silencing Og forever with a well-placed bullet. If I wished Og alive in the morning, I would be prudent to keep him attached by night.

Bernardo, as usual, was good for multiple perspectives. The *guardia*, he reassured, were severely disciplined by their own hierarchy and were dismissed at the first sign of abuse. "It is one of the most honorable systems in the world. Their function, which they fulfill, is to catch hardened criminals, to remove from society the *canalla* that endanger it. They are political only to the extent of uncovering occasional Communists who, in their wish to overthrow lawful government, are also, after all, common criminals. Strong police permit us the luxury of freedom. There are no *teddiboyce* in Spain because the Spanish police and a Spanish upbringing would not allow it. There are no packs of girls roaming the beaches, as in Italy and France, no teens gone berserk, sacking homes, burning cars. You can travel and pitch camp anywhere in Spain, unlike the rest of

Europe. Thanks to the *guardia* one is safe in the streets of
Spain, day or night. England and France and the United States
claim that Spain is not free, but their own people are not free go
about their business in safety. Where is the freedom in that?"

But it was always possible to go back to Bernardo for a
second opinion. Pouring us each a dark red glass of Valdepeñas
from a wicker-bound demijohn, he leaned forward, lowered his
voice and said, "There's a poem by García Lorca that you won't
find in the collections. It's about the *Guardia Civil* and it's the
one that got him shot." After a bracing swallow, he whispered,

> *Their horses are pitch black,*
> *With black the hooves are shod.*
> *Upon their capes reflect*
> *Stains of wax and ink.*
> *Incapable of tears,*
> *Those skulls composed of lead.*
>
> *With souls of patent leather,*
> *Along the road they come,*
> *Hunched over and nocturnal.*
> *Their whereabouts command*
> *A silence of black rubber*
> *And the fine sand of fear.*
> *They pass you, when they care to,*
> *Hiding in their heads*
> *A vague astronomy*
> *Of pistols in a blur . . .*

No one displayed overt fear in the presence of *guardias* any
more than they did when the *Levante* blew, but details were
telling. Only once was I stopped by the *Guardia Civil*, who
asked for my identification, seemed content with my driver's
license and sent me brusquely on my way. But my friends

reported being stopped regularly for their documents, particularly if it was late or the location was out of the way, and they lived in fear of losing or being caught without their identification cards. When I mentioned to Manolo how normal I found life on a daily basis, he reminded me of the price of tobacco. It was six pesetas—four cents—for a pack of Celtas. And look at the price of wine, which was set by law. Franco knew that the first step toward pacifying the citizen was to keep his vices cheap.

Franco himself, of course, was at the top of all this, and knowledge of him was subject to the same limitations. Personal experience of him was reduced to his official image, grim and pin-headed under his military cap, in every room of every public building. One would expect no personal anecdotes of the *Generalísimo* but I was actually treated to one, over the usual *fino*, by a man who helped round up deer for Franco to hunt. The animals were captured in the woods and mountains and the best of them were fed in an enclosure near the hilltown of Vejer, on the road to Gibraltar. Once a year they were let out and chased by helicopter to a field where Franco, installed in a chair, picked them off as they came. In the absence of further anecdotes, there were jokes. If Franco is at the helm, the *Guardia Civil* is on the prow, the priests are on the poop and the ship sinks, who is saved? Spain. And supplementing the jokes was graffiti. In 1964, to celebrate the first quarter century of the Franco dictatorship, the walls of public buildings were painted with the red capital-letter slogan 25 AÑOS DE PAZ—beneath which someone had often slapped, in shakier letters of a different color, Y HAMBRE. Twenty-five years of peace—and hunger.

Bernardo's double perspective continued. Franco retained power only because he was *muy suave*, very smooth, and to illustrate the quality he ran his palm over imaginary little waves. The Spanish were a peaceful race, but when provoked they rose to a very special savagery, not excepting the women. The Spanish Civil War was one of the most bitterly fought and thoroughly brutalizing experiences of modern times, and Spaniards feared a return of that violence even more than they feared Franco's police. Spain was a nation of individuals. Every citizen wanted something different and was willing to die for it. What they had most to fear was themselves. Franco retained power because he held a realistic fear of the Spanish character, and the unruliness of the Spaniard remained a check on his authority.

On a day when the *Levante* blew hot and dry, Bernardo got more personal. He had been born into a prominent family in Asturias, had embarked on a military career, had been dispatched to the Spanish colonies in North Africa, and over a period of twelve years had risen in the ranks. He endured intolerable heat, cholera, ravenous insects and the treachery of the Arabs without complaint. He met Franco when he first arrived, dismissed him as a loud pipsqueak, and watched with surprise his rapid promotions and appropriation of power. When Franco ordered Bernardo to execute a group of political suspects without trial, he quit. He bought farmland in Puerto Real, three years ago opened the campground, and here, amid the benightedness of peasants who hadn't mastered the Spanish language, he intended to spend the rest of his obscure life.

This patchwork of data about the police state was eclipsed for me by one overarching story from Sparkplug, who arrived alone one morning for coffee. The twins were working in the Bar Central, Skinny had been challenged to a high-stakes game of billiards and Sparkplug, having planned or not to tell me his personal saga, plunged into it like someone who had told it often before—sometimes, it turned out, to save his life. It lasted for two hours and whenever his cup ran dry, I boiled water for another Nescafé and served it to him without interrupting his flow. I was so caught up in the account's unfolding, even by what seemed to me a kind of perfection to the plot as narrative, that as soon as Sparkplug was gone I boiled up some more Nescafé, attacked the Smith-Corona and got down everything I could remember. By the end of a long afternoon it felt like I had retrieved all but the untranslatable Andalusian verbal colors of Sparkplug's voice:

I had served on the winning side of the war for five years, and when it ended I assumed my duties were over. I had not been a member of Franco's Falange but a Royalist, in favor of a republic under a constitutional monarchy, but we both fought what we considered our enemy, the Reds, and since the Falange was stronger than ourselves we willingly joined under their banner.

Of course we were not happy to merge forces. In my case the Falange and Royalist fronts had arrived at the same point beside a river, in their different uniforms. The Falange had a bag of their insignias for us to sew onto the left breast of our shirts, the cluster of five red arrows that is their symbol. Their captain handed the bag to our captain. None of us spoke; then our captain said, "Crabs belong in the sea," and tossed them into the water. All over Spain the Royalists refused to wear the uniform of the Falange, but they finally made a combination of the two, and even now traces of the Royalist uniform can be seen in our national uniform.

We never wore the arrows during the war, and in our hearts we remained Royalist, but we fought as hard as they did against the common enemy and many gave their lives. We thought military life was over with the victory, but then came the rise of Hitler, and orders for three more years of mobilization to protect the country from whatever might happen. I was already in my twenties, ready to begin my life, and was unwilling to let politics rob me of anything more. So after a few months I escaped from the army and headed for the mountains, where bands of the opposition were still holding out. Their only hope was to escape to France, and my hope was to go with them. I no longer cared whose side I was on; I was just a man in a desperate situation trying to get out. But I was caught on the way, branded as a deserter and sentenced to three years in a military prison.

They sent me to the concentration camp of Conil. There were many like myself who had tried to escape and been caught, and we were facing starvation. There was little food for the guards as well, and they took an unusually cruel way of giving us our ration—they merely threw it into our compound and let us fight over it. We lacked basic sanitation and had to perform all our functions in the compound.

But there was one who was much worse off than the rest of us. He was young, still in his teens, a Valencian rather than an Andalusian like the rest of us. He was cramped in a small solitary compound next to ours, given no food at all, and we were forbidden to give him any through the bars on pain of severe punishment. They knew of course that we would and were waiting to catch us at it, and meanwhile we could enjoy his slow death. His clothes had become rags; both legs of his pants were ripped so high that they were only shorts, and his shirt was in tatters. We were all deserters, but the reason for his special treatment was that we had fought for the Falange and he had fought for the Reds.

When it was completely dark we used to talk quietly back and forth, and one night I said, "I will get you out."

"How is that possible?"

"Don't ask me," I said. "But if you stay here you will die of hunger."

"That is certain," he said.

"We won't talk about it again, but be ready to move when I tell you."

The hunger was a danger to me too, for every few weeks one or two in our own compound died of starvation, and I intended to escape and take him with me. First I had to gain the confidence of the guards.

I began to talk to them during the day, just to be friendly, telling them about my experiences in the war, asking them about theirs, chatting about nothing in particular. Of course some were more approachable than others, but I made friends as best I could with the position between us remaining the same. Gradually a few took a liking to me. After all we had fought on the same side of the war, and my crime was no more than a peacetime desertion.

One day I asked two who were particularly friendly whether I might spend an hour on the beach, to bathe and wash off the filth of the compound. They did not seem particularly upset by the request, and the next afternoon they let me spend an hour in the sea while they stood watch, one with a rifle, the other with a machine gun. It became a daily event, and every afternoon I played in the waves, cleaned myself, chatted with them and gained more confidence before they returned me to the compound. There was no way to escape and I had no plan; I was merely looking around, taking in everything I saw, scanning for whatever I might seize on.

During the course of our conversations I let it be known that I was a crack shot, which happened to be true. Gradually they became eager to see me shoot, but were afraid to let me try. Finally they could stand it no longer and one day they took me far down the beach, beyond sight of camp, where nothing could be heard over the sea, and handed me the rifle. I made no move to alarm them, but merely shot at some white birds in the distance, felling one with nearly every shot. We began to have shooting contests. I usually won, but they didn't resent it. They respected me for it.

I became better trusted by more guards and started asking for more privileges: to warm myself by their charcoal fires at night, to use their latrine instead of the one in the compound, to smoke a cigarette with them. They used to do me special favors unknown to the rest of the prisoners, to give me a few bites of hot food if they had enough, to pass me a cigarette to enjoy while the others were asleep, to let me out for this reason or that. I was careful never to take advantage, and was under continual armed guard in any case; but gradually I became familiar with the camp and all their routines.

Finally I had my plan. I whispered through the grill to Fernando, "Be ready at ten tonight."

"What are we going to do?"

"Just what I say."

At quarter to ten, when the rest were already asleep, I whispered to the guard, "May I make a quick trip to the latrine?"

He was guarding the common exit to the compound. Without speaking he came to the door, unlocked it, let me out and locked it again. Then he whispered, "Make it quick!" and resumed his crouch by the pan of hot coals where he warmed himself.

I went to the latrine by the prison wall, spent the expected amount of time and returned. I crouched down beside him. "Mind if I warm myself a minute by the fire?" I said.

"No," he said, "that's all right."

"By the way," I whispered, "I happen to know that one of the guards put four potatoes under the kitchen coals around sundown, to eat on duty later tonight. I don't know if they will still be there, but if they are that's two for you and two for me." It was a lie, but in times of hunger men will believe anything about food, and steal what they can in secret. Potatoes would be hard to resist.

"Don't you go," said the guard. "I'll do the looking." We both knew that he ran no risk of my escaping, for the fire was just around the corner and I would have to run across a long

courtyard and climb over the wall; by the time I was halfway across he'd have sent out an alarm and I'd be caught. Still, the fire was around the corner and I knew it would take him a little time to sift through the coals and decide what was a potato and what was merely a piece of coal, before he figured that someone else had gotten the potatoes first. I had just enough time to enter the barrack, slip back the bolt of Fernando's cell and let him out. "Don't make a sound. Stay hidden," I said, and quickly went back to where I was leaning over the fire.

The guard came back and crouched opposite me with his rifle between his knees. "They've already been eaten," he said.

"Well all is not lost," I said. "One of the guards gave me a couple of cigarettes this afternoon. If you don't mind, I'd like to smoke one with you and warm myself a bit before I go back in."

"Fine," he said. I produced two cigarettes from my overcoat pocket and handed him one. He bent down to the fire to light it from a hot coal. In that moment I threw the rifle out of his knees to the ground with one hand and lunged forward and caught him by the throat with the other. He tipped over backwards and I tightened my hold with the other hand, pinning his head back so he couldn't talk. I have to laugh. I was a real terror in those days.

"Listen," I whispered. "Fernando and I are leaving tonight. He's out of his cell now. And you will let us go peacefully. Because if you don't, think what will occur. When you sound an alarm and have us caught, you will have to explain that you let us out of our cells. It will be worse for you than for us. But they change guard every hour. When they find we're missing in the morning, they will never know who was on duty when it happened. They can pin nothing on you. Understand?"

I felt the pressure of his nod against my hands. I put my foot on his rifle, then let him go and picked it up in one move. Fernando had followed my whisper through the open door and came out. "Go to the latrine wall," I said. "There are flat stones along the bottom. Pile them high enough to jump up and catch the top of the wall, then crawl over and wait." He left and I said to the guard, "You will put the stones back in place after we leave so the next guard suspects nothing when you go off duty." Then when Fernando disappeared over the wall, I said, "Here. Take your rifle. Fernando is already outside, and you'll be in enough trouble for that whether they catch me or not. There is nothing you can do for yourself but let us go." He watched me silently with his rifle in his hand while I jumped from the pile of stones and hoisted myself over the wall. On the other side I took off my military overcoat, gave Fernando a smaller coat I was wearing underneath, and we ran into the night.

We made it to the road between Vejer and Chiclana. I still had my complete uniform, for though a prisoner I was still a member of the army. But Fernando had only the overcoat I had given him, which did not cover the bottom of his bare legs, and his street shoes were eaten away. And neither of us had papers. We might have passed without notice from a distance or at night, but it was suicide to be seen.

Still, we had to get as far as we could, quickly; had to take a chance. We made our way parallel to the road, out of sight, and came upon a mail truck which had stopped. While Fernando hid in the shadows I went up to the driver, waited for him to finish urinating, and asked if he would take us as far as Chiclana. He would like to, he said, but it was a government truck and he wasn't allowed to pick up riders. I thanked him and walked away as he got back into the cab, then as he started the motor I scrambled up the back to the top of the trailer and helped up Fernando. We lay flat on the top. The road was even worse in those days and the truck went slowly. We seemed to lie there forever, and I kept thinking the driver would stop and we'd be discovered. But we made it safely though Chiclana to the other side.

About two kilometers beyond town the road meets the road from Cádiz to Sevilla, and at the intersection there was a control, as there is now, where all the trucks had to stop for inspection. But just before the control is a river that cuts across the road, and as the driver slowed we threw ourselves from the truck as lightly as we could. We landed bruised and dizzy from rolling on the pavement, but in our state of exhilaration we felt nothing. We crept under the bridge and collected ourselves.

When we had rested, we waded the ravine around the control, under the bridge to San Fernando, up to our knees the whole way. When we were beyond view of the highway we climbed up and saw San Fernando across the field a short distance away. Our only hope was to get on a northbound train from there, but dressed as we were, without papers, we didn't dare be seen in town.

We snuck up to the station. It was two in the morning now, and there was no one around. We waited near the tracks until a freight pulled slowly through. As it passed we leapt on the ladders that led to the top of the baggage cars. Again we found ourselves lying flat on top, this time a car apart. The train stopped in the field outside Jarana and I longed to get off, to see my parents, but knowing the chatter it would cause among people I grew up with, I didn't dare. We remained on top as the train pulled through Jarana, past Puerto Real and El Puerto, and on toward Jerez. When we approached Jerez I signaled to Fernando that we were getting off. We lowered ourselves down the ladders, waited for a flat place, and jumped.

Our destination was my aunt and uncle's farm, a few kilometers outside town, and we made our way through the fields to their property. By then it was around three-thirty, and I wanted to arrive as if it were a normal visit and not arouse their suspicions. We stretched beneath some trees a little way from the house and slept until dawn.

At sunrise we descended to the house. They knew that I had been in prison, but if they thought I escaped they might have acted suspiciously. I told them that we had been treated well as prisoners because we had fought for the Falange during the war, and we were given a two-week leave before we had to return to camp. I had no intention of staying two weeks; I merely wanted a little time to rest and think, for I had no further plans. I told them Fernando would be staying with a rich Valencian in town.

It was true about the Valencian, a man Fernando had known from childhood, who had settled on an estate in Jerez and was locally respected. As we counted on, the man took Fernando in when we arrived later that morning, and we arranged to meet on Calle Sierpes in town next day.

Calle Sierpes was a street entirely inhabited by gypsies. All that has been cleaned up since, but in those days you could buy and sell anything you wanted. The gypsies were, still are, entirely without shame, and will jump at a quick profit. We needed to get rid of our military clothes and disguise ourselves as people from the country, and after we met we approached a young gypsy on a burro. "How much will you give me for an overcoat?" I said.

"Are you crazy?" he said. "If they catch me in a military coat they'll give me a fine I couldn't pay in ten years and throw me in jail for dessert."

"Not to wear this way, idiot. Look at the thickness, the fineness of this material. You could make a splendid suit jacket out of it, and it would be strong against the cold as well. All you have to do is cut off the bottom, change the buttons and dye it blue. No one would ever recognize it."

He paused with interest. "What's it worth?"

"Five hundred pesetas."

"Try a different joke."

"That's what I paid for it, stupid, not what I'm selling it for."

"All right. What are you selling it for?"

"Two hundred."

He bought it for a hundred fifty.

We bargained off Fernando's coat as well. We entered a store and I sold the rest of my clothing, and we outfitted ourselves with old but decent shirts, overalls and boots. By the time we left you wouldn't know us from peasants in the fields.

I explained to my aunt and uncle that we had bought civilian clothes because we had two free weeks and wanted to forget everything military, and didn't want to show our papers every time we ran into a guardia. It was close enough to the truth that they believed it. Fernando and I arranged to meet in the Plaza General Mola in three days, which would give me time to rest and think. I spent the time on my uncle's farm, puttering around, helping with chores, catching up on sleep. I realized our only hope was to join the rebel bands in the sierra, as I had tried before, to make it to France.

I listened to local rumors. The bands were becoming more and more desperate as the government forces moved in on them, and ever more dangerous. They pillaged for food, lived in the few houses but mostly in caves, and even the guardia were growing frightened as they slowly closed in. Our only hope was to make it to Paterna, which faces the mountains, and somehow smuggle ourselves through the guardia into their territory.

Fernando and I met briefly in the square. I told him of the plan, he agreed to it, and we arranged to meet at the same place next day, ready to take off. I told my aunt and uncle that I felt rested and was leaving to visit my parents in Jarana. Fernando told the Valencian that he was going with me to Jarana. We were leaving with a plausible story and no suspicions.

As I waited for Fernando in the square next day I happened to see a member of my regiment who had stayed on after the war. I'd hoped he wouldn't see me, but it was too late. He was *grinning as he approached. "Taking a bit of a chance standing here, aren't you, José?" he said.*

"Then you've heard."

"Of course. They're looking for you in San Fernando and Chiclana, where I'm stationed, but I don't think they've sent the search this far north yet."

"You on leave?"

"Just three days."

"Have they figured out how we did it?"

"No, but they've thrown all the guardia *that were on duty that night in prison until you're caught so they can make you tell which one let you out."*

"You won't say anything . . ."

"Of course not. Good luck . . ."

A few minutes later Fernando arrived in the square. He was walking a girl's bicycle. I felt myself turn furious.

"What the hell is that for?" I said.

"To help us get away. It's a long way to Paterna, and with this we can get there faster. We can take turns peddling and sitting in the middle, steering."

I stood there speechless. *"You spent half of what was left over from your overcoat money for this thing? You bought it?"*

"Of course I didn't buy it. I only paid five pesetas. I rented it. For one hour."

"Then you have to return it."

"Return it, hell. We'll just take it."

"But how did they even let you rent it? You always have to show papers to rent a bicycle."

"Sure, they asked for my papers. I told them I didn't have them with me. I said I was a cook for the military barracks here, that I went to buy potatoes at the market and they were out, and I had to go quickly to the country to get some."

"They believed that?"

He shoved the bicycle in my direction for an answer. "Without any papers how can they ever know who took the bicycle?" He was smiling.

I felt like strangling him right there. When I helped save his life, I expected a least a little intelligence in return. "So after getting this far you want to jeopardize the whole thing by stealing a bicycle. Is that possible? They catch us for this and find out we've escaped from Conil."

He looked annoyed, as if I were making us late for lunch. "I rented it just after one o'clock. I've had it two hours already."

I grabbed it and we walked at a fast pace out of Jerez.

The road from Jerez to Arcos climbs through fields and olive groves. From two anonymous peasants we became two clowns balancing on a girl's bicycle. We went slowly, watching for guardia, and when we saw them we hid in the undergrowth by the roadside, hardly breathing until they passed. I knew from before where all the controls were, and we skirted them on back lanes through the fields.

We got to Arcos and took the road to the right, toward Paterna. When we were halfway there we dropped over the crest of a hill, and there was a guard station I knew nothing about. Because we were getting close to the sierra the guardia were probably doubling their number. We were already seen. There was nothing to do now but keep going and hope we wouldn't be stopped.

We passed the control, braking slightly, and gave the guardia a salute.

"Stop!" one of them yelled.

We kept going.

"Stop!"

The bicycle gathered speed down the slope.

"Stop or we'll fire!"

We pedaled fast onto the straightaway and shots rang out behind us. Whether they were shooting to kill or merely to

scare us I don't know, but we kept pedaling until we were out
of range.

We continued fast for two or three more kilometers, then I
jammed on the brakes. "Look, our only hope now is to get rid of
the bicycle. All they have to do now is radio ahead to the next
control and have us intercepted. Without the bicycle there's a
chance, just a chance, that we won't be recognized."

"No."

"What do you mean, no? What is there about this bicycle
that we have to get killed with it?"

"We've almost no money. We'll need money in the sierra,
where it's worth twice as much. We can sell the bicycle in
Paterna."

"Give me this thing!" I grabbed it from his hands and
heaved it off the road into a stagnant pond. It sank until there
was just one handlebar sticking out of the water.

"You can do what you like," he said, "but I'm going on with
the bicycle." I watched in disbelief as he waded into the pond,
fished it out dripping with mud and water, and wheeled it back
onto the road.

By now we were close to Paterna, after which it would be
a single dash to the mountains and safety. We hadn't eaten
since Jerez, it was unlikely that we would find much food in
the mountains, and it seemed reasonable that we spend a little
of what we had left for food. It would be dangerous to go into
town, but I knew of a little store in the fields above, where they
sold to farmers, and there should be no problem. I said only one
of us should go, in case the news had arrived of two people on a
bicycle. Fernando offered to go alone on the bicycle, and I was
so sick of both him and it that I let him go, knowing even then
that it was a mistake.

If anything happened to Fernando, the last thing I wanted
was to be outside where I could be seen. I went to a farmhouse,
spotted some bushes in back to hide in if I should need to, and

knocked on the door. An old lady answered, and I asked if I could come inside and rest for a few minutes. I told her I'd been let out of the military in Valencia and was making my way without money to work on my uncle's farm in Jerez. Seeing my condition she believed me and sat me down to bread and hot coffee.

Fernando, it turned out, arrived at the store, bought bread and some dried fish, and nobody paid much attention. But also in the store was a man who was fairly well dressed and looked like he might have money. Fernando approached him and asked if he might be interested in buying the bicycle. The man looked it over. "Looks in good shape," he said. "How much do you want for it?"

"Two hundred fifty pesetas."

"Cheap enough for one in such good condition. Actually I've been looking for a bicycle. Christmas is coming up and my daughter wants one very badly. But are you going to be here for a while? I have only a few pesetas on me at the moment."

"Well, actually I'm on my way to Medina, and need the money now. I should get going soon since I'll have to go on foot from here."

"If you can just wait long enough for me to go home and get the money, I'll buy it from you now."

"All right, I'll wait that long."

The man, of course, was in the pay of the guardia, and made the rounds of places people gathered near the mountains to prevent just the sort of thing we were doing now.

So I waited endlessly in the house of the old lady. It was getting more and more difficult, not only because of worry about what was happening with Fernando, but also because I had told the lady I only wanted to rest a short time. I kept the conversation going, asked her about her life, about the weather, anything to make it natural not to leave. At one point she looked out the window. "Are you expecting anyone?" she said.

"No, I'm traveling alone."

"*Because there is a young man on the way here, and with him are six* guardia, *two of them on horseback.*"

Without further word I pushed open the back window and jumped out. The guardia *were still fairly far down the hill, and there was a possibility they might not see me run into the shrubbery. Of course it all depended on the woman.*

When the guardia *reached the house she was outside to meet them.*

"*Is there anyone here with you?*" *I heard one of them say.*

"*No,*" *she said,* "*I'm alone.*"

"*Has anyone come by today?*"

"*Yes, a stranger came by to rest for a bit. He left a short time ago. I didn't know there was any trouble.*"

"*Then he must be still near here,*" *said the one to the others. With their pistols and machine guns raised they entered the house, then poked around the yard and beyond. It didn't take much to figure that the only hiding place was the bushes, and one of them saw me immediately.* "*He's in here.*"

They circled the bushes with their weapons raised. "*Come out,*" *they said.* "*There's no way to get away.*"

"*But I haven't done anything.*"

"*Nobody who hasn't done anything has to hide in the bushes.*"

I came out. "*It's just that I saw so many* guardia *that I got frightened and wanted to avoid any possible mistake.*"

It was useless, but I didn't know how much Fernando had told them and didn't want to reveal any more than necessary.

"*Where are your papers?*" *they demanded.*

"*I don't have them with me.*"

So we finally made it to Paterna, along with the Guardia Civil.

We spent ten days in the Paterna jail, which was just somebody's house used for a jail during the war. The guardia *still didn't know we had escaped from Conil, since we didn't have any identification, but we couldn't prove who we were or that we owned the bicycle and they held us on general suspicion. It turned out that Fernando at first said nothing to the guardia in the store, but they told him they knew there were two people with the bicycle, and that I would be caught anyway and it would be much worse for him if he lied. So he led them to me. After learning that I never spoke to him again, even though in that jail there were just the two of us in the room. But the window was open onto the street, people stopped and talked through the grill, women brought things to eat, and we were better fed than any time since the war. I remember that the people of Paterna were very fine.*

From Paterna I was sent to jail in Jerez, and Fernando to a jail in Valencia. By then of course it was known who we were, and we could only await the result. In any case we had escaped starvation in Conil and had no reason to regret what we had done.

I was transferred from Jerez to a succession of prisons in San Fernando, Cádiz, Chiclana and finally Madrid. In Madrid I waited over a year in jail for my trial to come up: in Spain you can spend that long waiting so that even if you are found innocent, or guilty of something with a ten-day sentence, you have been punished for a year. At the trial I told the whole story, since there was no reason not to, and I was sentenced to three years and six months. I spent two of those years in prisons outside Madrid, much of it in forced labor. Finally my sentence ended and I was brought before an examining committee. I was free, they told me, totally absolved of further punishment for the crime, and only had to report once a week for a year to the prison board in Madrid to show good faith. Also there remained one further unpaid crime: that of selling a military overcoat for less than its cost. I would have to pay a fine equal to the coat's value, five hundred pesetas. I replied that I didn't have five hundred pesetas, that I didn't know anyone who could lend it to me, and I would have to go back to prison by default.

"That may be so," said the examiner, "but you must pay the fine within a week or accept the alternative."

At that time my old regiment was paid their weekly wages. Wages are only half a peseta, as they still are, just a device so that Spain can say it pays its troops, for the only real payment is in daily necessities. But that night my friends explained my situation to the rest of the regiment, and each chipped in with his half peseta. The amount came to two hundred forty-five, just less than half, but the captain picked up the rest. They met me with it the next morning, I paid the fine, and the board presented me with a parchment with the complete details of my story, a list of all the time I'd spent in prison, and a concluding statement absolving me from any further punishment for crimes mentioned therein.

For the first time in ten years I felt free, and I returned to the normal existence that was all I'd wanted from the beginning. I was forced to remain in Madrid because of my weekly appearances before the prison board, but I found work there, fell in love and got married. We stayed there several more years, had children, then moved to Jarana to be near my parents.

One night when I came back from work my wife greeted me very quietly and asked if something had gone wrong.

"Why?" I asked.

"Because two Guardia Civil came by the house today asking for you. You are to present yourself at ten tomorrow morning."

I was calm, but calm. I had served time for everything that had happened before and was more than careful since. There was absolutely nothing they could want me for. As proof I carried with me the paper absolving me from everything.

When I arrived I was thrown in jail. I asked what the charge was, and they said I'd find out when my trial came up in Jerez. I waited three months.

When the trial came up, the accusation was bicycle theft.

I couldn't believe it. "But I didn't steal that bicycle. Fernando
stole it! I didn't want any part of it. I thought it was pure suicide to take it."

"There is no proof of that. The bicycle belonged to a rental
shop in Jerez. It was later found in the possession of the two of
you when you were caught in Paterna."

"But the paper I was given when I was released in Madrid
excuses me from any further punishment for all that happened
then."

"For escape from the camp at Conil, yes. For the incidental
theft of a bicycle, no."

I served one year in the prison of Jerez.

Three more years I lived a normal life with my family in Jarana.
Then once again my wife met me when I returned from work
saying the police had come, and this time she was pale as a
sheet. I presented myself the next morning. It turned out that the
police in Jerez had sent to Valencia for Fernando to try him for
his part in the bicycle theft, and Fernando was missing. Since
I had helped him escape years before, I must be doing so now.
I would either inform them where he was or remain in prison
until he was found. I had no news of Fernando since they took
him away from Paterna, and was personally indifferent to his
very existence.

I was held in jail for five months, then taken to the court in
Jerez. "Tell us," they ordered, "the exact circumstances of the
theft."

As I had done so often before, as I am doing now, I repeated
the story detail by detail. And this time I added that I didn't
know where Fernando was but would like to, only for the simple
pleasure of killing him with my own hands for all the trouble he
had caused me after I helped him escape from starvation.

This last pleased them a great deal in the courtroom. What
I didn't know was that Fernando had been caught, was in the

next room overhearing everything I said, and that my story co-incided with his exactly. They brought him in as I was taken out, and as our paths crossed there passed between us a look which shot straight through me. In that moment I realized how much of my life I'd thrown away on a total stranger.

Since that day I've lived peacefully with my family. I may be getting older, Bru, but I think the war for me is finally over.

10

One afternoon came a hard rap on my door. I opened it to confront an enraged Chinese lady. "Are you the owner of that horrible dog?" She spoke in clear English.

"I have a German shepherd."

"Your animal just ate my steak. I bought it in Gibraltar and it was the first decent piece of meat I've seen since Hong Kong. The old man in the office said the person accountable lived down here in the restaurant. Of course you must replace it immediately."

"I can sympathize," I said. "I'm a beef eater myself and the cuts in Spain are a lot less than I'm used to."

"I don't want your sympathy," she snapped. "I want a steak to replace the one your dog ate."

"I'll try."

I went up to Bernardo's office to ask what to do.

"*Nada*," grumbled Bernardo. "She left it on the ground with dogs around. Whose fault is that?"

"I already promised I'd try. Is there a market still open?"

"On Saturday? At this hour? Try Chiclana."

Chiclana was twenty-five kilometers away but I reached it just before closing. I explained to the *carnicero* that I wanted a piece of his best beef, so thick, demonstrating with my fingers. He started slicing a thin one.

"No," I objected. "Not five thin ones. One thick one. All one piece."

"Nobody eats it that way," he replied coolly. "You can't and I'm not going to slice it that way." He proceeded to slice four more thin ones.

On the way home I began to sum up the lost time, the burned gas, the energy squandered on anger and caprice, and the lady did seem more and more stupid to leave her prime steak out for grabs. She was menaced not only by Og but also by the two resident mongrels left by the gypsies plus the revolving zoo brought in by other campers. Meanwhile, it was past dinnertime. It was a long time since I'd had a decent piece of steak myself. By the time I returned to the campground I was starving.

I fried the first two in rapid succession, wolfed the first, and was about to share the second with Og when I remembered he had already eaten more than the rest of us would. I knocked on the lady's door and held out the remaining beef.

Her face congealed. "That does not remotely resemble what your dog ate."

"Tough," was the reply I thought of too late, but in any case it would have been some time before she could appreciate the pun.

Og did not always eat so lavishly, but he did live high on the food chain before Patrick and I discovered how dogs in Spain were fed. Finding no canned dog food and corrupted by years of walking into supermarkets, even drug stores, and finding a spread marketed for a pet's humanized palate, we treated Og to tins of stew, cuts of meat, viands no local dog would sample except by theft. We horrified the staff of the San Roque campground by emptying a can of *callos*—tripe in a seasoned tomato sauce, a treasured Iberian specialty—into Og's bowl, and it was an interesting sidelight on our own perspective that despite the elegance of the sauce and the fancy price, we considered it appropriate for dogs because it sounded so bad. Still more scandalous, we obligingly paid sixty pesetas—one dollar—to a butcher on the day of our arrival in Puerto Real for "food for the dog," the cause of much merriment when I later confessed it to the social quintet.

It was soon apparent that dogs in Spain were sustained by what was left over or unfit for human consumption. Og ate American when Teddy scored kibble at the PX, and when kibble ran out he subsisted on free scraps from the market. But just as the canine national dish in the United States was Gravy Train, in Spain it was chicken bones, a dog food considered by Americans second only to strychnine. When kibble and market scraps ran out, Og thrived on chicken bones.

Og didn't care what fueled him. Running to embrace every smell and stimulus, his encompassing zigzag resembled a unified field. As traffic sped through Puerto Real on its twin slots, Og lowered his head and charged the catwalk for pedestrians as if bowling a strike. A terrified old man once stepped into the street just in time to avoid a collision, and was only spared by a lapse in traffic from being run over by a truck. I worried that Og might kill someone and get deported.

Og's response to beasts of burden was untested on his arrival in Spain, but he blankly ignored all horses, donkeys and burros, from the car and on foot. When he was in possession of the Lung, the sight of another dog would turn him into a fury of bared fangs, but once when the social quintet flung the door open with the car parked, the motor running and Og in full snarl, he dropped his head in chagrin and pretended not to notice the several pairs of hands urging him out the door. On foot he ignored other dogs whenever conceivable, complied with the niceties of bottom-sniffing only when pressed, and dodged encounters with his species like an American avoiding fellow tourists.

Rodents, chipmunks and lizards were his greatest delight, and the faintest disturbance of dry grass could set him prancing from pose to pose, braced and puzzled as the creature under scrutiny slipped away without risk. One needed only to point

to a random patch of terrain and remark in a terse undervoice,
"Og . . . it's a lizard . . ." or "Og . . . it's a rat . . . GET IT!"
and he would leap and freeze, pounce, give chase, then collapse into a look of familiar betrayal. Yet "Og . . . get the kitty"
produced a vague and wondering gaze toward the sky. Had he
confused kittens with birds? Or did they climb the nearest tree
whenever they caught sight of him?

While Og did chase cats over our helpless shouts of protest,
the end result was usually no more than a little quick exer-
cise. Once, however, when Teddy returned from the PX and Og
needed distracting from an overweening interest in the Gravy
Train, Teddy pointed without looking and yelled, "Og, get the
kitty!" To our collective horror, he had pointed at an actual
cat. Og, instinct and command in unusual conjunction, was
launched like a cougar. "Og! Come back!" Teddy, Flo and I all
yelled. The owner of the cat, a fellow camper, charged over and
confronted Teddy. "You bastard! You cruel malicious son-of-a-
bitch!" Teddy stared tongue-tied at the cat owner while Flo and
I watched Og in breathless dread. Og and the cat circled and
looped around the campground in a dead heat. At last there was
a fusion of stopped fur in a field beyond the cut grass. The cat
lay on its back with Og's paw on its neck, hissing and spitting
in Og's face. They remained motionless and Og seemed caught
in a misty concentration. It was so prolonged that I began to
wonder what went through his brain. *Is this victory?* perhaps
he was thinking. *Is this all? Is something further required of
me? Some goal?* Was it possible, in that stare of consummated
aggression, that he was looking deeply into himself? There was
no peering into the interior of that existential moment, but we
were all relieved when Og lifted his paw and sauntered sadly
away, the cat fled, and Flo and I defended Teddy to a camper
who lacked Og's conciliatory nature.

Og's relation with humanity was always more of a collabo-
ration than a dependence, and in the security of El Pinar his

parallel existence took him farther afield. He seemed aware of the perils of the highway, and I had no more than a mild curiosity about his lengthening disappearances. Then came news from Bernardo: the bitch two ranches toward town was pregnant.

The small ranch, with its scattering of chickens and goats, turned out to be the domain of two ladies who invited me in for tea. The older—fiftyish, stout, sheathed in black—had a baritone voice and level humorous eyes that seemed amused at all situations while the other—more shapely and brightly dressed, some fifteen years younger—extended that cheer. "Yes," said the older with mock disapproval, "your German shepherd has been having a little sport with our girl. We usually charge a fee for such liberties . . . ." As the repartee became bolder and the Andalusian more colorful until it veered beyond my grasp, it became apparent that the ladies were supplementing their income from hens' eggs and goats' milk.

The crowning surprise, however, was not the profession of the ladies but the identity of the bitch: she was a full-blooded American-born German shepherd, complete with papers, who had been left in gratitude by a client from the naval base at Rota. Patrick had told me that Og, whom he had bought by answering an ad in a San Diego newspaper, had come with papers declaring him a pure German shepherd, which Patrick proceeded to lose—and given Patrick's truthfulness and carelessness, I believed it. Used as I was to Og's ingenuity, I was nonplussed that at a ranch of dubious repute in the Andalusian countryside he had consummated a union that could have been blessed, with due registration, by the American Kennel Club.

I returned often to banter with the ladies over tea and follow the pregnancy, and we were frequently joined by a young Guardia Civil they referred to as *el Niño*, who occasionally disappeared with the younger lady into the back room. From that strategic crossroad, news of the issue spread up and down

the line. The ladies reported that requests for pups came from
Cádiz and Sevilla. The chief of police of Puerto Real wanted
one and could not be refused. Two of my own friends asked for
pups, and I was promised two males in payment for Og's services. My enduring mistake was not to take a pup for myself,
but at that point my hands were already full with father.

I took Ramón to see the expectant. As we approached the
house, a large grey Mercedes pulled into the drive. Ramón
pulled me behind some bushes and motioned me to be still.
A large self-assured looking man parked and walked into the
kitchen. "That's Amalia's father!" he whispered. Amalia was
the fiancée of a guitarist with the group that was reforming
around the dying Starfis, and her father was manager of the fish
market in El Puerto where Chano and I had bought our stock.
The potential for scandal was large.

Ramón and I quickly withdrew and later I returned alone.
The older lady invited me in with a penetrating look. "I saw
you earlier, when the car pulled up," she stated in her baritone.
"That man is extremely important in El Puerto. Pivotal. You
must not say anything. The repercussion would be terrible. *Nos
gusta el focki-focki.* Some wine?" The spark returned to her
eyes and we clinked to discretion.

Despite the mounting excitement, I had unspoken doubts
about the impending whelp. Og had fathered one litter before,
in Aspen: one pup was born dead and the other had lived but a
few hours. The problem could have been the mother's, but Og
was cryptorchid, possessed of a reticulated testicle. Skinny had
noticed it right away. "Og has only one ball!" Bernardo woke
me gruffly one morning and told me to go immediately to the
ranch. When I arrived there were eight perfect pups.

The dogs grew swiftly into sturdy, strong, lively animals,
and several developed coats of burnished silver like tarnished
mirror, more lustrous than either parent. By the time they were
given away or perhaps, on the part of the ladies, sold, several

were already larger than Og or the mother. It was an unexpected disappointment to watch none grow to maturity.

Of the six distributed by the ladies, I saw none again. One of my own choices was lost to view when my friend moved elsewhere. The fate of the other was sadly visible: his owner had apparently only wanted him as a gesture of friendship on my part, or for mistaken status, and perhaps in the misconception that a puppy involved no obligation. He was fed little, exercised seldom, and left heartless days in a dank, reeking bodega, tied to a barrel of sherry. He hardly grew after he was taken from his mother, and when I went to reclaim him, my friend told me the dog had disappeared. What disappeared was more likely the courage to live.

Yet however sad the dispersal of that litter might be for many on both sides of the Atlantic who have wanted descendants of Og, not to mention myself, there was no sense in the euphoria of the moment that the litter was to be Og's last. And from the standpoint of subsequent generations of the Andalusian dog, doubtless it wasn't.

11

Over one of his first coffees at the campground, Luis informed me he was having the padre make me an amulet of Our Lady of Carmen to wear around my neck so that if disaster struck I wouldn't be dispatched to Hell. One dawn a couple of months later, after I had been picnicking all night with Starfis, Manolo woke me an hour after I had crawled into the sleeping bag. What steps was I taking to turn myself Catholic?

"I just got to sleep!" I protested.

"Why are you so touchy, considering the consequences?"

"Go! Come back when I'm up." When he maintained his crouch outside the tent flap, I lobbed a shoe at him in a manner meant to be playful, yet persuasive.

While I was playing a gig in Jerez several months after that, a nightclubber probed my background, then asked if I didn't get mad when people called me Protestant.

"Why?" I asked.

"Because it's such an *insult*."

In what was now over a year of living in Spain I had inspired only those three irruptions of the Word, far fewer than I expected. Sparkplug and Skinny never mentioned the Beyond, nor did Bernardo, and as for my friends in El Puerto de Santa María, the Holy Spirit had entered Mick Jagger, not Jesus. The only truly religious

person I had encountered was Flavio, the Starfis singer, but he
was so swamped by the melodrama of aspiring toward monk-
hood while singing in a whorehouse that it never occurred to
him to redeem someone else. Nor was there ever a follow-up
from the twins. During Sunday mass they were at the campground, helping prepare our afternoon feast. The lobbed shoe
had found its mark and the dread amulet never appeared.

The religious baggage I carried to Spain was, in any case,
light. I never mentioned that the Protestantism I grew up in was
Christian Science, whose tenets would have disqualified me as
a rational being. Looking back on childhood, I could see that
I had tried to hold onto Sunday school theology in the way one
clings to the atmosphere of a dream, even when that dream is
not entirely pleasant—but it was hard to believe in the non-ex-
istence of matter when the tweed I was forced to wear itched on
my neck. In my first encounters with the college bull session,
Mary Baker Eddy's assertions, already stretched thin, burst
like a soap bubble. The joys of unbelief were fortified by books
circulating the dorm. I sympathized with the protagonist of
Somerset Maugham's *Of Human Bondage*, club-footed Philip,
who had sat through long services "when every limb itched for
movement" and, once disabused, "could breathe more freely
in a lighter air." His relief was echoed by Leslie Stephen, now
chiefly remembered as the father of Virginia Woolf, who wrote
of his loss of faith, "I did not feel that the solid ground was
giving way beneath my feet, but that rather I was being relieved
of a cumbrous burden. I was not discovering that my creed was
false, but that I had never really believed it."

Even though, like Maugham's Philip, I "lacked the religious
temperament," I thought I should at least learn about other
religions, even allowing them to persuade me if they could,
and I duly made the rounds of New Haven church services.
Mass, with its darkness full of candles, its acrid censers and
its chanting in Latin, appealed to my taste for the exotic, but I

was put off, as always, by the agony on the cross, the flesh and blood we were supposed to partake of in what struck me as symbolic cannibalism. There had to be something wrong with a religion that had organized around a meat rack. Protestant churches offered the boredom of Christian Science without the vaporous metaphysic, and though their crosses were only intersecting planks, I could see the tortured flesh hovering like a watermark where horizontal and vertical met. Judaism wouldn't let me in. My favorite flavor was Russian Orthodox, a whiff of pre-revolutionary Russia with its screens of saints unburdened by Western perspective, their stylized, dimensionless faces framed by dinnerplate haloes—effects that summoned Yeats's "Sailing to Byzantium," a poem I had learned at the time that the home of my imagination settled into Durrell's *Alexandria Quartet*. Even as I sampled churches I realized that I was embarked on religious tourism, not seeking, and that organized religion didn't interest me any more than team sports. Perhaps atheism needed to be disguised socially so one wasn't taken for a monster, but as far as I was concerned the choice of creed, like the gender of one's beloved, merited a grand existential *who cares?*

Spain, whatever the secularity of friends, was an insistently Catholic country and it committed me to more religious tourism. If I was an achieved atheist, I was only an aspiring writer, and I felt I should be exposed to everything if only to have experience to draw on. I popped into churches and found them to be empty, or dusted with figures that were middle-aged to old, female and dressed in black. Inquiring over sherry in the Bar Central, I was told that Protestants and Jews were now permitted to practice their witchcraft freely if they avoided public display. Jokes about lecherous priests were standard fare and a crane operator told me that the Church was the Devil's Iberian castle. Unperturbed by such cynicism, the Mother of God, cushioned in gilt, watched over nearly every home and

sometimes over every room. From the music syndicate to the
train station, the meat rack hung in every government office
flanked by dictators. Over the sweating bodies of the ironworks
floated the Virgin. On every postcard spindle Mary competed
for stardom with the comely bullfighter El Cordobés, regular
size and jumbo. During Holy Week, the climax of the liturgical
year, with or without Child, she was shouldered lifesize through
the streets.

The most famous Holy Week celebration was in Sevilla,
and Patrick and I had found ourselves in town for it while
evading our doom in Africa. Famous Catholics were said to
have converged from all over the world, and we spotted Teddy
Kennedy when he was gifted with both ears at a bullfight.
Patrick wasn't interested in Holy Week itself, and I left him
to read Rimbaud at the campground when I headed daily
downtown. It's one-hundred-twenty processions of costumed
penitents and shoulder-borne floats all intersecting and over-
lapping, Holy Week played out its symbolic drama of the
Passion from Palm Sunday to Easter. Pedestrians poured
through the streets; traffic came to a halt. Those who could
afford it bought bleacher seats, while the rest craned from
packed sidewalks and mobbed intersections, seeing little of
the hooded penitents that suggested to me a rainbow-hued
Ku Klux Klan. Peering through fellow members of the mob,
pedestrians caught glimpses of Jesus, Mary and the saints
bobbing overhead. Bands of brass and drums beat out modal
dirges more chilling for being vaguely out of tune, while the
holy figures glistened with gold, silver, silk, lace and gems. I
jostled with the crowd for an occasional flash of painted skin
crusted with glitter, and sensed I might be moved in some way
if only I could see. As spectacle it quickly grew all alike and
it was soon obvious that Holy Week in Sevilla was, *in excelsis*,
a tourist attraction. I would be more likely to witness citizen
immersion in the mysteries if I were the only tourist.

Settled into Puerto Real, I realized that one didn't have to
wait for Holy Week, for processions occurred at random intervals throughout the year. One March morning when the
town was breathing a quiet due to relief from transport trucks
blasting their way through donkeys and pedestrians, I came
upon an unexpected crowd. Above them, a pale apparition,
rode the Virgin on the shoulders of schoolgirls in simple blue
and white uniforms, singing a soft hymn. Her shiny plaster face
was jelled in a maternal smile and the crowd stared as if at an
adored aunt.

She was followed by a band of schoolboys in Muslim robes,
giggling as they shoved each other out of line, then an orderly
band of girls in dark uniforms. Next came the first of three
floats, a pickup truck arched with a lattice of palm fronds that
shaded a dozen children near the age of twelve. Elegant and
serene in back stood two genuine Blacks, the first I had seen in
Puerto Real, while at their feet a small Spanish girl with enormous hooped earrings parodied them in blackface. Next to her
squatted a girl yellowed to an Asian pallor, eyebrow-penciled
with angry crowsfeet and a cruel drooping moustache: a jaundiced Fu Manchu. A raven-haired girl in buckskin stood next
to the Blacks with shoe-polished cheeks and a single feather
poised above her leather headband. Gathered at random were
a small leprechaun with a green suit and a peaked felt hat, a
teenage Franciscan in white robes and a rope belt, a girl in a
white habit, a small girl in a common white street dress and
finally an adult nun, no doubt there to keep order. Thinking
this might be Brotherhood Week, I turned to the man next to
me and asked if he knew the occasion. He shrugged, bored:
"*Una procesión.*"

I could see ahead to the third float containing children
in peasant costumes of Central and South America, but the
second float was boarded solidly on the sides, with a mysterious
backdrop behind the cab so that its burden wasn't visible until

it had passed. But you couldn't miss the laughter that exploded like a breaker as the crowd saw into its sanctum, nor could you avoid collision with the many others who followed in its wake without wasting a glance on the poor Latin Americans.

The truck was lined with red velvet. Seated to either side on sumptuous red benches were eight miniature archbishops, and raised to an eminence on a velvet throne, flanked by twin sets of golden keys, further hoisted by a monumental overstuffed pillow and surmounted by a golden crest, sat a four-year-old pope. His thumb and forefinger pressed into a delicate oval and the other three fingers fanned out like wingbones, he made the sign of the cross with the air of a gastronome informing the waiter that this was, indeed, the wine. About his air of containment hovered the suggestion of a smirk. He stared at the crowd provocatively, as if about to demand something of them, then motioned them forward with the faintest of gestures. The crowd surged, howling, and the pickup hauled him around a corner.

When I intercepted the procession several blocks later, he had tasted popular acclaim. Too restrained to overplay his role, he studied the crowd with a vague smile, as though he found them mildly amusing as long as they kept their distance. He let their shouts reach the breaking point, then made a sign of the cross too fast to follow. He studied their faces as if watching the result of a chemical experiment, and a slow smile spread over his lips. He made a long, intricate, drawn-out cross, then three quick ones, the merest blur. The sidewalk went wild. A man leapt into the truck to take pictures and three grinning priests shouted advice from an open doorway.

Suddenly the pope removed his crown and shook loose his unruly black hair. He glared at his worshippers defiantly, daring them to make him put it back on. Slowly he let it settle, making it clear he assumed his office only by choice. He made one stately, majestic, canonical cross to accept the public acclaim, then the floats veered off in separate directions, the crowd dispersed and quiet rolled back through the empty streets.

In my desire to observe, if not penetrate, the Catholic mysteries, I had in mind such imponderables as communion, mortification, transubstantiation and resurrection rather than the mysterious parody of a religion's own trappings. Transubstantiation into laughter was religion I understood. Puerto Real's Palm Sunday procession was a hilarious contrast to the dirgelike observance a year before in Sevilla, but I didn't imagine that even Puerto Real would play the actual Passion as farce. Still, during the build-up to the biblical weekend, the only change in citizen behavior was that members of Puerto Real's single rock band, Los Vampiros, were doubling their time at the pool tables to earn extra spending money for towns they were to play during their Holy Week tour of the province.

The procession on Tuesday night was bleakly impressive, a commemoration of Christ's climb to Calvary. A crucified Christ was carried through the streets, pausing in front of fourteen illuminated altars representing the fourteen stations of the cross. There was little gilt and no music beyond the bare roll of the drums. At each altar a priest delivered a brief explanation of the station and its relevance to daily life, then the procession's followers repeated a section of the litany in Latin. The simplicity seemed classic, and could have been involving if friends hadn't materialized from all sides to ask if I'd heard that the old drunk who danced to the juke box at El Chato, never paying for the music or the wine, had been hauled off to jail for the night to give him a good scare. Should we take up a collection and bail him out or let the lesson sink in? A glance around confirmed that anyone who was not a matron looking fierce stood no chance of dodging the debate about the dancing drunk, dueling volleys embellished with wit, tangential gossip and friendly insults. Even though the chatter was ultimately about mercy, I gave up on religion and had a *caña* of beer at the Bar Central.

Wednesday night there was no procession in Puerto Real, so I drove to El Puerto de Santa María to catch the last of theirs. It seemed treasonous to set foot in that town without stopping first for Ramón, but I couldn't share this mission with a rocker sensibility. The Virgin, back from her tour of the streets, was about to scale the cathedral steps. Like all such effigies in elaborate settings, she lay heavy on the shoulders of her bearers, their anonymity under the brocade draped from the sides only betrayed by the chance flash of a sneaker. By now the men were exhausted and more than a little drunk, and this was their most demanding maneuver. The crowd shouted *Up! To the left! Heen! Heen!* as if directing a tug of war. The Virgin wobbled and rocked precariously step by step to the top, turned and came to a rest facing her onlookers. An old man broke into a *saeta*, literally an arrow, a wailed seizure of adoration, his falsetto quailing passionately in semitones. Several men shouted *olé*. The Virgin backed into the cathedral, unexpectedly stopped, returned to the step and dipped forward in a wooden bow. The crowd burst into applause. She moved back, returned, dipped again and received another ovation. With what looked like a last curtain call she withdrew for the year.

The next night I made a point of getting to Puerto Real just as the procession began, in hopes of seeing it before I ran into irreverent friends. No luck, for just as I caught a glimpse of Jesus bobbing between the walls two blocks away, I was grabbed by a welder who had already had, by his estimation, seven beers. As I steered us toward the crowd he regaled me with calamities at the boatyard, then asked if I knew that the dancing drunk had spent the night in jail and, now sprung, was cavorting again without paying at El Chato. A still drunker friend that my boatyard companion was trying to shake, a drunk's drunk, caught up with us, shouting *olé* as the Virgin went past. The welder was concerned because it looked like any moment the other might break into loud flamenco, which might incur a steep fine

for himself and, worse, bode ill for anyone with him. When the
drunk's back was turned we ducked into a bar, a tenable move
since I wasn't seeing much of the procession anyway.

After a quick beer I mentioned wishing to return to the procession. No fear, said the welder, we would have an unmolested
view right from the door. After two more beers I heard the bray
of advancing trumpets and stationed myself on the curb, but
by the time the Virgin arrived, a friend of a friend was trying
desperately to engage me in a conversation about whether it
was easier to learn Spanish or Italian. The Virgin stopped for a
rest, the velvet cloth beneath her went up and several roguish
faces grinned out. I exchanged jokes with a couple of regulars
from the Bar Central, sweating in old shirts and jeans as if they
had been caught in a *cachondeo* that was getting out of hand.
The cloth went down, the Virgin groaned up and the drinking
resumed.

It was one o'clock by the time I next saw the procession.
I had moved on to the Bar Gallego and was getting unsteady.
Drums sounded, hooded penitents passed, the Virgin glided
forward and Jesus tottered in the distance. A third of the clientele went out; the rest drank on oblivious. A group of women of
all ages followed the Virgin in black dresses and head cloths.
Some were barefoot, no doubt fulfilling a promise of penitence,
and with a couple of exceptions their features were serious,
even tragic. If there was an authentic look on the face of Holy
Week, this, for a sobering instant, was it.

Did the procession always choose to rest in front of a bar or
did Puerto Real offer no alternative? Drunken onlookers gossiped with drummers and trumpeters. A couple of penitents
ducked inside, lifted off their hoods, shook their hair briefly free
of their sweatbands and bought bottles. "Join us," shouted one
who knew me, "there's plenty to drink!" Desire for experience
warred with my own drunkenness and distaste for religion and I
blurted, "I can't!"—then instantly regretted the lost opportunity.

As they rushed back to the float, friends slapped them on the back with a conspiratory *Te la beba!*, a friendly taunt meaning *May you drink it!* A small boy passed a bottle of coñac under the Virgin just before she lurched forward once more.

The drinking redoubled, and when someone down the street began singing a *saeta* I was the only one to duck out and listen. The younger men, restrained in their flirtations earlier in the evening, were shouting, "*Ai*, you're a gorgeous cunt!" As I left for the night, a garrulous old drunk was still holding forth. "The Virgin of Puerto Real is the most beautiful in the world. It's wrong to make comparisons between saints, and I won't, but next to the Virgin of Puerto Real, the Virgin of San Fernando is worthless."

By the climax of Holy Week on Saturday night, I'd given up looking for any mysterious dark powers and accepted an invitation to Jerez from two friends whose stated intention was to get drunk. Our mission was accomplished within the first half hour and we barged noisily into the crowd, one friend paying obscene compliments to every girl of passable appearance within range. I still naively thought we might enrage the rest of the spectators, but it was a crowd we couldn't very well stand out in. A soft drizzle began and the procession gradually gained speed until it nearly ran through the streets. Suddenly the Virgin flew by on twenty-four pairs of revealed sneakers. When we returned to Puerto Real, we learned that the procession had been called off because of a downpour, and one man complained, "You pay all year for a good show and then don't get to see it."

During Holy Week post-mortems at the Bar Central, I was told that the frivolity of Holy Week in Andalucía was far different from the piety and solemnity of the North. One man made the point that God is not necessarily best celebrated with a long face. Another told of the procession in Sevilla in which the followers of La Macarena, the gypsy Virgin, sing and shout her praise en masse. He watched a young man who stood entranced before an image of Jesus, his black locks streaming over his sweating face. He stretched out his arms to Jesus, his features in agony, and cried, *"M'cago en tuj muertoj qu'erej bonito!"*—I shit on your dead but you're beautiful! The point most generally made, from which there was no escape, was the baldness of the hypocrisy. Having given birth to a savior who asked us to sell all we have and give to the poor, the Mother of God was shouldered through the streets in gilt and velvet, dressed in brocaded silks, crying crystalline tears. The man who told us to beat our swords into plowshares rode through town flanked by the Guardia Civil bearing bayonets. It was hard not to be cynical when this same man on the cross, who died that we may be redeemed, was bleeding rubies.

By default, my touchstone for serious religiosity remained Flavio, the Starfis' St. Anthony, who drank too much and acted drunk when he wasn't, who danced a wild and spidery twist, who squeezed a love song to the last quiver of melodrama then growled into a jazz lyric like a dirty sax, who mimicked the King of Jazz to his very shadow, who envisioned girls in dreamscapes of moons and still rivers that collapsed into cascades of adolescent profanity. One picnic near dawn he told us:

"I was sitting before the altar one evening praying, which I did from time to time, being a good Catholic. I was singing in a club then, involved in the olive business by day and engaged to be married. All I wanted was for everything to go on just as it was, and I directed my prayer to the box under the cross where a bowl with the bread, the Body of Christ, is kept. Suddenly I heard a voice speaking to me. There was no one around and I was frightened. But the voice continued and I listened. It was telling me to give up the cares of this world and come to Christ. I didn't know what to do but I left the church feeling changed.

"I went to my girlfriend's house, as I always did. As soon as she saw me she said, 'What's the matter? Is something wrong?'

'No,' I said, 'nothing's wrong. What could be wrong? It's just me.' 'No,' she said, 'you didn't kiss me when you came in. You're cold, you're not Flavio tonight.'

"It continued that way for two months. I went to see her every night while she became more and more worried and I kept denying everything, telling her nothing had changed. But the moment I stepped out of the church that night I didn't love her anymore. I knew there was only one direction for me, only one I wanted, and I finally told her. She cried much, said that life would never be the same for her, and wished that all would go well for me if that is what I wanted.

"In four months I go to Sevilla to begin my studies. In nine years I will become a *sacerdote*, a priest. I am through with this world and don't want any part of it unless I can help my fellow man. I still have my mother to support so I keep singing and selling olives, but I am doing it only for the money, not because I enjoy it. My mother receives a small widow's pension because my father worked for the government, and she says it will be enough if joining the Church is what I want. Meanwhile, I am studying the catechism and the history of the Church, and only wait for the day I can head for Sevilla."

12

The absence of godheads in my life left, as far as I could tell, no gap, for much else—classical music, revered literature and, above all, the natural world—lifted me beyond myself. I thrived in Spain without those secular miracles as well, for I neither heard nor made classical music, I barely read, and I had no contact with wild nature as I knew it in the United States. I went on no camping trips and my only hiking trail followed the railroad track to town. To the east lay the mountains Sparkplug had tried to escape to with his callow friend and the girl's bicycle, but they were hunched blurs, kilometers off, and no one cared to explore them with me. The land around me was flat, an expanse of geologically recent lake deposit that dipped below sea level to form the Bay of Cádiz. Since no one was interested in the sierra, I tried to stir up curiosity about a blank area on the map. Stretching northward to the Portuguese border, it lay between the towns of Huelva, Sevilla and Sanlúcar de Barrameda and appeared to represent the delta of the Guadalquivir. This mysterious triangle was labeled *marisma*, swamp, and the map had filled it with schematic plants that looked like five-pronged yuccas. On a Sunday sherry-drinking excursion we drove to one of the triangle's points, to sample some manzanilla in Sanlúcar, the town that made it. Standing near the mouth of the Guadalquivir, on the spot from which

Columbus launched his third expedition to the New World, I gazed across at the low vegetation and sprinkle of white buildings, and asked fellow members of the quintet what lay beyond.

"Just *marisma*. Just swamp."

"But isn't the swamp interesting?"

"Interesting? It's *swamp*."

"Is there a way to get there?"

"You can't cross the river. You might get there from the Sevilla side on some little road, but there's no point because there's anyway nothing to see. It's just swamp."

Forced to give up any notion of fleshing out the schematic plants, I let nature invade me subliminally by living in a pine grove. The wind seethed in microtones and unknown birds flashed through the shadows. Lacking binoculars or any knowledge of European species, I let them call to me in gibberish or vaguely penetrable corvid. And I knew I was still on Earth, for often I saw the black-and-white streak of the black-billed magpie, identical in Spain and Colorado—the all-purpose, global magpie. As for encounters with wild species, I had a memorable one in Puerto Real and another in El Puerto de Santa María.

One morning as I was blinking awake over coffee, a tiny face like a bright green Winston Churchill appeared in front of my nose. A wooden stick and a brown arm led to Skinny's grin. He had brought me a chameleon.

We named him Hon Bie-nay, the Andalusian pronunciation of John Wayne, and Skinny told me that to keep him as a pet I should wear him on my shirt, where he wouldn't fall off, rather than suffocating him in a jar. At least for the morning, I did want to adopt the little green creature scuttling between cups of coffee.

The most notorious local fact about chameleons was not their shifting colors but their weakness for cigarettes, a spectacle I had heard about but not seen. Skinny had just lit up a Celta and suggested we give John Wayne a drag.

Fear for my new friend lost to curiosity. *"Como no?"*

Skinny picked up the chameleon, squeezed his mouth open and plugged in the cigarette. The chameleon darted around the table waving the white tube like a flag. The cigarette was half his own length and he puffed it like a fiend. His eyes were fired coals on their tiny green cones and his mouth revealed a cavern of ferocious white pricks. He slowed down and began to wobble. He was getting drunk. Skinny was laughing uncontrollably while my own amusement was short-lived. "Maybe he's had enough," I suggested.

"Nah, he'll sleep it off."

The chameleon staggered to a halt, his face darkening. Skinny removed the cigarette. Bits of loose tobacco clung to the mouth. Skinny tried to pick off the tobacco with the paper end of a match, but the chameleon clamped down as if Skinny were trying to steal his favorite toy. "Wash it out with water," I offered.

"Chameleons don't drink water."

"But maybe it would get the tobacco off."

Skinny took him to the washroom. When he returned, the chameleon's head was an ugly lump of carbon. Skinny set him on the table and he dragged himself along with a bent, darkening body. The half-paralyzed claws on one side dug in vain for a grip on the oilcloth, and the claws on the other side couldn't reach past the distended belly. Small puffs of smoke still curled from his mouth. For a fleeting moment I wondered whether this was how they made monster movies. The end appeared close. "Do you think he'll pull through?"

"Ah, he'll sleep it off," Skinny reassured me.

By now the chameleon had stopped moving entirely. He lay curled on one side, his beady eyes closed. "Is he dead?"

Skinny touched the tail and received a faint response. "No. We'll put him in the bushes for a while." Skinny laid him under some shrubbery. We parted the foliage and looked down. He was entirely black, a lump of charred meat, the small replica of a smoker's lung. He looked the same an hour later. I touched the tail: he was inert. It was the end of John Wayne.

I realized the ubiquity of this trick one day when we were walking through Las Canteras. A group of children were showing me how they set traps for small birds. A five-year-old who was looking for ants to use as bait found a chameleon instead. He put it on his shirt and fondled it, folding his arms and swaying as if to make a cradle.

"Give it a Celta!" shouted one of the older children.

"Let him keep it, idiot," said the boy's brother.

"No, let's see it smoke."

"Yeah, give it here, give it here!" chorused several more. The little boy glared.

"Quick, who's coming over there?" snapped the oldest child, and when the little boy turned to look, the trickster grabbed the chameleon.

Soon the chameleon was steaming bug-eyed in a circle, puffing frantically, turning black as John Wayne. "Whoo whoo!" shouted one child. "He looks like a train."

"He's getting drunk!"

"He loves it."

"*Que cachondeo!*"

The lit end of the cigarette was nearing the mouth. "Leave it in! Leave it in! We've never seen that before."

A circle of heads bent around the expiring chameleon. The first flake of burning tobacco touched the mouth. The strange green face remained stoic as the color darkened. Bit by bit the whole flame entered the mouth.

"He'll die."

"Of course he'll die."

By now the flame was consumed and nothing emerged but wisps of smoke. One of the children grabbed the chameleon by the tail and tied it to a barbed wire fence between the pines and a cotton field. Another child took aim with his air rifle and blew the head off.

"Hit him again!"

The boy fired again and the body separated. "Hey, let's see if we got anything in the traps," shouted another child and they were off like a flock of starlings, leaving the lower half of the chameleon to swing by its tail in the morning sun.

I tried to remind myself that children all over the world behaved like this—some sort of urge from the brain stem, the instinct to mutilate, kill and move on, was universal, and Spain was only adding its coloration. And as with other children of the world, all Spaniards didn't all grow out of it. For weeks Diego and Manolo, the guitar-playing brothers of Starfis, had invited me to go bird hunting instead of picnicking some night after work, and I knew I would have no peace until I consented. I was more numb than usual by the time we finished the last set, for I was just drying out from a cold, the sky was stormy, and every fiber rebelled. My own urge to new experience, no matter how unpromising, found me dutifully changing clothes, and by 3:00 a.m. we were loaded into the Lung.

We picked up a couple of the brothers' friends, started north on the road to Jerez, then pulled off on a two-lane track through some trees. Low branches brushed the car in the darkness. As the surroundings turned mysterious, I started to get into the mood. We stopped in a grove of young eucalyptus, doused the lights and piled out. The air was dank and fragrant.

Flashlights were taped to the barrels of our party's two lead-pellet rifles and Diego trained his upward, scouring the branches overhead. We moved slowly so that Manolo, on braces, could keep up. Suddenly Diego excitedly touched my shoulder. "See that!"

I followed the shaft of light and located a sleeping finch. There was a quiet pop and the finch fell to the ground with a thud.

The trees were loaded with birds that were picked off one by one by Diego, Manolo and their friends. Birds continued to sleep on the branch where their fellows were killed. Other birds flew off, wounded, beyond range of the flashlights, and chirped in the darkness. A few more swung around when they were hit and hung upside down by their dead claws. Now and then a bird seemed to sleep peacefully through all the pellets fired at him, and one of the brothers' friends would mutter, "What's with him? Is he having a little *cachondeo* with us?"

A gentle rain began and I retreated into my coat as the hunt continued. There was a sudden cloudburst and a mad dash to the car, with Manolo struggling on his braces to keep up. *Cojones*, the night was over too soon! Diego totaled the catch: thirty-three finches in all, at least a respectable hors d'oeuvre salted and fried in olive oil. But this was nothing. Once they had stayed out all night and bagged nearly twelve dozen. Some night when the band didn't have to play we would see if we could beat that record. Of course we would have to stay alert, for hunting this way was illegal and the *guardia* didn't mess around.

It was dawn by the time I returned to the campground, warming at last to Franco's police.

At El Oasis the next night I went up quietly to Diego when he was alone, said that I had enjoyed our jaunt to the country, but wasn't the bird population put at risk by so much indiscriminate shooting? Diego immediately struck back. Hadn't I seen how many birds there were? How could we dent such multitudes? Besides, Manolo was crippled. This was a way he too could enjoy nature. Should the handicapped be deprived of the privilege? My question, which I had tried to couch with tact, was apparently rude enough that I missed the invitation to next Sunday's sherry with finch, despite being compliant chauffer for the hunt.

As the putative owner of an animal, I was always alert for human threats to Og. The conventional Andalusian response to an unknown dog was to sizzle a rock to its feet while shouting *fuera!*—go away. The dog's response to an unknown Andalusian was to slink sideways, then bite if the spirit moved. This cycle perpetuated a race of furtive and semi-vicious dogs that justified further rock-throwing, further bites. My life's only dogbite was delivered by Charlie, the stray deposited by the gypsies at El Pinar, an alumnus of such schooling. But German shepherds, I noted, commanded a fair amount of awe, and Og had transcended his own category. A Starfis groupie, in El Puerto de Santa María he had been seen chauffeuring us through the streets wearing his dish like a kepi while I, shoulders beneath his paws, steered by squinting through the sub-windshield vent. In Puerto Real it was more accurate to speak of our social sextet. More important still, he could match any Andalusian beer for beer. Og had turned himself into a minor celebrity and no one, in my eyesight, ever chucked a rock in his direction.

Og, credited with a brain and a drinker's joy, had crossed the line below which non-human creatures, even driven by such legible emotions as hunger and rage, either lacked feelings at all or suffered passions that didn't count. Because it was the natural world rather than theology that lifted me beyond myself, I couldn't help seeing a larger continuum. I had seen religion as paraded through the streets and I had watched the dismissal of animals as sentient creatures. Jesus hung in agony somewhere in nearly every Spanish interior, dogs were stoned daily for existing, birds were slaughtered as they slept. I had discounted Christian Science for its denial of physical reality, but Catholicism seemed no less out of touch. Mistreatment of creation was global, but its very casualness seemed personalized in this country that filled its coffers by displaying nailed flesh during Holy Week while founding an aesthetic on the ritual slaughter of bulls. Beyond setting a counter-example, there was no way of resolving the tension between belief and abuse, and I contented myself with the realization that even under the Generalísimo I was just the species to be: a human being.

13

A young regular at the Bar Gallego bought me a sherry, then thrust a paper full of handwriting at me. He was returning from a family visit in Málaga, he had stopped in Torremolinos, he had met this English girl, he had her address in Manchester . . . Would I translate this letter for him? I picked it up and scanned it for legibility. "I can, but it's fairly long. Can I take it home and give you the translation tomorrow at the same time?"

"Sure."

I gave it my best shot, handing over the original and the translation while accepting another sherry. He looked at the versions side-by-side and annoyance darkened his face. "But I wanted you to translate the whole thing."

"I did."

"You can't have. It's only half as long."

"That's the way it came out."

"All right," he said, exasperated by the obvious fraud. "I want you to tell me, word for word, what you wrote."

"This is going to sound a little weird," I warned, taking up my handwriting, "because English word order is different from Spanish. But you should be able to follow it." I proceeded to give him the Spanish equivalent of every English word, sparing no absurdity. When I finished, I found him staring at me wide-eyed. "So you see," I concluded, "it's all there."

His stare persisted. "English is like a telegram!"

Translation into English was illuminating, a literary bank shot that revealed new aspects of my own language as I took in Spanish. After learning *contrario de las manecillas del reloj*—contrary to the little hands of the clock—I newly appreciated the compactness of the English *counter-clockwise*, and *my neighbor's plumbing burst* seemed more forceful than *a mi vecino se le reventó la tuberia*—to my neighbor it burst itself on him the plumbing. Eventually a connoisseur of such differences, I would savor such collectibles as the Boston subway's *Sistema de intercomunicación para pasajeros en caso de emergencia situado al extremo del tren*, which the English reduces to *Passenger emergency intercom at end of car*. Spanish was roundabout: the passenger emergency intercom was a system of communication for passengers with cases of emergency on a very long verbal train. But the train, as spoken, went by fast and patience with it paid off, for sometimes Spanish found the word, the precise *cachondeo*, that was missing in English. I let my ears swell with the logorrhea around me as the brevities of English receded to my notes and my letters home.

Everything I did—playing with the band, selling fish, shopping, going to the movies, especially drinking—doubled as a lesson in language. Listened to for sheer sound, Spanish crackled like dry kindling. Occasionally I just let it combust around me. But mostly I listened for sense; I wanted to know that fire, and what it was burning. As I did so, language lessons doubled as lessons in life—for no matter how wordless an experience may be, as soon as it enters consciousness it refashions itself in speech. Language is falsely viewed as some intervening screen between inner and outer reality; it is part of reality itself, a full participant in experience. Visually, a new country merely shifts the scenery; new vocabulary transforms it. Every instrument receives a new jab of attention. Knife, a single cutting syllable, may ultimately be the more vivid term for that object, but reseen as *cuchillo* it inspires new caution. It doesn't draw blood, it draws *sangre*. It lies less submissively on the table, glittering with new possibilities.

On my inner track, Spanish started edging out English. Dreams were increasingly in Spanish, with language itself— particularly the battle with language—the real subject of those dreams. New labels became a magnifying lens, slowing the sense of time. With heightened self-awareness I drove a *coche*, I played piano with a *conjunto*, I ate with a *tenedor*, Og my *perro* ate scraps that were *huesos* and *sobra*, and one hundred pesetas was *veinte duros*, twenty-five peseta coins, even if one paid with a paper bill. I was literally on new terms with my routine. Hands on the *volante* of my Citroen *Dos Caballos*, or on the *teclas* of a piano, or on the *cuchara* that got the *gazpacho* to my *boca*, days were sagas and seasons became years. Eventually the sensation would wear off and the novelty die through repetition, for a *cuchillo* was ultimately no sharper than a knife. A good recipe for a long life, I decided, would be to travel from country to country, culture to culture, language to language as ever the new resident, the ear ever affronted by fresh sounds, the senses ever sharp and attention honed. Sustained linguistic focus returns the newcomer to the absorption of childhood, when all was huge and fresh. It is hard to go to sleep on a world you are struggling to pronounce.

The sounds of Spanish seemed displaced rather than out of reach. The difference in vowels was subtle, the *oo* deeper, the *ee* keener, the *ay* less of a diphthong, the *ie* more so: *ai!* The consonants too had shifted: the *t* more a *d*; the *d* halfway to a *th*; the *b* and the *v* alike, meeting somewhere between their English counterparts. Rolling an *r* between vowels, easy enough, proved nearly impossible before a *d* or *t*. Puerto Real, El Puerto de Santa María: how embarrassing to mangle the names of where I spent my life. And then there was the *double r*. How long did one roll it? How did one roll the single and the double in the same word without rolling the tongue instead?

When I drove alone between the two unpronounceable
Puertos and only Og could hear me, I slowly screamed the word
for highway. *Carretera! Carretera!* The vowels going from *ah*
to *ay* then back from *ay* to *ah*, one of each kind of *r* between
them, the whole thing pivoting palindromically around the re-
assuring *t* in the middle: *Carretera!* My friends, seeing that
I was trying, taught by example and let me work it out, but
the waiters at El Oasis were ruthless. *Why* did I talk with my
mouth closed? Just open it and say *puerto! Puerto puerto.* They
had been saying it with no problem from birth. What was the
matter with me? Encouragingly, there were good verbal runs,
times when I made that fine crackling sound, and was both the
combustion and the dry wood. At other times my mouth froze.
I gained fluency with sherry and lost it with a hangover. On
days when I couldn't make the sounds at all, it was consoling to
remember that there were days in English when I couldn't say
brewery or *cottage cheese.*

Remembering words themselves was no problem, for I was
so eager to absorb the new system that I had only to look up
a word once for it to stick. As for the notorious Spanish verb,
I respected its complexity in the belief that all those tenses
and shades of tenses meant something. However it worked in
practice, I liked to imagine a chromaticism of flux, particularly
in the past tense, through all the degrees of having occurred,
a minor palette of receding events wasting through some kind
of grammatical red shift into oblivion. Was it a spice rack of
Proustian nuance one could master, then translate back to
English? Was it a potential weapon for the writer? Secure in
my daily exchanges, now and then I cracked the second-year
grammar I bought in Barcelona and boned up on my endings.

Tolerance of the baroque Spanish verb didn't extend to grammatical gender. For no reason I could fathom, *books, pianos,
plates* and *envelopes* were masculine while *cameras, tables,
stoves* and *sheet music* were feminine. *Cults* were masculine but

sects were feminine. The *police*, including the *Guardia Civil*— as male as it got—were feminine. I knew both masculine and feminine words for *erasers* and *eyeglasses*. Except for a few abstractions, all nouns were gendered and required that the articles that preceded them, along with the adjectives that followed, agree in gender and number—irrational nonsense that plagued every sentence. Grammatical gender was not unique to Spanish, for English alone among European languages has had the wisdom to remove gender from the inanimate, but I resented having to memorize malarkey to speak correctly.

One day in the Bar Central, when I was laughed at for crossing the genders of *puente*—bridge, which is masculine— and *fuente*—fountain, which is feminine, I struck back. This whole absurdity of assigning a sex to objects that didn't have one was idiotic. Bridges and fountains don't have a gender; they're just *things*. They *do* have gender, came the loud objection. They do, but only in your heads, I persisted, because you've been talking as if they did since you learned to speak. It's not in the real world, it's in your minds. It's *association*. When they held their ground, I escalated. "Let's take the extreme case. Let's take the most gendered thing there is: *Genitalia*. Let's start with *el pene*, which is also *el carajo*, *la picha*, *la polla*, *el chorizo*, *el bicho* and *la verga*. Half the words for penis are feminine. Then there are *los cojones*, which are also *las pelotas* and *las maracas*. Now let's look at *la vagina*, more commonly called *el coño* and *el chocho*."

"And *el tunal!*" shouted one of the drinkers.

"*El conejo!*" shouted another, and now the whole bar was laughing and screaming obscenities.

"You've proved your point," a man said when the vocabulary was exhausted and the voices calmed down. The others nodded, then concurred out loud. I took a swig of masculine *fino* from my feminine *copa* to hide my stunned face. I was *right*? Not that I doubted my evidence, which was beyond dispute, but

that I had never won an argument before in Andalucía, never
expected to and, as it turned out, never would again. A handful
of half-drunk Andalusians admitted that they were wrong and
I was right. I blessed the idiotic genders for handing me this
triumph.

But my little victory didn't last the duration of a sentence,
and if I was going to speak correctly I would have to master
everything from past perfect subjunctives to the sex of fan
belts and carburetors. And what kind of Spanish was I actually
learning in Puerto Real? Paul Bowles, an American writer I
hadn't yet heard of who was living across the strait in Tangiers,
refers in one of his travel pieces to "a corrupt Andalusian version of Spanish." To my American ear, the difference between
Castilian and Andalusian was the difference between Oxford
elocution and a Mississippi drawl on speed. My friends in the
Puertos accepted that their Spanish was debased, and certain
corruptions were obvious. The s at the end of a word was either
absent entirely or was reduced to an almost inaudible little
breath, so that plurals had to be deduced from articles, verb
forms, context. Manolo assured me that they never miscommu-
nicated because of this; I was unique in hearing incorrectly. In
Andalusian speech, Cádiz routinely shrank to Cádi, which the
gypsies further shortened to Cái. You didn't have to be a gypsy
to skip your d's, and words like escuchado became escuchao.
When I mentioned that one to Manolo, he told me the story of
an Andalusian who was headed to Bilbao, was trying to shape
up his Spanish for the north, and told his friend, "Mañana voy
a Bilbado."

I didn't trust being understood if I didn't pronounce the
entire word, and even though I aspired to speaking like everyone around me, I sounded all the letters and made my
plurals clear. "You speak better than we do," I was told by
people who actually meant it, and I wasn't always sure it was
a compliment, for authenticity seemed a function of speed.

The regular alternation of consonants and vowels in Spanish, with no clustered consonants to slow it down, propels the phonemes forward with nothing to stop them. I marveled at a petulant bit of Andalusian slang that often concluded a negative sentence, a bit of fill that meant "or anything." Consisting of *ni nada* with the *d* left out, the expression fluttered the tongue in automatic fire five times: *ni na ni na ni na ni na ni ná!* I tried it and usually messed up by the third *na.* The inability of English to attain such speeds is demonstrated by the patter songs of Gilbert and Sullivan, which gain their comic effects by pretending to clip along like an aria out of *The Barber of Seville* while colliding with Saxon verbal clots. The headlong rush of sounds revved my attention to a pitch that was sometimes exhilarating, sometimes exhausting. Because English by necessity goes slower, its speakers' mouths don't shape themselves for speed during the formative years, and when ears don't mature hearing language at that velocity, the neuron networks don't develop to deliver meaning that fast either. Hearing, speaking and processing at warp speed are powers best built in as a child. Starting in my twenty-seventh year, I trained myself as best I could, listening fast to catch the half-spoken, the plural that was only a breath, the implied, the omitted.

Andalusian speech stood out in its full corruption whenever I heard a speaker from the north, a customer from Madrid at El Oasis or an announcer on the radio. I was always struck by the clarity, the smooth delivery of meaning. Spanish didn't *have* to go so fast, or be that incomprehensible: why did I struggle so to learn bad speech in Andalucía when it would be so much easier to learn decent speech in Madrid? It seemed paradoxical that the educated, with their broader knowledge and more extensive vocabulary, would be easier to understand, but it was the uneducated with their slang, their omissions and their shortcuts who made the educated sound simple.

There was, however, an underside to Castilian clarity, for ears attuned to the ship builders of Puerto Real found the speech of Madrid snobbish and self-conscious, too sibilant with all its plurals pronounced and its articles and adjectives in agreement, one *s* after another. People from the capital hissed like cats. The *th* sound for which Castilian is famous, the macho lisp, was also more luxuriant. When I ran this effect by Manolo, he enunciated, "*Los lienzos de Velazquez gozan de una luz fugaz,*" which means, "The canvases of Velazquez enjoy a fugitive light." Concocted to sound absurd even to Spanish ears, in English transliteration it might read, "*los lee-enthos day Velathqueth gothan de una looth foogath.*"

Immersed in these new sounds, I had no interest in speaking English, and did so only during the three months I played at the naval base or at the campground with Teddy and Flo. But I was, to my knowledge, the only native English speaker who circulated in Puerto Real, and was therefore sought as a teacher by the few who wanted to learn. I had no interest in instructing, but piano jobs were far between and when the principal of Puerto Real's secondary school sent word that he was looking for an English teacher, I presented myself. What were my teaching credentials? None, I said. I had a B. A. in English from Yale University, but that was a degree in literature. Well, that could be waived. What accent would I be teaching? I said that I was American. Correct English was British, not American, he pronounced. I could have retorted that correct Spanish was Castilian, not Andalusian, but I held my tongue. Would I teach with an English accent? One of my bar tricks, as it happened, was to do an impression of BBC English for those who understood not a word of it, and whom the sounds sent into gales of laughter, but that was the only British in my repertoire and I couldn't inflict it on the young. I would teach correct American English. The principal held that there was no such thing and dismissed me.

A few individuals, mostly friends of friends of the Bar
Central, asked for instruction, and while I did nothing to solicit
pupils, neither did I turn anyone down. Least to benefit was a
middle-aged lower official at the boatyard, who came into contact with crews from all over the world and thought it would be
bonito to learn some English. I picked up a beginning text from
a shop in Cádiz and we plunged in. His structural incapacity
for English sounds defeated the most patient repetition. *Thunk
you*, I pronounced, then wrote out the sounds: *Tenc iu*. Thank
you, thank you. It eluded him. Simple syntax might as well
have been the calculus. We tried to gain ground twice a week
for several weeks, but the dim fire in his eyes died, and when
his wife turned me away at the door because he had a cold,
which over the next couple of weeks worsened to the flu, I took
the hint. He knew where to find me. I think he only wanted a
little novelty in his life, and English proved a dead end.

Far quicker on the uptake was the young owner of a bar on
the edge of town. He had already acquired a grammar, had made
inroads on his own, and we got through a chapter a week, which
he fully absorbed and pronounced well. He always began our
sessions with a discussion in Spanish of international politics, a
rare topic in Puerto Real, and when he praised me for knowing
the word *clandestino*, I refrained from telling him that I'd never
actually heard it before; I was just reversing my usual process of
forming Spanish adjectives by adding an *o* or an *a* to the English
and hoping for the best. Our lessons would have helped a future
English speaker on his way if he'd had an assistant in the bar, but
he could only focus on our lessons in moments when he wasn't
attending to customers, and the novelty of our lessons actually
attracted them. Like all bars, it was open to the street, where the
Lung was parked with its French tourist plates, advertising that
something exotic was in process. Passers-by called in their gossip
or their smart remarks, children popped in to gawk, and customers crowded my student's table after he poured their drinks.

Once as I was explaining the formation of English plurals—change the *y* to *i* and add *es*—a family of goats came leaping and sidestepping toward the bar. The parents paused a moment while several juniors spiraled around them, bucking in swirls of golden dust. Two of them spotted the Lung, leapt onto the hood, looked around a little breathlessly, bounced onto the roof and, seemingly from sheer delight, began to screw. Their mother let out an *a-a-a-a-a!* like a muffled machine gun, and they sailed to the ground in a single plunge. This was the ultimate in being upstaged and I set down the grammar book and laughed. My pupil looked at me satirically and said, "You Americans aren't the only ones who know how to form plurals."

I regretted but understood when these lessons were canceled, reducing me to my star pupil. To my surprise, this was a twenty-nine-year-old monk who taught at the boarding school run by the Silesians on the way to Las Canteras. Its students received five years of industrial training in return for working a required amount of time for the companies that sponsored them. Tall and bespectacled, with a brusque but worldly polish, the monk was already proficient in French and Italian, taught literature, mathematics, geography, religion and physical education, and was adding English and shorthand to his arsenal.

Brother Martín's English was already absorbed into correct but colorful structures that he extended into monologs, and his lessons flowed without effort. He granted me a tour of monastic life, showing me the refectory, the chapel, the dormitory where forty monks slept on cots twenty on a side, and the lavatory where all the urinals were enclosed in little stalls for modesty. He had begun his language study with Italian, he said, because it was required of all members of the order, but personally he didn't like it. It was soft, too like the buzzing of bees. English was now his real love. He had started less than a year ago, took two months of classes with an English couple living in Sevilla, and had gotten the rest from books, language records and old copies of *Newsweek*. As he spoke, his jaws opened wide and bit the words from the air, as if wrenching tough meat off a bone, and when a word escaped he clenched his teeth, squinted and braced for the endurance of unavoidable pain. Every new word was a toy to be repeated, tasted in different contexts, admired from shifting positions, and he told me that before going to sleep each night he lay on his cot rehearsing consonants: *Probably, probably, probably— make the* b *more explosive—probably probably, probably* . . .

"Doesn't that keep the other brothers awake?" I asked.

"No, they're just bothered because they can't tell what I'm saying."

About his childhood in Sevilla, the consuming interest of his monologs, he was most vivid: "When I was ten I would leave home for school in the morning and usually disappear into town for the day, and my father finally sent me to a strict Jesuit school. The priests there kicked and beat and slapped me every way they could think of. Once I came home with the shape of a hand red on my cheek. I was afraid to tell the truth for fear my father would think I was blaming the Jesuits for one of my street fights, so when he asked what happened, I said, 'I was tired and took a nap with my face on my hand.'

'And the print on your neck?'

'That was when I rolled over.'

'For a lie like that, young Christian, you can turn the other cheek. I'll give you a hand to match,' said my father. And he did."

The text for the lessons was always something he sprang on me, whatever interested him in English at the moment. Once he produced an article on Einstein's Special Theory of Relativity from *Scientific American* and asked for an explanation. We pored over each sentence while I unraveled the grammar, the quirks of phrase. I was fortunate that the vocabulary of Western science is easily converted from one language to another, for

I had no idea what the words meant. The experience of successfully explaining something I didn't understand reminded me eerily of the way quantum physics dissolved our obsessive brains to pattern and probability.

When Brother Martín summarily canceled our lessons, I consoled myself that I had added something to an already bright mind, despite having no vocation for teaching. I had nearly forgotten him by the time I ran into him again, on my way to Las Canteras. I greeted him enthusiastically in English.

"Me alegro verle, amigo," he said, *"no sabía que todavía estaba aquí."*

I was startled because we had never spoken Spanish before, and was even more surprised by his use of the formal pronoun than by his assumption that I was no longer in town. I persevered in English. "How are your studies coming? You should be speaking perfectly by now."

"Inglés?" he continued in Spanish. "I passed my exams in Madrid with the highest marks, but that was months ago and I haven't spoken it since. After all, that was all I needed it for."

And I don't need to teach it, I thought, saying goodbye to this person for the last time.

Divested of my last pupil, I devoted myself to the language I was learning for its own sake. Instead of dulling it, familiarity only deepened its romance, its personality. A *zaguán* might only be an entryway, but its two Arabic syllables resounded so that I heard the clanking shut of a large door, leaving me in a cavernous antechamber where the air was cool and dank, and a farther door led to who-knows-what. A *jinete* was just someone riding a horse, but such English equivalents as horseman or horseback rider were too clunky to conjure the lean and swift figure who bore down on me, cantering on his mysterious business. Less sublime was a very Andalusian word pronounced *bah-tay* and spelled *water.* This was slang for WC, watercloset, and I loved excusing myself to go there, for it always gave me a good laugh at the derivation along with the relief. Most usefully there was *guasa*, almost as versatile as *cachondeo*, with whose meanings it overlapped. Something with *guasa* could be funny, difficult or a hassle, a *guasón* was a practical jokester, and *guasa* installed itself permanently on my inner track. Even a globally known word like *adios* had to stretch to mean hello as well as goodbye. If you were greeting a friend from a car, or one riding by on a bicycle, or a cantering *jinete*, you didn't shout *hola* or *buenos días*. Prolonging the final vowel and ignoring the *s*, you yelled *adios*.

Finally, I had to relearn my own name. All foreign names were converted to Spanish if there were equivalents, so that even the quite pronounceable Teddy and Flo became *Teodoro* and *Florencia*. But what to do with Bruce? It derived from a Scottish surname and had no Spanish version. Bruno came closest, but not close enough. All Spanish names were taken from the saints' calendar, and all men were supposed to buy drinks for their friends when their saint's birthday rolled around. *What day is St. Bruce?* I was sometimes asked.

"There is no St. Bruce," I would reply, "and I'm not about to be the first."

"Then you never have to buy drinks?"

"Apparently not," I would reply, smiling.

By not appearing on the saints' calendar, I was literally off the chart. Since Andalusians never pronounce a final sibilance, I was called Bru, with an *oo* sound so pure and deep that for the rest of my life I have started, as if by a summons, if I hear the sound in a crowd. The only exception was Bernardo, Castilian to the last phoneme, who called me Broo-thay. As for Og, his ears snapped up on hearing Ack, Ock, Ah with a glottal stop, a whole range of vowel sounds sharply pronounced. I was only sorry he couldn't have savored Flo's note: "Don't waste your kibble, I've given a bowl of stew to Arque."

But my favorite exchange about language occurred with
Ramón. Every now and then someone would say, you guys are
always together, a Spaniard and an American. What language
do you speak when you're alone? The first time we answered
together by accident, and after that we timed it to speak in
unison: "French."

14

Ramón remained the other half of my split existence: there was Spain, as represented by Puerto Real, and there was Ramón. Back and forth we went, he to Puerto Real, I to El Puerto de Santa María; he sluicing unseen through my town on its twin one-way chutes, as indifferent to my town as it was to him, while I remained a circulating presence in his. Rock music, for Ramón and his friends, was all there was; intoxicating in its own right, it was increasingly seen as the fuel to launch its players beyond home turf. Andalusian bands, I learned, had roughly a two-year lifespan, and Starfis, already a middle-aged one-year-old when I joined it, had run its course. Los Simbroni was forming in its wake, with Ramón as its drummer. The group's new members had been Starfis groupies, hangers-on at El Oasis or members of expired rival bands, and I was its pianist if we landed a gig in a club with keys. In the absence of a piano, my instrument had become the Lung, and I drove players and guitars to and from Jerez and one-night stands at farflung roadhouses while the drums and speakers rode the van for distributing beer.

The only person to launch himself as far as the campgound was, ironically, the non-musician who delivered beer. Older brother of a Simbroni guitarist, Javier was sometimes manically exuberant, sometimes sullen and withdrawn, capable of getting drunk, dancing swishily, pointing to his male dancing partner and shrieking in fractured English, "He iss my hossband!"—behavior unknown among local rockers—and going on a quite conventional movie date with a girlfriend the following night. Who was the real Javier? All we knew was his situation. His father owned a small bodega that made sherry for local consumption, and Javier's beer deliveries were its non sequitur. His duties, light enough, gave Javier a bit of disposable income, and he began inviting me to elegant three-course dinners on the Puerto de Santa María waterfront. While everyone occasionally ate at a restaurant that served salad, paella and flan for twenty-seven pesetas—roughly forty-two cents—not even Ramón considered sitting down at a sidewalk table, ordering with leisurely anticipation off a menu, selecting an appropriate sherry and engaging in civilized talk. When I tried to reciprocate or help pay, Javier brushed me aside. "There's not a single restaurant where you can offer me a decent meal in *your* town, and in mine you will be my guest."

Javier had usually been drinking for hours by the time I reached his sidewalk table, and he would be in rare form. Did I know about El Puerto de Santa María's famous poet, Rafael Alberti? Just as he feared. Alberti was born in El Puerto in 1902, spent much of his youth at sea, catching boats with fishermen in that dock right across the street, and he paid his way with verses drenched in brine. He was a star of the famous Generation of 1927 that included García Lorca. Like the rest of the poets, he fought for the Republic in the Civil War. Unlike most of them, he survived, and now lived in exile in Chile. But he wasn't forgotten in El Puerto. Javier's curly brown hair tumbling over his twenty-year-old pout, his diction a little slurred, he would quote Alberti's poems about wind and salt and wandering clouds that were the sky's islands. Refilling our *copas*, steadying his gaze, voice pitched to project, he would recite *El Grumete*, "The Cabin Boy":

Don't you touch liquor!
Don't you drink!

Drinking sailors
who work the port,
don't let him drink!

Fishermen, don't let him drink!

Always clear-eyed,
his lips ever awake
to the sea and not to liquor!

May he not drink!

As our second bottle of Terry seco neared bottom, dessert would arrive—an orange or a banana for each of us, chaste on its white plate beside a small knife and fork. Having no idea what to do with the utensils, I would peel and eat the fruit by hand. Javier, suddenly a craftsman, would pare the orange so as to leave a perfect globe of meat beside a spiral of peel that could be returned to a seamless sphere enclosing a globe of air. Or he would prong the banana near the stem, slit the peel lengthwise, free the flesh, then part it along its longitudinal seams, leaving three strips of banana in elegant parallel. Setting his implements aside, he would rip the orange apart with his hands and cram as many sections as possible into his mouth, or squeeze the banana strips into mush and shove them in whole. Eyes watering, cheeks bloated, masticating hysterically, he would choke down dessert in spasms like a snake. Lubricating it all with an emergency draft of sherry, he would lean back philosophically in his chair and pronounce, "Once you've shown that you *know* proper form, it doesn't matter what you actually do."

As he put on and discarded roles, lurching between hooliganism and intellectuality, he let the real Javier leak through. His father was an ogre and his father controlled his life. His father wanted him and his brother to take over the family bodega. Fine for his brother, if that's what his brother wanted, but it wasn't what Javier wanted. El Puerto de Santa María was provincial. It was boring. There was a further world out there and Javier was determined to reach it.

One evening he turned up at the campground. He was running away to Algeciras and my digs were his first stop. I lent him my sleeping bag and we talked through the night. Algeciras seemed a paltry destination. While larger than El Puerto de Santa María, it wasn't really extended enough to get lost in. Its ferry to Tangiers made it the port of entry for all of Africa and therefore a funnel for the drug trade, and it was green with Guardia Civil. Plus it was only a few hours drive away. Nonetheless, Javier saw it as his only option, and he caught a ride southward at dawn.

A couple of hours later his father, the ogre, arrived at my door looking sad-eyed and bewildered. "Where has Javier gone?" he asked. "Why has he done this to me?" I too was intimidated by this man. I knew how he had tried to encage his son's numerous personalities, and had brought this on himself by freezing Javier in a role without ever taking an honest look at his son to see if he fit. And yet a wave of pity overcame me for a man who had only wound up caging himself. "I don't know where Javier is," I told him, and he got back in his car and headed south. He found Javier hitchhiking outside the town of Vejer, halfway to Algeciras. The ride Javier caught was merely a return trip with a shaken father, and that was that.

But the whole rock subculture felt trapped by these towns around the Bay of Cádiz. It was so provincial, so traditionally Spanish, so Franco. The real sounds were coming out of Liverpool and the good clothes were coming from London's

Carnaby Street. Zealots of the new from all over Europe were converging on the nonstop international beach-party blowouts of the Mediterranean coast. Los Simbroni's trump card was a bass player whose family owned a summer home in Altea, a town in the province of Alicante, and the group snared a contract to play dances several nights a week at its outdoor movie theater during July and August. There would be no piano but I was automatically included as a unit with Ramón, not to mention owner of the beloved Og, not to mention the possessor of wheels. Javier, the most desperate to leave, was not a musician and would not be coming. Now into my second year at the Puerto Real campground, I was as restless as the others, ready for fresh horizons. Assured by Bernardo that my room at the boarded restaurant awaited my return, I collected Ramón and we were off.

As Ramón, Og and I in the Lung trailed a rental van bearing instruments and other Simbronis, I had misgivings about the horizons we had committed to. When I traveled the coast from Barcelona to Gibraltar with Patrick a year and a half back, I had a good look at the high and mercenary tourist precincts that were encrusting the Mediterranean like the bathtub ring of a reservoir. I had no specific memory of Altea, but we had necessarily driven through it. Our approach avoided the coast, for we took an inland cut-off that took us past wind-scoured sandstone hoodoos, an expanse of dunes, jagged blue skylines beyond hard scrub, an unexpected quick tour of the American West. Though it didn't make me nostalgic, I felt somehow reassured, confirmed. Here, said the bass player during a rest stop, was where the action sequences of the Italian-made Clint Eastwood films, the so-called spaghetti Westerns, were actually shot, and I commented to Ramón, "Perhaps they should be called paella Westerns."

At midnight we arrived at our quarters for the summer, a raw new apartment building that confirmed my worst fears.

Our three-room suite was unfurnished except for a scattering of bare mattresses in the two bedrooms; we tossed our sleeping bags upon them and passed out.

In the morning we staggered onto the balcony to take stock. Only a field of stubble separated us from the sea, and the only true eyesore was the one we were in. Walking the kilometer into town, we discovered that Altea was a sunbleached village packed onto a small hill, a cone that had erupted in salt crystals, so self-contained and compact it seemed blind to the newer growth below it. That lower world, our new domain, was a wobbly string of newer apartments, shops and modest residences along the coast highway. The new horizon wasn't so fearful.

Los Simbroni's duties weren't fearful either. Three nights a week it played at La Terraza Costablanca, replacing the movie screen, backs to the sea. The folding chairs had been moved toward the projection booth, where they joined little drink tables and left a clearing to dance in. I helped set up the instruments and haul them at the end of the evening to the storage room, and otherwise had no duties. I always listened to a couple of sets to show support and to socialize during the breaks, but music I barely withstood as a player became intolerable when I was reduced to a mere listener. How far into the night could I wander and still hear it? I walked the coastal highway, heard the voices and electric guitars trail away and pinch out, then lost Ramón's drums, and all the way to our apartment the long waves of the bass pursued me like a seismic pulse, mercilessly drilling its two-note phrase a fourth apart, *doon*, doon-*doon*, doon-*doon*, doon-*doon* . . .

Time spent at La Terraza Costablanca was fortunately slight compared to the hours and days—finally measurable in months—spent at Altea's one-stop all-purpose bar and social center, La Bodega. Its street entrance opened onto a high cavern of rough wood, wicker chairs, and walls full of paintings and *objets d'art* created by the clientele, an artistic penumbra that spilled onto a terrace of beachside tables. Unless it was actually raining, both doors were left open to a breeze that transported a cool salt smell from the sea and the rhythmic wash of the tide. The bar offered the standard array but its specialty was the *porón*, a glass pitcher with two spouts, one fanning upward for air, the other a cone that pinched to a hole, so that when you leaned back and held the *porón* overhead with both hands, the cone jetted a stream of wine into your open mouth. Drinking from a *porón* demanded a steady hand and good aim, and if the drinker was new and the wine was red, the shirt was instantly ruined. Often we drank from the standard array, but when we knew we were to brave the *porón*, we arrived in a pre-ruined shirt.

La Bodega's customers were the expected northern Europeans, but they were hardly the disco set. There was a pair of young English writers who lived with the kind of artist-collecting woman who would eventually hold salons. There was a mad German painter Wolf, who spent most of his time running off other males from his Ursula. There was the personable young Norwegian, mysteriously supported by a Norwegian three times his age who never ventured past their front door. There was a teenage Dutch boy who complained that his mother kept stealing his girlfriends. And there was a quite normal English family that drove to Gibraltar every month to withdraw money from the Bank of England. These folk lived, many of them year-round, in rental farm houses and newer structures tucked away in the hills beyond town, improvisations often connected by walking trails that followed the irrigation canals, and no one plied the arts seriously enough to interfere with closing La Bodega. This floating world was unrestrained, but it was also low-key. Altea only appealed to quality people like themselves, they maintained, because its beach was composed of pebbles; inartistic trash types required great stretches of sand.

La Bodega, alluring in its own right, was also a welcome alternative to our apartment. The only furniture we supplied it was the record player, which endlessly broadcast the Beatles' *Rubber Soul*; in the livingroom we simply joined Og on the floor. As Simbronis we maintained possession of the mattresses, but we allowed a succession of drifters and fugitives from unpaid bills to sack out elsewhere in sleeping bags, blankets, whatever they could scrounge. After the rent and the tab at La Bodega were paid, there were few pesetas left for anything else, even food. Og fared the best, feasting on hand-outs from all quarters, working it off on long walks, passing satisfied hours on the balcony staring over the sea. The rest of us often subsisted on no more than a sandwich a day, a tough white roll stained by the merest lichen of ham. My American concept of the sandwich, whereby the bread was merely an edible device for holding together the meat, cheese, lettuce, onion and heaped condiments, gave way to the Spanish principle by which the contents were the minimal flavoring that allowed one to choke down the bread.

I realized that we would not actually starve and that if things got lean enough we would just go home, but it was on my conscience that I was sharing what little food we had without kicking in. Altea had no pianos in public places, leaving me a rocker without portfolio, so I looked for work in the nearest appreciable town, fifteen kilometers down the coast. Through a selection process no one understood, a given coastal town might appeal almost exclusively to the French, or the Swedes, or the Belgians, and Benidorm had been annexed by the Germans. None of the German-leaning restaurants or bars could use me, but a couple of spots that catered to the English minority were interested, particularly if I sang as I played. The owner of one bar told me that I passed his test if I could jump up and down at the keys and sing "Knees Up, Mother Brown." Alas, I could not. The most promising spot, a restaurant called El Cortijo that catered to the English—and, they proudly added, the Spanish—might have an opening, eventually, I should keep in touch. When I reported this job failure to the Simbronis, they assured me that I was of equal value as a translator, an instrument grip, a taxi to occasional one-night stands along the coast. I was relieved at these extra jobs, because along with the sandwich money they put me at the wheel of my instrument by default.

Aside from transactions in stores, we had little interchange with the local population, which found Andalusian rockers as foreign as northern Europeans. We worked bits of their Valencian dialect into our vocabulary for spice—calling each other *chicón* and saying *no vale res* instead of *no vale nada* for "it's worthless"—and while they understood our corrupt version of Castilian, their speech was opaque to us. But when we got wind of a local experience, we didn't hesitate. Someone at La Bodega mentioned stumbling on the ultimate paella at a hamlet called Abdet and we piled into the Lung to investigate. A thread of pavement took us through a winding valley to a sign and a gravel road, which we followed a downhill kilometer and across a bridge to three inhabited streets. There were no signs indicating a restaurant, or anything else, but a woman pointed to a door, which opened on a bar and the town's male population. We ordered the red wine that the rest were drinking, and when they paid for it, we reciprocated. We told the bartender that we also wanted to eat paella. He shouted, "Mari!" A woman appeared and asked if we wanted chicken or rabbit; she had several of each in the back yard.

"Rabbit," someone replied after a moment of hesitation.

She looked us over and remarked, "One should be enough."

While she dispatched the rabbit, a teenage son lit some wood in the back-room fireplace and let the coals die down. We had more rounds. The woman returned with a vast cast iron skillet. She laid it on the coals, poured in a dollop of olive oil, then ladled in rice, onions, pimento, garlic and saffron. We followed her beady-eyed and half drunk as smells from the fireplace blossomed. Suddenly the door opened and a half dozen women accompanied by twice that many children burst in, swept past the men and disappeared into an inner sanctum off the back room. The men picked up their drinks and followed. We too followed to see what it was about. There was no room for us but the mystery was revealed. On folding chairs, on the floor or standing, all were staring intently at a small black-and-white TV where the Western *Bonanza* was just beginning. Said a man by the door, "This is the only TV in town. We wait all week for this. The whole village is here." Beyond him we could hear Hoss complaining in perfect Castilian.

Mari detached herself and stirred the paella, and her son pulled the diningroom's two tables together. As Andalusians we required sherry with our meal, and the boy brought us a bottle of Tio Pepe. At last Mari removed the skillet, so heavy she merely slid it onto the floor, and she spooned the paella golden and steaming onto six waiting plates. One rabbit was indeed enough, adding more texture than flavor, and the richness cut through even palates bludgeoned by alcohol. This feast cost us no more than bad sandwiches in Altea and we returned every week.

Our other favorite Altean experience—the running of the bulls—occurred almost on our doorstep. Hemingway wouldn't have cared for it. To celebrate mid-summer, a ranch that raised fighting bulls brought their most valiant specimens to Altea's beach and turned them loose one at a time. No one owned a proper red cape. Local young men and a few tourists peeled their shirts off and shook them in the bulls' line of sight. It took considerable shaking to catch a bull's attention, but eventually it would charge. Since bulls stop running as soon as they reach the water, a fleeing provocateur merely had to get there first. The bravest were those with the closest calls, and even I enjoyed nerving myself to remain on the beach as the bulk with lowered horns bore down. None of the Simbronis were notable for their *cojones*, and though I savored doom as long as I dared, I always found myself in the first breaker of cowards to hit the waves. With a safety net that stretched to the horizon, this was tauromachy that the valiant, the gutless and the bull could all enjoy.

It wasn't until a week before the end of the Simbroni contract at La Terraza Costabrava that Restaurante El Cortijo informed me that they did want me as a pianist for a run of two months. Ramón and I were faced with a decision: we could go home with the band, or we could move rent-free into the house of departing Belgians. What were we missing in either Puerto if we stayed on? The rest of the Simbroni loaded guitars, speakers and themselves into a rental van, and Ramón and I settled into a five-room house in the hills.

After a teeming apartment with no furniture, it was eerie to move into a suite of whitewashed rooms full of oak furniture, brass beds and Moorish sabers on the wall. Surrounding the house were several acres of orchard whose oranges, lemons, tangerines, figs and pomegranates were ours. The panorama from the terrace swept over orchard, hill and sea, always pulling the eye to Altea itself, a far scoop of vanilla. Towering unexpectedly over our domain was an iron windmill whose tail was lettered, like my birth certificate, *Chicago*. Ramón set up his drums in the livingroom and banged away with no one to bother but me. The bother wasn't great, for trails beckoned in all directions. Evenings off, I climbed the windmill and watched Altea turn from vanilla to peach.

The other novelty of the new life was El Cortijo, rendered on English menus as The Farmhouse. A bar and restaurant with a small performing space, its walls were hung with coiled ropes, spurs, riding crops and iron rings holding pots of geraniums, an effect that was aristocratically horsey. During the dinner hour I rambled through my favorite Gershwin and Porter, then took an hour off while a bad local guitarist hammed it up from table to table. The guitarist and I then threw off our remaining taste for an hour of such classics as *Adios muchachos* and *Juanita Banana,* building to the Uruguayan tango *A media luz.* Separately and together we filled requests that we hoped would fill the tip jar, but too often we were paid in drinks that customers insisted we consume. On such nights it was a challenge to get through the program's climax, my arm-flinging rendition of Lecuona's *Malagueña.*

For the owner, the highlight of any evening was the birthday or anniversary for which he could stack champagne glasses five or six high, pour champagne into the top glass, and let the ones below fill in slow sequence, the champagne clinging by surface tension to the undersides of the bowls while I played "Three Coins in the Fountain"—an innovation for which he sincerely expected a place in cultural history. I made my own dubious history the night I was tipped with *bacalao,* dried cod, the most expensive tapa and the only one I could not stand. When the waiter handed it to me, I nodded to the customer and set it on the piano.

"Enjoy it now," the customer called.

"After work," I smiled.

"No," he repeated, "enjoy it *now.*"

Hoping professionalism would see me through, I speared some with the little fork and stuck it in my mouth. Immediately my eyes watered, I started to gag, and I dashed to the men's room, where I hoped the ensuing noises couldn't be heard. Perhaps the waiters warned subsequent customers not to tip in cod, for it never reached me again.

That was the only bad food experience, for I was always served some nourishing plate while the guitarist yucked it up if customers didn't treat me themselves. The real highlight of each evening wasn't "Three Coins" or "Malagueña"; it was the doggie bag. When I returned each night, Ramón and I rescued whole pork chops and barely sampled steaks before turning over the grosser remains to Og, and our only mistake was to mention this practice to La Bodega's Spanish bartender, who gasped, "You mean you eat after the *English?*"

At first it seemed that nothing could touch this idyll. Ramón drummed at home and grew shoulder length hair I didn't mention disliking, and Og rambled through the orchard. Then Og did something wholly uncharacteristic: this individual who never left home or showed the least interest in his own kind took off for three days. We weren't concerned for his wellbeing, for we caught occasional glimpses of him tearing through the countryside, leading a most unselective pack of crazed local hounds. On the third night he returned with a scarred face, and subsequently refused to recognize the least ally of that aberration. It was as if he had wanted the experience of leading a Spanish pack, had satisfied his curiosity, and could now return to a life of reason—but his lapse anticipated threats on the human front.

Occasionally Ramón came to work with me, but usually I deposited him at La Bodega, then joined him for a nightcap when I returned. On one such occasion, the owner of El Cortijo told me between pieces that an American was waiting for me in the bar. I knew no Americans on the coast, and no acquaintance but Ramón had ever joined me at El Cortijo. At first I didn't recognize the shaggy person with locks, a trenchcoat and two days' growth, holding out a hand, though something about the eyes . . .

"Don't you know me?" he asked, offense in his voice.

"Frank!" I exclaimed.

"Tony," he replied. "I've changed my name." This deserter from the U. S. Navy had also changed his looks.

"But how did you find me here?"

"I had to move on from where I was. Someone told me there was a young American playing the piano in Benidorm." He smiled. "Who else could it be? I need somewhere to cool it for a while. They said the pianist was living in Altea."

As I drove Frank nervously back with me after work, he filled me in on his career since I left him at the Algeciras waterworks. He had lived up and down the Costa del Sol, traveled to France without a passport, passed some time in the Riviera chateau of a movie director, returned to Spain still without papers, and most recently settled in Marbella with two statuesque English girls. Through this entire time he had been ignored by the various kinds of police, and he assumed that his desertion from the American Navy had been ignored or forgotten. Two days back, the English girls had returned from shopping to report that a cordon of *guardia municipal, Guardia Civil* and American military police was stationed a block from the house in every direction.

"Then how . . . ," I began.

"I shaved my face and my legs as close as I could, put my clothes in a huge handbag that belonged to one of the girls, and dressed myself in her blouse and skirt. The shoes didn't fit, but all the foreigners in Marbella go barefoot. The girls walked out of the house on either side of me, we smiled at the police, the girls said hello, and we kept on walking all the way to the train station. I wasn't sure where to buy a ticket to, but someone on the platform told me there was an American pianist in Benidorm." I couldn't wait to reach La Bodega: I wanted a drink and I wanted to be with Ramón.

As soon as I walked in, the bartender said, "There's something you need to know immediately. Ramón is in jail."

I felt as if I'd been stabbed. "On what charge?"

"No one seems to know."

No one else in the bar knew either, though worried friends had already been to the police station to press for details.

I dashed there myself. "I wish to see Ramón Talamantes Ayala."

A man at a desk looked up. "He's had enough visitors for tonight."

"What's he charged with?"

The man's annoyance hardened. "I'll let you know when they decide."

With memories of the concert Starfis had played for maximum security prisoners beyond a succession of bolted doors, I drove the fugitive Frank to our house, mostly for something to do. The Vietnam War was underway and I knew that it was an honor to harbor an American deserter, but Frank had defected purely for kicks. "You can stay tonight," I said when we arrived, "but it would be better if you found another place after that."

I expected an objection, but Frank replied calmly, "I already got a lead on that when you were trying to get your friend out of jail."

At dawn Ramón appeared at the house on foot. After a fearful night in a cell, he had been released with the demand that he cut his hair or leave town. He was indignant. Shoulder-length hair might be avant-garde for Spain, even in 1966, but it was common enough in the rest of Europe, where life was moving ahead. Foreigners were allowed to dress as they pleased. Why were only Spaniards deprived of their liberty in their own country? He wouldn't think of complying.

Superficially, life returned to normal. Frank's lead turned out to be a Danish girl, and he moved in with her the next day. I continued my job at El Cortijo, dropping Ramón at La Bodega, joining him for the last call or two. But peace of mind was gone. Ramón's father had fought on the wrong side of the Civil War. That was why he had fled to Morocco, why Ramón was born in Casablanca, and the Talamantes Ayalas would be there still if the Moroccans hadn't nationalized and kicked

them back to Spain. This jeopardy was compounded by the
association with Frank, for the police of two countries were
after him. His natural insouciance, engaging when he first went
AWOL, had turned arrogant during his successful year on the
lam. In kinky detail he retailed his nights with the Danish girl
to the crowd at La Bodega. Bernardo, scowling over his wine
at the campground, had pronounced him a negligible speck
of the flotsam pullulating through contemporary Europe, and
while I wouldn't put it so grandly, I now concurred; my fellow
American was just the sort of disco-culture trash I had dreaded
in Altea and not found. Now he threatened calamity.

Two or three times a week the police came up to Ramón:
cut your hair or leave. Ramón's hair counterattacked. These
fiats about his appearance were inane, yet serious—for Franco
was on top of it all. Was anxiety about it the reason I woke up
at night choking? I couldn't sleep for more than three hours
before I was awake and gasping for breath, remembering that
my grandfather died from inhaling particles in a grain elevator
and my father of complications from chainsmoking. Was I fated
to pulmonary insult? I mentioned it to friends at La Bodega.
"Is your house whitewashed?" someone asked. "Check your
walls." I trained my eyes on our air and found it hung with
a fine talcum. I ran my finger along a wall and it came off
chalked. My lungs were being whitewashed. Our pastoral in
the hills was turning deadly. Stubbornly, I hoped to finish my
gig at El Cortijo.

My alliance with Ramón had so far consisted of my fitting into
his world, and once the novelty of rock-and-roll culture wore
off I was wholly bored with it. I knew that it was hopeless to interest him in books or classical music, but perhaps he could be
lured into the landscape. All he had known, after all, were the
city of Casablanca and the town of El Puerto de Santa María;
if he broke into open country, he might like it. I had a two-day

break from El Cortijo and the perfect destination hovered in plain sight, a formal white glimmer on the escarpment over our terrace. It was a Moorish castle, we were informed by the Dutch widow of an American painter, and one room of it had been fixed up by the Alpine Club of Alicante. There were platforms for throwing sleeping bags, cooking utensils, a small cache of food and a fireplace. On one of La Bodega's flimsy cocktail napkins she drew a map with such features as *Alhama Springs, zigzag trail, well in the rock, long climb* and the goal, *castillo.* She concluded her directions in two languages with the same menacing phrase. *On ne peut pas le perdre.* You can't miss it.

With thin French sleeping bags, no packs and no coats, we were ill-equipped for the late October cold. We stuffed ourselves into as much clothing as would still allow us to walk, wadded three blankets into a sleeping bag that sagged like a bladder, and dumped some sandwiches, a flashlight, a saucepan and a jar of instant coffee into a blue wicker picnic basket. Bristling with self-consciousness we set off past a construction crew, Ramón wound in a scarf and padding like a teddy bear with pajamas under his jeans, I swinging the blue basket, Og careening from bush to bush, a gourmand of smells.

Ramón had once mentioned a heart condition, some sort of murmur or arrhythmia I had forgotten about, and on the first switchback he announced it was kicking up. We inched uphill, aware of each step, visualizing a jumping pulse under his unraveling green sweater and his pajamas. "Should we go back?" I asked.

"We'll make it," he gasped. "We'll rest often."

"Let me carry the bladder."

Humiliated, he handed it over and accepted the basket.

We plodded and paused, then Ramón gained his second wind and the heart condition vanished. No longer our terrace's blue backdrop, the mountain was a gnarled mass rising through a deep meadow to stone ribbing that cut the skyline like a great dorsal. We pulled out the napkin: it showed the trail angling left. The trail, in reality, disappeared. We veered left anyway, spirited on by game trails through the high grass.

The meadow broke into terraced olive groves, revealing a cabin with adjacent pens and shelters for animals, a complex crumbling with disuse. For us, it was a rest stop. We visualized olives rocked to the valley by mule, return trips with supplies, failure, loneliness. The defeat was invigorating. Ramón grabbed the bladder, handed back the blue basket, and we pushed into some briars beyond a splintering grove.

The following pitch was a delirium of boulders, thorns, nettles, crashing, backtracking. *"C'est un cauchemar, ce camping,"* muttered Ramón. *"Merde."* This camping was a nightmare, and we weren't even camping yet. By late afternoon we reached the *well in the rock*, where Og had a drink, then began the *heavy climb*. We treaded upward through fine scree poised at the angle of repose, so that the weight of the stuffed sleeping bag rolled back the gain of Ramón's each step. *"Merde, merde, merde. Carajo!"* The sun was nearing the horizon. We gained the stratum we aimed for and I ran to a lip to see the castle. It wasn't there. We trudged along a limestone shelf, up and down drainages, past one withheld view after another. After a half-dozen false arrivals I spotted a pile of rocks with a few tumbled arches. There it was.

As we descended the stones took shape. From the murk gathered a scattering of roofless walls, four surviving arches and a grassy declivity suggesting a moat, beyond which the valley blanked into dusty purple. Any disappointment to find no dominance of ramparts and turrets was lost in our anxiety to find the room furnished by the Alpine Club. We circled the pale stones, at last located a small wooden door, hesitated, then pushed it in.

"Buenas tardes," came a voice.

The greeting's very quietness made us jump back. *"Buenas tardes,"* we returned. By the gloom of a small fire sat an old man with close-cropped white hair. He invited us to sit down. We zealously took in the room while exchanging identities. "I'm herder here," he said, "but only in the daytime." Og and his small dog sniffed nose to bottom. The floor was soft with charred dust, and next to a small fireplace lay a pile of brush, kindling and a few larger trunks.

"Is this the room fixed up by the mountain club?" I asked.

"A room of theirs? I've never heard of one. This is the only habitable room in the castle. They did leave this." From the wall the shepherd unhooked a plastic envelope containing a one-page history of the structure and greetings from the Alpine Club of Alicante. "You're not thinking of spending the night here."

"Yes."

"You'd be much better off at my house. It's only around the corner. I live there with my wife, daughter, son-in-law and grandson. There are two other families next door. There are folks; it's civilized. It will be cold here. There you can sleep in a bed . . ."

We expressed our gratitude, but we had come to spend the night in the castle.

"You're making a mistake. Anyway, would you like some wine?"

"Very much."

He produced a small wooden cask like those in pictures of Saint Bernards, with a metal spigot on top. Adepts from La Bodega, we tilted our heads back and jetted the home vintage down our throats, dark, rich and sweet. When it was drained, the shepherd suggested a tour of the castle. "Be careful of the bulls," he cautioned as we stooped out the door, "because they go into the chambers for shelter and some of them are mean."

"*Bulls?*" we said together.

"Fighting bulls. I tend bulls, not sheep. Most of them now are only cows. The young males are taken below every spring to raise them for the ring. I look after the ones here in the daytime and at night they fend for themselves. I think most of them are out in the field now."

We inspected more slowly what we had already seen in pursuit of the furnished room, then returned to the smoky warmth. The shepherd rolled a cigarette, invited us again to his house for the night, repeated that we would regret our decision. Again we politely declined. "In that case, I'll say farewell until morning," he said, and vanished out the door with his dog.

How strange, we thought, a family living so close, and two other families as well, with drinking water, perhaps a school the children could get to. Pondering this mystery, we threw wood on the fire, ate our sandwiches, then read the one-page history of the castle. It was not Moorish but Christian, built by Philip II to hold the Moors that remained in Spain after they had been officially thrown out ten years after the consolidation of Catholic power in 1492. It was, then, not so much a castle as a prison, "perhaps the most impregnable fortress in Spain", and had been leveled less by time than by the thoroughness of fortune hunters who demolished entire walls in search of gold fabled to be secreted here by the Moors. It was suddenly cold. We heaped more wood on the fire. When the room was warm enough for comfort the air was ripe with smoke, our eyes watered, our lungs seized and we dashed outside to breathe. Instead of a night's relief, my lungs were condemned to a new insult. Apparently we would divide the night between weeping and freezing.

"What time is it?" asked Ramón.

"Eight o'clock."

"Is that all? Feels like eleven."

The wood was shrinking. Og gave up on the smoke and settled outside the door, his ears quivering and alert. We imagined the evening in the shepherd's house, the fire crackling, the broth steeping, wine easing the fissures in the veins . . .

I stepped outside. Radiance hovered over the ridge, then the moon burst free, an enormous flat circle near the full. The rocky soil, the castle walls, the olive trees in the moat broke into silver, emerging in a slow but discernable advance like a photograph slanted into developer. Solidity stopped cold at the cliff. I moved forward cautiously; the empty expanse was filled with a delicate mist made luminous by the moon, through which Altea, the seacoast, the Rio Algar, the fields, groves and wooded rises traced themselves like a valley just thought of. I felt composed of cold spray.

The roomful of smoke was newly welcome, but the brush was dwindling and by eleven it gave out. We ran out with the flashlight to look for more. Before we found it, the chill fingered our bones and we dashed back in. We put off feeling guilty about using up the shepherd's wood, transfixed by our own discomfort.

We arranged the sleeping bags in the dust and crawled into them. Should we heap the blankets on top of us, mass a defense against the floor, or thin our insulation by dividing it? We debated, staring into pitch blackness. "At least there's no one here to hassle you over your hair," I commented, to no response. We would never camp again; I was condemned to a life of rock and roll. We were still quaking in our blue nylon when we heard the shepherd and his dog approaching the door next morning.

"*Buenos días.*"

"*Buenos días.* How did you sleep last night?"

We grinned sheepishly. "It was cold."

"I told you you'd be better off at my house."

"I'm afraid we used up all your firewood."

"That doesn't matter. I'll get some more."

"We'll help you."

"No, stay where you are. It will just take a minute."

Propelled by curiosity as well as guilt, we leapt out of our bags, jumped into clothes and followed him out the door. A few paces from the room he gathered an armful of brush. Only a Moorish curse could have kept us from stumbling over it during our search farther afield, and within five minutes our arms were spilling with piles as thick as the ones we had burned.

"We can give you some coffee," said Ramón, "if you don't mind instant."

"Thanks, I just had coffee at home. I'll get the fire going."

We had trusted the Alpine Club of Alicante to furnish the cups, and had to wait for the pan to cool before we could bring it to our lips. Still, the fire and the warm liquid rekindled our bones, along with our interest in seeing the settlement where the shepherd lived before starting back down.

"Come, I'll show you the way," he offered.

The old man set such a brisk pace we nearly sprinted to keep up, but the circulation was welcome. The dawn was heavy with clouds turning black where they touched the mountains, as if the rocks were bleeding into the sky. The valley remained a suggestion through the mist.

We entered a basin that funneled toward the valley, then into space. Here and there, singly and in pairs, dark bulls wandered about, grazing or staring blankly into the distance. A few of them stared at us instead, their horns, long, sharp and trained forward. The shepherd stopped now and then to point to certain individuals, to comment on their ages and comparative meanness.

"Don't they ever attack," I asked.

"Only a single male will attack. A bull will never attack from a group, or even a pair."

"So that's why they turned them loose on the beach one at a time," said Ramón. "Were those bulls from here?"

"Here they were born."

The trail rounded the end of the cliffs, then continued around the back of the ridge. The new vantage gave way to farther ridges and valleys flecked with the white pools of towns. "There's my house," said the shepherd.

It was some time before we saw where he was pointing. In a small valley at the foot of the mountain, surrounded by fields and orchards, lay three houses in a broad triangle. Through the mist we could make out little detail, but we wished we had known, as we lay shivering, that we never could have made it in our exhaustion. "It's a long way," said Ramón.

"Everything is," said the shepherd. "There's a town several kilometers from our house, which you can't see from here. We go there to buy food. We walk there, and a taxi brings us back in exchange for an occasional chicken."

We returned to the castle at a near jog, ready to roll up our bags and start back. "You must stay and eat," said the shepherd when he saw our preparations.

"No. We don't have food we can share and don't want to finish yours."

"Nonsense." Without waiting for an acceptance, he began cutting up tomatoes, green peppers, onions and a vegetable we didn't recognize. His hands appeared now here, now there like a badly spliced old movie, an abruptness of gesture that differed from nervousness in an utter conviction that he could never miss. He simmered the mix with saffron over the fire and we scooped it from the pan with bread. It was mild-flavored, satisfying, and we assumed the meal was over, but now the shepherd produced a tin of sardines from his pocket. We ate them with more bread, the shepherd tossing alternate bites to his dog with an unmeasured backsnap of the wrist that required no glance at the dog that stared so intently back at him. Now and then we rested from our chewing and the shepherd passed the flask of wine, which he had refilled. When the meal was finally finished, the shepherd reached into his shirt pocket

for cigarette papers, shook a string of tobacco from his pouch,
then a blur of fingers produced a flawlessly machined white
tube, which he passed to Ramón. He conjured another for me,
then for himself, and settled back to talk.

Spain. The trouble with Spain is that Spaniards have never
learned to get along with each other. It's not because Spain
is poor, for it's not, but because people are too busy robbing
each other. The disease comes from the big cities. In the little
towns like the one where we buy our food, the people will still
return a lost wallet to a drunken stranger. But the cities are
crawling with thieves and one must carry one's money in an
inner pocket, beneath layers of clothing that a clever hand can't
pierce.

"Dans tes pyjamas," I whispered to Ramón, who smiled.

The shepherd delivered himself of more opinions, his hands
leaping like electrons from one orbit to another with no inter-
mediate position—but as finely honed as he was, I sensed that
his own experience merely reinforced a view held in common
by his community, the vast one that was rural Spain. Only
petty thieves bother with the streets, he went on, for you can
steal bigger in the factories. If one wants a decent product one
must buy something foreign, for the Spanish one will fall apart.
Still bigger thieves sit in public offices. Country people work
all day so office workers can lie around doing nothing, and
they've arranged it so we can't make a move without paying
for their papers. If a well-dressed man walks into an office, he
gets quick service, nothing but smiles, but a man like me has
to wait hours before anyone sees he is there, and often we give
up first. But worst of all are the *Guardia Civil.* The rest of the
thieves merely rob us from a distance, from their cities, but
the *guardia* come out to where we live to have fun in person
with us shepherds. They always show up in pairs and show off
for each other. They demand identification, ask unreasonable
questions, pry into our lives, and if they are in a frisky mood to

find that something is "not in order" they will strike us, maybe beat us up, just because they are the lucky ones in uniforms. Yet more than one *Guardia Civil* has made the mistake of molesting some shepherd who turns out to have powerful friends, or relatives with influence, and has wound up being expelled. I once got revenge against such a Jew myself.

"Jew?" I said. Nearly a half millennium back Ferdinand and Isabella had kicked out the Jews, followed by the Moors who were incarcerated in this very castle, and there had scarcely been a Jew with authority in Spain since.

"Jew. The police, the bureaucrats, the crooks who sell you things that don't work, the people who own all the land you can see and don't live here, they're all Jews." *Jew* was the word for overlord, for the people who dominated and interfered with and preyed on the shepherd's countrymen, and what sounded like anti-Semitism was class loathing. During the course of what turned out to be a two-hour rant we had moved from the smoky room to a stony perch from which we could see Altea self-enclosed on its little hill, long ago complete, along with the new buildings full of foreigners strung incoherently along the coast. To the shepherd, the overlords were well-defined, immemorial. He hadn't guessed at the new ones beneath us, but there they were in their fresh constructions, spending pounds and francs and kroner on food and drink, vacation and retirement homes, playing plug-in guitars, trawling the back country for paellas, ruining their shirts with wine, sporting on the beach with bulls meant for the ring. Ramón and I, a non-practicing Catholic and a vaporized Christian Scientist, were the new Jews, along with artists, hedonists, drifters, Brits on pensions, army deserters and other new vermin infecting the immemorial poor. Native Alteans were already laying tile, mopping apartments, washing pots and linen, selling swimsuits and scrubbing toilets for these intruders, and before long the shepherd's sons and grandchildren would join them, abandoning the family hovels in the middle of nowhere, because a little money was better than none. Dribbling amorphously along the coast highway, the future lay before us and Ramon and I needed to get back to it.

The old man joined us as far as the talus slope, then sat on a boulder to watch our descent, shouting corrections when we veered from the trail. I looked back and later saw him crossing back to the castle, a small rock set in motion. Stumbling, inept in our exhaustion, we traded off the sleeping bag full of blankets and the tattered blue basket, noting with detachment the point where we'd lost the trail on the way up. We didn't care about the gapes of the construction workers, and even Og, surfeited with smells, held to our single-minded march toward sleep.

Our own revelation on the mountain was that it was time to leave Altea. I gave notice to the owner of El Cortijo, who agreed that the season was winding down and paid me in full. A German girl talked us into lingering long enough for a farewell party. We postponed departure for two days, one for the party and another for the inevitable hangover. The day of our recovery we stopped in town to collect a blanket we had lent out, and another party developed. The morning of our departure, our hangover now compounded, our possessions crammed in the Lung and Og restless on top, we paused at La Bodega for a quick farewell. The young Norwegian was waiting with a bottle of Bacardi and an array of Cokes. We couldn't insult him by the refusal of one drink. We complied, bade farewell, walked out the door. Two of our tires were flat.

It was Sunday and all the garages were closed. We had lingered a week past the latest haircut deadline and were marooned on the central downtown block with all we owned in the car. The Norwegian shrugged. "What to do but drink?" All afternoon and through the evening the Norwegian invited. It wasn't until midnight that he admitted letting the air out of the tires because he loved us and didn't want us to leave.

We let Og out, trudged back up the hill and crawled into our empty house for what remained of the night. The next morning, greeting no one, we had the tires pumped in the rain and pulled away in silence. Thus ended the quieter of our two summers on the coast.

15

I had expected to slip back agreeably to a life divided between the two Puertos, which is to say, between sides of a split self, but neglected formalities began to catch up. My room at the restaurant awaited me, as promised, but Bernardo greeted me with unexpected news: Teddy and Flo had taken off. Shortly after I left they had loaded everything into the trailer and settled up, saying they were going to San Roque for a while, and hadn't been heard of since. Ramón, tired of commuting to Puerto Real, was meanwhile pressuring me to move in with him in El Puerto de Santa María. I put him off, partly because it meant also living with his parents and grandmother, partly because I was sure it would mean seeing little of Puerto Real and the social quintet. As I stewed over these turns, in the murk of my wallet my Colorado license expired, making my driving illegal all over the world.

Not knowing what might follow from a minor infraction, I drove cautiously into Cádiz, parked around the corner from the *Jefatura Provincial de Transito* and inquired what I would need to secure a *permiso de conducir*. A man in a suit heaped me with more official forms than I had ever held and told me to report when they were completed. The Spanish I learned from dockworkers and adolescent rockers was suddenly confronted with officialdom at its most Gongoresque. "In order to record that, in complying with the requirements ordered by His Excellency the Administrator of the Department of Vehicular Licensing of Cádiz in Document No. 862, dated 29 of November, 1966, this Special Service of Fiscal Vigilance represented by the Provincial Subdirector of Cádiz Don Federico Nieto Pino and Inspector D. Antonio Martínez Trigo, require that Bruce Nicolas Berger present himself to said functionaries in the office of the Service . . ." ran the first fifth of one single-sentence trans-syntactic stew in which it took several readings to determine who was to do what to whom. I complied as best I could, and the first stamped document I received commemorated my surrender of the Colorado license, but appeared to stop short of serving as a temporary driving permit. Though I'd had no accidents in Spain, I became paranoid, stopped driving into Cádiz, and became a regular on the ferry from El Puerto de Santa María. As I threaded the ancient labyrinth with my papers, stopping pedestrians for directions, I realized that each office had its forte: one specialized in being closed, another in referring me to someone else, a third in requiring previous completion of a form from a fourth office which would not release its paper without my first presenting the document from the third. In every office two constants held, my payment of a small compensation in pesetas and eventual receipt of a small rectangle of pulp affirming that I had complied, stamped with a seal featuring laurel leaves and a crown encircling a Maltese cross, signed with a *rúbrica*. These latter, dashed off at great speed, were scribbles of combs' teeth surrounded by spirals and whorls of ink. Signatures not meant to be read, they were hieroglyphics, some of them quite beautiful, and I became more resigned to the chase when I thought of myself as a collector of *rúbricas*.

I understood the eye test requirement, but I was surprised to find no chart when I arrived at a third-story walk-up for my appointment. A meticulously tweeded gentleman cast a malevolent eye and demanded, "Do you speak Castilian?"

"I speak Andaluz," I replied, intending a pleasantry.

He didn't smile back. With a covert snort he ordered me to the window. "Cover your left eye."

I did.

"See that lighthouse at the end of the pier?"

I followed where he was pointing. "Yes."

"Cover the other eye. Can you locate the tugboat leaving the harbor?"

I located the tugboat. "Yes."

"Completed. You may pay my secretary." He could have played a trick by switching the tugboat and the lighthouse, but I knew the lighthouse well, for I could make it out across the bay from my room at the restaurant.

I arrived for the final examination at eight in the morning with certificates, photographs and pesetas in hand, and was herded in a high state of adrenaline with sixty other people into a basement auditorium. We submitted to a one-sentence literacy test, then were instructed to fetch our vehicles and line them up at the performance course. With an official in the passenger seat we performed a succession of simple turns, backing and parking through a matrix of ropes whose Euclidian clarity bore no resemblance to streets full of pedestrians, bicycles and mules. However tortuous the course to the license itself, when I held at last the handsome grey credential that folded three ways, stapled with a photograph of me looking suited and serious, authorizing me to chauffeur up to nine passengers at a time for ten years, I felt the surge of pride that had eluded me at previous graduations.

But what was I reauthorized to drive? Years of rough roads and rougher passengers had reduced the Lung to a seizure of rattles, stopped wipers, trick door handles and cracked mirrors, while the headlights were incurably cross-eyed, the right staring uselessly lower-left into the pavement while the left wandered upper-right into the trees. The Citroën's most notorious feature, its suspension, engineered to the structural limit on my model, appealed not only to frolicking riders but to street children who climbed onto a pair of rear-end protrusions when it was parked and bucked it like a trapped pony. Many times the Lung barely gasped to the Citroën garage in Jerez, where it had to be left overnight while I hitched home. On more serious occasions it had to be towed.

Yet Lung complications seemed survivable until the gas cap was stolen. Not wanting to leave the tank open to the elements until the cap could be replaced, I made the mistake of plugging the hole with paper. Unsurprisingly, kids pushed it inside within the hour, and the system required a major emetic. The paper was officially removed during another overnight in Jerez, but the afterpulp was beyond recovery. Throughout the car's remaining career, the fuel line to the carburetor clogged every few kilometers, requiring me to pull over, lift up the hood, disconnect the tube, suck the gas and spit it out to remove the offending wad, then drive a few more kilometers in a state of nausea until the procedure had to be repeated.

The Lung's most flagrant offense, blazoned in red and white fore and aft, was a license plate that read 547-TT-1965. The year was 1966, and I was surprised not to be stopped until late May. Even then the police ignored the obsolescence of the license, a French one that came with the car, and were concerned instead with a regulation I was unaware of, that all foreign vehicles had to cross the border every six months. I had no proof that I had ever done so and I was given a week to comply. Portugal was only one hundred thirty kilometers west of Sevilla and I took off.

As the customs officer at Ayamonte stamped my passport, I asked him for documentation that the car too was crossing into Portugal.

"That is not necessary," he replied. "The stamp on your passport is enough."

"Enough for my person, perhaps, but the officials who stopped me in El Puerto de Santa María want proof that I crossed with the car."

"We have no form for that."

"Then perhaps you could write a note . . ."

"That would be illegal as well as needless. The stamp on your passport is sufficient."

To sample another country, I continued to the Portuguese coastal town of Faro for the night, and though the Spanish police went back to ignoring my brazen plates, six months later I returned to Portugal, this time farther north, to the little interior town of Serpa. If these border crossings hadn't been forced upon me, I would have missed the difference between Spain under Francisco Franco and Portugal under its own dictator, Oliveiro Salazar. I had expected a continuation of Spain with a change of language, but Portugal was no such thing. As soon as I crossed the border, litter disappeared and fields were orderly and green. No jaywalkers, motorcycles or burdened beasts choked my passage through the towns, for the streets were nearly empty of inhabitants and the few pedestrians walked correctly on the sidewalks. Faro's waterside buildings, spaced out on lawns in dress white, suggested a British colony, while Serpa's were drab but fixed up, with the population safely within them. The adolescents in Serpa's pension did not respond to Andalusian kidding and the street outside remained silent until midnight, when the crack of boots on cobble reported through the stillness—clatter that repeated itself at two and four. Though Spain was also a tyranny, and by comparison a mess, I was relieved to return to it from both overnights in Portugal.

Shortly after I returned from Serpa came the moment I had expected all along. As I was parking near Rámon's apartment, an officer pounded on the door and demanded to see my car papers.

I produced the registration and my passport.

He inspected the documents. "Your passport proves that you have been in Portugal, but there is no evidence you crossed with the car."

It was the observation so coolly, so frustratingly foreseen. There was no recourse but to repeat what I had been told at the border. I had done what I could.

The officer was unmoved. "In addition to failure to prove compliance with the requirement to cross the border twice a year with the car, the car itself has exceeded the limit for operation with a foreign license. Furthermore, the license itself is out of date. If you do not license your car properly within a week, it will have to be confiscated."

He was right, of course. He could even charge me with schizophrenia for having subjected myself to *rúbricas,* eye tests and geometric ropes to become the legal driver of an illegal vehicle. But the cost of a Spanish license was the difference in purchase price between France and Spain, roughly $350. Spain had every right to protect its automotive industry with an import tax, but my Yankee upbringing balked at paying a full third of the car's original cost for a mere license plate. Instead, I accepted the wayward alternative, which was to keep driving and ignore the consequences.

Three days later in El Puerto, while I was still collecting opinions on what to do, a summons appeared under my wiper. I was to appear next day with the car at the *Jefatura* in Cádiz.

The official in charge was politeness itself. I would license the car now or lose it.

"How much would the license cost?"

"Twenty-one thousand three hundred pesetas."

I thought hard for a moment. I had arrived in the usual manner and my mouth was full of gasoline fumes. "I'm afraid I will have to relinquish the car."

The official ordered an assistant to accompany me to the Lung. "You drive it," commanded the assistant when we reached the street. He installed himself in the passenger seat and directed me to the ancient walls of the city of Cádiz. Set into the base of their heavy stones was a phalanx of hemispherical double wooden doors, a feature I hadn't noticed until now. He motioned me toward one of them. "Park." He got out, inserted a key in a padlock, swung the doors open, then motioned me to drive forward to one side, into the darkness.

When I got out I felt a rush of cold air, as if from a cave. Next to my car stood another Citroën, the aerodynamic luxury model, and between them tilted a motorcycle. The dust on both vehicles was so thick that I could not determine their color. I gave the Lung a farewell pat, whispered, *"Merci pour ta compagnie,"* then returned to the sunlight. I glanced down the row of padlocked wooden doors: the walls of the city of Cádiz, built six centuries back to enclose the oldest continuously inhabited site in Europe, were filled with the rusting hulks of improperly licensed vehicles. This was not just another scrap heap; the Lung had entered history.

We returned to the *Jefatura* on foot. I signed a paper acknowledging release of the car, then boarded the ferry to El Puerto de Santa María. The divestiture had happened quickly. I stood on deck, watching the blocky profile of Cádiz recede, the lower contour of my new hometown take shape. No more autonomy to go where I liked, and when. No more motor trips for Og, no more life under the pines for either of us. No more flats, breakdowns, tow trucks, mouthfuls of gasoline, emergency errands for friends, parking to contend for, close calls on the highway, children to scream at, mechanics to be ignored by. The loss felt light. Ramón would be pleased. The marathon of offices and garages that had set me on an obstacle course through a bureaucratic maze within an urban labyrinth, with side trips to the Salazar dictatorship, had led a mere ten kilometers, from my room at the boarded-up restaurant to Ramón's parents' apartment.

16

I was now a fulltime inhabitant of the world Ramón and I created together. It was a land with its own language, for in our year and a half of speaking French in Andalucía we had evolved a private speech that compounded French-Moroccan slang with pillage from Spanish, English, German and Arabic, an instrument we adapted to mood and topic. It amused us that shopkeepers shut their ears to both of us as soon as they pegged me for American, never registering our nasals and throaty *r*'s, always assuming we were speaking English. Even our Spanish among friends set us slightly apart, for Ramón's was too correct to pass for Andalusian and mine was still in process, but the breach we relished was our own idiom, which gave us the sport of being private in public.

Mostly we were public in private, for as young males among elders we overwhelmed the Talamantes apartment. Og's and my outdoors, recently our own pine grove over the Bay of Cádiz, shrank to a balcony over vegetable stalls, and the shrieks of ravens and magpies were now the cries of vendors and housewives haggling over onions. Our indoor space, on the other hand, expanded from a cement cell to a second-story six-room sweep of cool tile along two sides of a glass-roofed courtyard, the atrium of a bar that made a persistent off-white noise. Ramón's bedroom, too confined for anything but sleeping, contained us only when we were truly in bed; otherwise we exploded into the next room, which was the kitchen, or into the livingroom, now also known as Og's room.

There were five of us human beings, but two seemed like wraiths rather than presences. Ramón's grandmother, ailing inhabitant of the room to the other side of ours, never ventured from the apartment and took her meals on a tray in the livingroom. Ramón's father, a lean fiftyish man who endured life in bitter silence, came and went wordlessly, breakfasted before we got up and took the rest of his meals on the road. Having fled the Franco regime to build up a forty-employee shoe factory in Casablanca, only to lose it when Morocco nationalized and sent the European businessmen back where they came from, he now found himself owner of a two-truck hauling company and drove one of the trucks himself. The dozen children of his first marriage all had lives in Morocco, if they had lives at all; one, also a truck driver, drove in the opposing lane straight into cars that didn't dim their lights, swerving at the last instant, and was killed in a head-on. In Puerto de Santa María, Ramón's father was reduced to the one child of his second marriage, a wastrel who drummed instead of getting a job. My exchange with this man was little more than a minimal greeting in the hall, but aside from the occasional argument in which Ramón refused to cut his hair, that was more contact than Ramón enjoyed.

The house's other vibrant spirit, Ramón's mother, was goddess of the kitchen, ally of the many dinners I had already eaten with Ramón. Plump and voluble, she made the best of us. Untiringly she turned out saffron rice with onion and garlic, potato omelets, breaded fish, lentils, cous-cous sent by a relative in Rabat and, when the larder was lowest, garlic soup. Ramón's and my contribution was to make endless trips around the corner to refill unlabeled green bottles with sherry or red wine, and to keep the kitchen marbled with smoke. "Put the cigarettes *out*," she would cry. "You're coughing like tubercular patients and I can't breathe. Stop it!" I felt for her, knowing we were repaying her generosity with insult, yet callously kept lighting up with Ramón, drunk on our mutual capricious will. Knowing her only recourse, she would dice pale, bland, resilient pieces of lettuce stem into the lettuce, adding onion, tomato, olive oil and lemon juice, then plunk the bowl down so we would stub out our Celtas. That was our signal to grab our forks to see who could harpoon the most pieces of lettuce stem. Tines cocked for each pale eruption, we feinted, stabbed, missed, breached and stilettoed, keeping score as over and over we narrowly missed each other's flesh—a drummer and a pianist seemingly bent on goring each other's chops.

It was in our room that we had to tone it down, for the wall between us and Ramón's grandmother didn't reach the ceiling and her deafness was only partial. Light from the outside barely reached that windowless sanctum, having to filter its way through the courtyard and the hall windows and over the transom to where we slept. Usually I woke before Ramón and was anxious to begin the day. Ramón, sometimes facing the other way, dozed on, and on one such occasion I passed the time by staring intently into the back of his head, willing him awake. A nonbeliever in telepathy, I was shocked when he stirred, turned in his sleep so that he faced me, then opened his eyes to find my own boring into them. "Don't *ever* do that again," he commanded.

"You deserved it," I shot back.

"Why?"

"Because when you woke me last night I was eating roast beef. *Tu sais ce que c'est, manger rosbif?* Roast. Beef. I can only eat it when I'm asleep."

Our eyes were still locked and we burst out laughing. Such was the pillow talk in our not-quite-private room.

Any fears that adventure would stop when I moved from Puerto Real to El Puerto de Santa María were misplaced, for it came

to town with the spring fair. I had been to these weeklong celebrations of sherry and flamenco dancing already in the two
Puertos, in Jerez and in Sevilla—whatever we could reach in
the Lung. Clubs, businesses, families and town fathers set up
little ceremonial houses where they invited friends and passers-by to *copas* of sherry, tapas and a sit at a table with guitars
and cigarettes, and those who didn't host these *casetas* only
needed to bring stamina and enough self-discipline to make it
home. Without car, we were confined to the fair in El Puerto,
and it was quite enough. *Quieres ir a la feria?* we would ask
Og. *Tu veux aller à la foire?* Dervishing amid leaps and yelps,
Og would dance toward the door.

Once we were in the street, Ramón and I had our arms over
each other's shoulders while holding our free hands in front,
a position that had to be mastered to navigate a sidewalk, but
we were no different from other pairs of young men and young
women except for the German shepherd reeling around us like
a satellite running amok. *Caseta* tenders who offered us sherry
would ask, sarcastically, whether our dog would like a *Fino La
Ina* or a *Sandeman amontillado.*

"He'd prefer a San Miguel," I'd reply, naming a beer, and
often Og would be served.

Attached to these traditional celebrations were carnival
midways of the sort to be found in any part of the world, and
sometimes we sobered up amid the game booths and rides.
Crowds surging through the warrens of improvised streets
made it difficult to keep track of each other, let alone our short
companion, but Og did his best to keep us in sight. Patrick had
given him a call as personal to Og as his name, an undulating
whistle that might be graphed as a sine wave, and it was usually enough to establish contact. If Og were stranded farther
afield, he simply remained where he had last seen us and we
retraced our steps until we found him. His loyalty earned him
the dubious privilege of joining us on such ground-level rides

as the Shaking Cage, which reproduced the thrill of dice being rattled in a cup, and hand-steadied horseback rides on the merry-go-round, but his attempt to join us in the Octopus was nearly his undoing.

Instructing him to wait, we paid for our tickets and climbed into an empty car. The engine cranked into gear, the central pivot rotated at a tilt, the arms gathered speed in a careening spiral, and the eight cars spun in place, so that we swept to the ground and back in the air in a series of unpredictable accelerating spins. Og kept track of our car even when the Octopus was reeling and gyrating at full speed, and each time we spun to the ground he lunged toward us and tried to leap in. We sat helpless in a suspension that turned to panic as each swoop threatened a haphazard but fatal blow to his skull. The operator of the ride yelled at Og, paced in frustration, and at last dove under the pinwheeling cars, nearly getting brained himself, grabbed Og by the leg and hauled him yelping backward. Yelling at an assistant to stop the ride, he gripped Og like a vice until we were back on the ground. With his leftover adrenaline Og left a measles of tooth marks all over our right arms.

We felt more relaxed about leaving Og to his devices when we reached a plywood building advertised by a young man in black and white prison stripes, a wordless barker staring sullenly into the midway, luring people in. A large sign over the ticket window proclaimed CARYL CHESSMAN. Ramón had never heard the name and I explained that Chessman was a petty thief and alleged rapist who had been executed several years ago in the United States, provoking a campaign against capital punishment. Five pesetas parted the burlap.

The tent filled, the light dimmed. The curtain opened on an alcove with a plain chair in an oversized telephone booth. A loudspeaker welcomed us in Castilian and gave us a resumé of Chessman's career: the legal tangles, the sentences, the reprieves, the agony of death scheduled, death postponed.

The young man in prison stripes entered stripped to the waist.
He was followed by a fat executioner whose head was covered
by a red cloth bag, his eyes leering from sagging oval holes.
The condemned sat; the executioner mimed the strapping of
his wrists. In somber tones the voice-over explained that the
condemned needed to be strapped in place to keep him from
thrashing, that cyanide pellets were dropped into a vat, that the
resultant vapors invaded the condemned's lungs. Steam rose
in the booth. The young man twitched, his torso began to twist
and writhe. He lurched forward and back to free himself from
imagined shackles, his face straining as if from constipation.
The voice spoke in a hush. The end was coming. There was a
final gasp; the man's head heaved forward and hung.

The victim remained motionless for several minutes while
the voice, dark with social conscience, lectured on the irony
of the state committing a crime the condemned had not been
accused of: murder. The booth dimmed, the voice droned to
a stop, a luminous skeleton appeared in the chair. The voice
resumed, heavy with tragedy. Protests had come from around
the world. Albert Schweitzer, Pablo Casals and the pope implored the state of California not to do it. The condemned himself had written four eloquent books in his behalf. All in vain.
Lights reappeared in the booth and the chair was miraculously
empty. The voice shrank to one word, repeated in a whisper. It
stopped, exhaled the word once more: *Muerto.*

There was a moment of silence while the crowd waited for
the house lights. Suddenly three screaming men in luminous
prison suits lunged from the darkness, firing blanks. They
shoved the front row, which shrieked, then vanished the other
direction. The lights flicked on and we filed out. Back in the
midway, I said to Og, "You didn't miss anything."

After a week of crowds in the dust, costumed locals dancing
the *sevillana*, darts at balloons, gypsies selling shish-kabobs,
copas of sherry for me and Ramón and dishes of beer for Og, I

was ready for the fair to be over and was not impressed that one
end of it was dominated by a vast metallic globe proclaiming
the uniqueness of one Raphael Blounde. I assumed, without
much reflection, that all it took to ride around the inside of
an iron cage so that one crossed the summit upside down was
speed, centrifugal force and a certain courage not overbur-
dened with brains.

Carmelo, however, the lead singer of Los Simbroni, had
struck up an acquaintance with the great Raphael, and invited
me to join them for lunch. The trim, fine-featured Raphael arrived in a neatly tailored suit. Originally Rafael Rubio from
Madrid, he had changed the *f* to *ph* and converted Rubio,
meaning blond, to Blounde—doctoring the French for effect—
in recognition that Spaniards, like most people, expect of their
artists the glamor of being from somewhere else.

I had thoughtlessly underrated Raphael's act. There was, to
be sure, a rabble that rode motorcycles around such constructions as the Infernal Sphere with some pretense to daring, but
Raphael was the only one in the world to risk himself between
the four deadly wheels of a car. Yet the public was obtuse to the
distinction. Raphael, meanwhile, had become tired of traveling from fair to fair. The Sphere had seemed like an inspired
means to stake his return to Formula One, a race he had once
nearly won, but it barely paid his living expenses. Audiences
were poor because there were too many competing attractions.
The crews that mounted and dismantled the sphere, a complicated procedure on which Raphael's life depended, were
holding him for ransom. And the very circumstance of being
an appendage to these regional blowouts was humiliating to an
act of his quality. He had come to a decision: after this fair he
was striking out on his own.

We arrived, now, at the reason for my invitation to lunch.
Raphael, with assistance from Carmelo, had put together a
show for which the Infernal Sphere would supply the climax.

The audience would be primed first with a full variety show: rock group, singing sister act, stand-up comic, recitation of narrative poetry, gymnast, female vocalist, flamenco serious and flamenco parodied. The location selected for the first performance was the *plaza de toros* at Rota, near the American base, where a great potential American audience co-existed with the Spanish. Would I translate the flyers and programs into English, as well as assist Carmelo in his position of general manager, for a respectable fee? Possessed of the normal American urge to join the circus, I leapt aboard.

The acts were ready to go, the tickets printed, the bullring committed. I rendered the flyers literally, producing a Victorian effect that mirrored the Spanish extravagance:

Plaza de Toros de Rota
Saturday 18 at 10.00 PM
THE INFERNAL SPHERE
The world champion automobile acrobat
has arrived in Spain for the first time.
RAPHAEL BLOUNDE
The man of audacity and cold blood without rival
in the Twentieth Century.

———

Accompanied by his racing car, he will give a public
Acrobatic Exhibition
with fireworks in his Infernal Sphere
with his Artistic Group and varieties
Don't miss this unique world-famous spectacle!!
One day only

———

We had it printed in five colors and plastered it on every blank wall in Rota. All that remained was to dismantle the sphere at the fair in El Puerto and reassemble it in the Rota bullring.

Raphael had severed relations with the fair, the crew that packed and transported the rides was no longer available, and the assignment to round up an alternate crew fell to Carmelo. His efforts to improvise a work force in El Puerto and Rota came to nothing and he was forced to fall back on his reserve, a labor pool in Jerez that was mostly gypsy and reliably desperate. Afraid of further delay, we sped to Jerez in his borrowed van. Within an hour of arrival, Carmelo had rounded up as tattered, pungent and hostile a selection of humanity as I had smelled up close, several of whom joined us in the van; the rest piled into an old truck of their own.

Under Raphael's manic supervision they dismantled the Sphere, wedged it with cunning into a truck that swallowed it like a clam, and our several vehicles sped to Rota. By late afternoon the unpacked pieces lay in the center of the Rota bullring, poised for assembly in triangular wedges like the rind of a sliced melon. Carmelo faced a dilemma: should he pay the gypsies on the spot and risk their being satisfied with a single day's wages, or should he wait until the job was done and chance their defecting in fear they would not be paid at all? He felt he had no choice. To establish credibility, he paid them for their day's efforts, impressing on them the urgency of their returning next morning to assemble the sphere for the evening performance.

To no great surprise, the next morning they didn't show up and by noon it was clear the show would have to be canceled. The afternoon was devoted to staving off disaster: radio announcements that the show was postponed, assurances to the variety acts that the tour was weathering only a minor setback, arrangements to secure a few more days of bullring for the sphere.

Three days later the Sphere was assembled by surer hands and the show went on. But disaster had found its mark. Half the variety acts sniffed the end and disappeared, a suspicious

public saved its pesetas, and a pitiful show played to forty individuals caught between anger and embarrassment. Raphael,
for the last time, entered the great cage to a flourish of fire-
crackers. He revved his beat-up Ferrari with a sequence of
throaty growls. As he began to spiral in low turns around the
base, the sphere began to wobble, then to swing, and it was
immediately obvious that bullring sand lacked the stability of
midway dirt. "Grab the supports!" Carmelo yelled to the tenders of the arena. They converged on the Sphere's foundation
and bore down on it with their weight as Raphael accelerated
his way up in steepening circles. I was terrified that the Sphere
was going to keel over and crush an attendant, never mind what
happened to Raphael. But the Sphere stabilized as Raphael
continued working his way up and finally ringed the Sphere
vertically, touching four wheels to the top in several shrilly
combusting passing taunts to gravity. He worked his way more
swiftly back down, survived the next round of wobbles, stepped
out to ragged applause, and the show was over forever. The ex-
pense of paying the last crew, renting the bullring for four days
and rewarding the loyal variety acts was so great, and the take
so scant, that Raphael contacted a Rota ironmonger and sold
the sphere for scrap. The next morning the pieces lay together
for the last time, bizarre and pitiful remnants of ballyhoo that
returned, like Raphael, to anonymity.

We didn't really need fairs to distract us when Og was our daily
live-in adventure—and we were his. Several times a week we
lured him onto the bed, threw the four corners of the spread
around him and carried him through the apartment like Santa's
ninety-pound sack. We hid in closets, behind full-length shut-
ters or on the balcony, and called through the intervening
rooms, *Quieres dar un paseo? Tu veux faire une promenade?*
Want to go for a walk? while he spun from room to room in
a gathering frenzy, at last caught smell of one of us, yelped

and clamped his jaw repeatedly on hand and forearm, lunging for better grips, while we tried to defuse him with unctuous caresses and croons: *sweet doggie, petit chou-chou de chien, perro precioso!* Nor did we confine our mental torture to the house. Ramón and I would duck into a movie and leave Og to wait patiently for two hours by the door. Once when the film was over we left by a side door and circled around until we could watch Og from the shadows across the street. He stared at each person to leave the theater with an intensity that grew darker as the crowd thinned and stopped. There was a long gap, an attendant came out to change the poster and close the ticket window, and finally the owner locked the front door and went home. We watched Og gape heartbroken at the empty façade. Softly, we floated the sine-wave whistle from the shadows. He wheeled and charged across the street, leaping and yelping, and savaged our hands with his fangs.

It was only fitting that Og found an effective way of taunting us back. Javier, the beer-delivering brother of the Simbroni guitarist, had acquired an old Paris taxi that he and several raffish friends painted black, and so mobilized they tested the already tolerant local standards of drunkenness, slept off their binges in the seats, and only touched home for occasional hot soup. Og soon showed us he was born to be one of them. At first he merely caroused with them in our company, but soon he was ditching Ramón and me when he caught sight of them and only scratched back at the door after his binge—an honor he conferred on no other strangers. Still more humiliatingly, the ruffians would arrive at our door and invite Og to a night of drinking, neglecting to extend the invitation to Ramón and me, leaving us to stay home or proceed by ourselves—abandoned by our friends and our dog. On such occasions we sometimes caught sight of the Paris taxi making the rounds with six young drunks inside and Og up on the luggage rack, yelping at the world or bestowing a calm mayoral gaze.

So Og-besotted was our life that he invaded my very dreams. One night I was a super—an extra in an opera production—a scenario no doubt suggested by an evening I spent as a one-dollar walk-on priest in a San Francisco Opera production of *Boris Godunov*. As the dream proceeded through a crowd scene in *Aida*, where I stood onstage as a robed attendant, I noted that Og, unknown to myself, had landed a job playing a leopard. As I admired his stately bearing, the ferocious cat head hooked over his snout, the hide stretched over his back and attached with bands at the legs, the sweep of the wired tail, he suddenly recognized me, broke character and started prancing in my direction. His head began to slip off, beneath the leopard fangs broke the familiar nose, the toothsome grin, and the entire costume started sliding backward. I fired off a stage whisper. "Cool it, Og, you're blowing your act!" Onward he came, oozing out of his leopard skin, until with a joyful bound he leapt toward me free of all encumbrance. I woke laughing, and Ramón demanded to know what was going on.

Like most unusual behavior, Og's deportment did not pass unnoticed by the authorities. In charge of dog control in El Puerto was a Chaplinesque little man who had been demoted from parking tickets because he couldn't handle the math. Perhaps out of pity or to allow the man a moment of glory, Og contrived to be caught. Rumor of his capture reached us immediately and we stormed in pursuit.

El Puerto's dog pound, to my horror, turned out to be located in the slaughterhouse. We reached the gate and began to yell. As soon as the little man unlatched for us, we demanded, "Where is he?" The man pointed at a door across a courtyard. We charged across, peered through the slats, and found a frantically leaping Og fastened with a rope and iron collar in a roomful of nasty little yappers that scampered about him like sparrows in the lion cage. When we demanded Og's release, the man stood his ground. The dog would have to remain locked up a minimum of twenty-four hours and would be turned over only upon presentation of medical papers plus payment of a modest fine. Og had received his rabies shot at the campground, but the campaign to inoculate all dogs in Spain produced no documents. From the slaughterhouse, we took off for the vet. Persuaded by our hysteria in insisting that Og had been covered by the rabies program and was in perfect health, the doctor backdated a series of certificates. With nothing more we could do in Og's behalf, we distracted ourselves with a round of errands.

We were at the fish market when a friend came up and informed us that our dog was at our door and scratching to get in.

"*Ojalá*," we answered sadly, "if only that were true. But he's locked up for twenty-four hours."

"That may be," shrugged the friend, sauntering off, "but anyway he's at your door."

We finished buying fish, aware we'd been victimized by the usual flying misinformation, but couldn't help returning home for our disillusionment. At the top of the stairs we were leapt upon and bit in paroxysms of joy. Our dread replaced by curiosity, we locked Og in the apartment and raced to the pound to find out how Og had pulled it off.

The dogcatcher's daughter gave us the account. While her father was out rounding up more strays, Og slipped out of the iron collar and lunged at the door with the slats until it came off its hinges, letting all the other dogs out as well. The dogcatcher's daughter raced about the courtyard trying to catch a dozen yipping, scrapping, squealing and defecating little mongrels while Og looked for the way out. When the returning dogcatcher opened the gate, Og tore past him and made three great circles around the compound's perimeter. Drawing a bead on the Talamantes apartment, a free meal in his stomach, he tore home through two previously untraveled kilometers to the east at a dead run.

Neither the dogcatcher nor any other official made any effort to verify Og's papers or collect the fine. To seal Og's deliverance, Ramón's mother ambushed the terrified dogcatcher several days later in the street, shook her finger in his face and commanded, "You leave that dog alone!" Og's freedom of expression was, by extension, our own, and it suffered no further restraint.

17

The girlfriend of one of Puerto's rockers arrived at the
apartment to return a record, poked her head into our
bedroom, saw the sleeping arrangements and said, "Uh-
oh, I know where that leads." I happened to know that
the young woman's father was a regular at the ranch of
ill repute where Og had sired the puppies. I also knew
that she and her boyfriend had copulated standing
up in the vestibule of his apartment. Still more to the
point, I knew that this same boyfriend had once made
a pass at Ramón, who rebuffed it with indignation. I
felt like saying, "Look to your own house, Mila," but
Ramón and I let it pass without comment and never referred to it afterward, even to each other. The incident
was notable not because it happened but because it was
the only critical remark we ever received about the life
we shared. Our freedom to live as we pleased was no
more threatened from outside than Og's was by the dogcatcher. Any threats to our alliance could only come
from ourselves.

Alas, they did. As Ramón and I passed a newsstand
in Cádiz, having come over on the ferry so Ramón could
buy new drumsticks, my eye snagged on a spindle of
books. They were used paperbacks, in English, and my
hand landed on a beat-up edition of Virginia Woolf's
The Waves. Ramón watched without comment as I paid
twenty pesetas and walked off with it. We rode the ferry

back to El Puerto without either of us inspecting, or even referring to, my purchase.

Books! My mother had taught me to read before I reached
first grade and I had been doing so addictively ever since. But
books in English had given out even before Patrick had taken
off two years back. When I was first learning Spanish I bought
Juan Ramón Jiménez's collection of miniature essays, *Platero
y yo*, plus an anthology of modern Spanish poets, and lay long
hours on the roof over my room at the restaurant, dictionary
at hand, picking up vocabulary as I read great writing—but
since exhausting those slim volumes I had read nothing at all.
Like everyone around me, I lived a purely oral life, not real-
izing that my brain was out of ink. From *The Waves'* first pages
I felt a surge of reconnected energy. This was voice; this was
genius. I kept the book close to me, read it when Ramón went
to the bathroom or around the corner for cigarettes. I wasn't
just living with Ramón and Og; I was also living with Virginia
Woolf. When he discovered me squinting into *The Waves* in the
thin light that fell over the transom as he awoke, he asked why
I was so obsessed by that book.

"You don't want me staring into the back of your head and
waking you up," I said. "This distracts me." He didn't look as
amused as he should.

I had worried that life in Ramón's apartment would reduce
me too strictly to a rocker's priorities. Simbroni had run its
course and a new group was coalescing around the two of us
and some guitarists from Jerez. As we became regulars in their
houses, our own house filled with the dance routines Ramón invented to amuse ourselves with. I was indeed amused, loved our
life. But one day I said to him, imitating our line to Og, "*Tu veux
faire une promenade?* Shall we go for a walk? In the pines?"

"Why the pines?" he asked. "There's nothing there."

"There's green there. I'm tired of nothing but buildings."

"Buildings are where the people are."

"I'm going there anyway," I said. "I'll be back in an hour."

The first few times I went walking on my own, Ramón let it pass, but eventually he said, "I don't get it. Are you meeting someone there?"

I froze; there had never been a remark like that between us.

"I go there precisely because there's no one. You're the only one I want with me, and I've asked you, but you refuse."

"So you're leaving me for a bunch of trees? No, I'm not going there."

Ramón had poisoned the pines for me, and now I merely took circuitous routes when it was my turn to buy cigarettes. On one such detour I was detained by an incident in the street; some ten-year-olds were hurling rocks at a wounded dove trapped on the high windowsill of a bodega. The elements began to resonate: the dove was a symbol of peace; the street was named for General Mola, an ally of Franco's; the children were innocent of these associations and were merely throwing rocks at a bird in the manner that they gave cigarettes to lizards. I hadn't written a poem in two years but one began to take shape. It would be in ballad stanzas, somewhat in the manner of Lorca, and to avoid mawkishness about the bird, it would be a cold recital whose very objectivity delivered the impact. When I returned home, I grabbed pencil and paper and headed into the most private space, which was our bedroom.

Ramón followed me in. "What are you doing?"

How to explain a poem to someone who didn't read at all? I described the scene in the street and declared I was writing a poem about it. "But it won't be sentimental. It's not about a wounded bird. It's about the way people behave."

"Why do you do stuff like that?" said Ramón. "It takes you away from people when you should be connecting."

There was more than one way to connect, I thought, but I didn't answer. I finished working out the poem in pencil, typed it up, then put it away.

I could better have tolerated music I could see through if I also had access to the densities I preferred, but again Ramón tried to expel from my life whatever he couldn't share. He tolerated it, though declined to join me when I was invited to the house of opera buffs who had chanced to be in El Oasis the night the lights went out and I wound up accompanying Puccini arias by candlelight. To honor our two countries they played me the Leontine Pryce recording of Falla's "*El Amor Brujo*." I marveled at the voice, they laughed at the accent, and I was reassured that Spain had more to offer musically than the "ye-ye" of ersatz Brits. After a pair of such evenings the music lovers arranged for me to meet Carlos Terry, twenty-year-old scion of the family that owned El Puerto's leading bodega. In town for a few days from Madrid, where he was studying classical piano, he had many people to visit in a short time, but I would be welcome from eleven to twelve on Sunday. This was, as well, an invitation to the house of El Puerto de Santa María's leading family, and I invited Ramón to join me.

On the morning of the appointment I showered first, then turned over the bathroom to Ramón. When he took longer than usual, I poked my head in. "It's twenty to eleven."

"I'm not ready."

It was nearly eleven when he emerged, dripping. He toweled off, leisurely selected his underwear, lingered over a choice of shirts, perversely chose the naval pants with a complicated twelve-button flap in front, which took an age to line up and fasten. "We're going to be late," I said. He returned to the bathroom to comb his hair. When he emerged ten minutes later, I said, "You've won. We're not going."

"What's the point?" he replied.

The point was that I was furious. Did he think that just because I shared a musical taste with the unmet Carlos Terry, I was going to take off with him to Madrid? Disappointment over a missed event was nothing compared to my resentment over Ramón's underhanded sabotage of an accepted invitation.

Chafing at these imagined threats, one day I set up the type-writer in the livingroom and began pounding away. Ramón appeared immediately. "Another letter to your mother? I thought you just wrote to her."

"I did. These are notes about the Infernal Sphere. I want to get it down before I forget it."

"Is your memory that bad?"

"I'm not worried about now. I'm thinking ahead. If I ever come to write about my time here, there'll be all this stuff about Puerto Real and nothing about El Puerto de Santa María, even though I've spent just as much time here as there."

Ramón congealed. "Write a book! Are you here to live the life we have together here, right now, or are you just planning to retail it all later somewhere else, in another language?"

Ramón struck a nerve I didn't know I possessed. However irrational Ramon's drive for total control, his question dove to the heart. Was I immersed in our life for its own sake or was I salting away material for future use? I'd taken my assorted motives for granted, since they all seemed benign, and never stopped to consider them. When I gained perspective, I accepted that the writer stands in a predatory relation to life. Everything is lived for its own sake and everything is potential material, and any writer who can't accept a nonstop double motive needs to put away his pen. Eventually I also realized that if I had simply faced Ramón and said, *You let me have my writing and my music or I move out*, anyone so desperate to hold onto me would have relented, and we would have returned to the untroubled communion we shared when we lived in separate towns. But neither clarity nor ultimatums had entered my repertoire. Ramón left the room, I put away the typewriter, and I never again tried to write more than a letter home in the Talamantes apartment.

Nothing but Ramón's own chimeras threatened his peace, but I was found out from a greater distance. In the middle of the night came a rap on the door. A messenger bore a telegram from the American consulate in Palma de Mallorca: *Patrick McDougal in hospital, condition serious, call for details.* There was no telephone in the apartment, calls from a public phone were a snarl of misconnections, mashed voices and denials of the existence of said consulate, and a return telegram of my own went unanswered. Two and a half days later, by train, boat and taxi, I arrived at the Hospital Provincial de Baleares.

Patrick's parents had already arrived from San Diego. Patrick had apparently been returning to his pension at night in Ibiza, had stumbled over the old city walls and had fallen to the rocks below, breaking his spine. He had lain unnoticed into the following morning, when he was found by the police. They had flown him to a Catholic charity hospital in Palma where, by a stroke of luck, one of the world's great neurosurgeons, a doctor from Madrid vacationing on Mallorca, performed at no cost as fine an operation as Patrick could have received anywhere. He was paralyzed from the waist down—a condition not necessarily permanent, since there was still feeling in his legs. Alone with Patrick, I learned that he had been taking LSD on Ibiza, and though he didn't remember the fall, it might have occurred during an acid flashback.

I spent three weeks in Palma, most of it with Patrick's parents, visiting the hospital, helping them arrange complicated ambulance and airline reservations for the trip home. At last the three of them boarded the first of the flights that would deliver Patrick to Scripps Clinic in San Diego.

Finding myself a free agent in an unexpected place, I decided to lift my spirits by investigating the one Mallorcan connection I knew of, the bleak and remote monastery where Chopin and George Sand had spent a tubercular winter in 1839, Sand smoking cigars while Chopin coughed and knocked out a prelude for each key and each emotion. As the only discernibly foreign passenger in the bus from Palma to Valldemossa that rainy Tuesday in February, I planned to talk the guard into letting me play a few preludes on the Pleyel Chopin had waited for in such agony—the very keyboard on which the pieces were composed. I was startled to be let off in a vast parking lot full of rental cars, taxis and international buses. Tours awaited me in four languages. I waited for the crowd to clear at the silk cord, glimpsed the famous Pleyel, inspected the little plastic replicas of it with their busts of Chopin in the gift shop, and took the bus back to Palma. Chopin out of reach, I returned to Ramón.

The outside world next summoned me in the form of a letter from my mother. She hadn't seen me in two and a half years, didn't know what I currently looked like, couldn't imagine my life. She and my grandmother were coming over.

How would this play out, I wondered in alarm. The fact that the two of them and my Andalusian friends were all sherry drinkers only pointed up the differences between suburban bridge parties and all-male stand-up zinc bars. The scenarios I imagined led to social disaster and I was relieved to learn, next letter, that they had booked a Mediterranean cruise whose last stop was Málaga. They would linger in that town for a couple of days to visit before their flight home. It seemed they merely wanted to touch base.

Ramón declined to come with me to Málaga. I reached the Hotel Miramar by bus, rented a car, drove my mother and grandmother into fields of daisies, invited them to paella on terraces, took them shopping in Gibraltar. I inveighed against Torremolinos, through whose clot of third-rate tourist high rises, discos with fractured English names and cafés full of flotsam we had passed: Torremolinos for the moment was uniquely horrible, but it prefigured the future of the Spanish coast.

My mother interrupted me. What was I doing with my life?

"Living it," I declared with what I hoped was finality.

"That's no answer," replied my mother. "We all live our lives. What are you doing with yours?"

On the bus ride back to El Puerto, the two days of home values receding like a hallucination, that question rang in my ears. I was cynical about the notion of people finding themselves, so much in the air. Had they tried the mirror? But what did my own mirror show?

An outsider might have seen a person who had struck out on his own, setting his life on an original, even eccentric path. I saw a curious passivity. A friend had lured me to Europe; when the friend left me, I headed to the nearest familiar campground with the car and the dog; when I lost the car, I accepted an invitation to move to the next town. From the inside, this looked like adventure by default. Even if it was a series of retreats, I had been given options to try on like new sets of clothes: nightclub pianist, fish salesman, carnival assistant, member of a Spanish-Moroccan family and—the most important role of all—adolescent. As an actual teenager, immersed in books or the family Steinway, alone or with adults, I hadn't been young at all, and perhaps it was important to get it all in even if it was out of sequence. This putting on and discarding of roles, at least in theory, put me on the track of that grail of Western industrially developed post-Freudian culture: the discovered self.

A more dashing version of my life came to light when one of the Simbroni guitarists remarked, "You know, most of the parents here are afraid of you."

Given my shaky self-image, I was startled. "Why?"

"Because of what you represent. You set the example of someone who left his family and his country and is perfectly happy doing what he pleases somewhere else. Every day you're here, you show the possibility that we too could leave home, go to another place without the support of what we grew up with, and do just fine. Our parents don't like that." I had no idea that those cordial and generous elders saw me as a threat and a subversive. Of all the new selves, that of social menace pleased me most. But this self-interrogation, stirred up by my mother's question, was precisely the turmoil I avoided in my contentment to be the unexamined person who loved his friends, loved Spain, loved Ramón. As I gazed out the bus window at forests of cork oak, their boles debarked like the legs of shorn lambs, I could not help wondering: was I finding myself, or did I merely find myself in Andalucía?

The wallow ended as soon as I got off the bus, for Ramón informed me that we and the guitarists from Jerez had landed a summer gig at a club called El Top-Ten, in Torremolinos. A season in the one Spanish town I despised would, I was sure, be the nightmare we had been spared the previous summer in Altea. To confirm my fears, I would be playing something called a Farfisa, a little fifteen-note electronic keyboard that would choke off jazz riffs and impromptu filigree, not to mention the arpeggio and octave practice I worked into rock-and-roll piano. Lacking a car, we would not be able to take Og, who would stay with Ramón's mother. The name of our new group, Los Everplay, suggested the time element of this hell.

El Top-Ten was an underground cubicle of cigarette smoke, speakers at the threshold of pain and international youth with progressive hairstyles, bellbottoms and wide collars from Carnaby Street. The owner, a man in his early thirties, had the finest hair and widest collar of all, and cheated us out of a night's wages when he moved us across the tunnel to his smaller, louder, smokier cubicle called The Band Box. At this second club, for a month and a half from nine-thirty until four in the morning, seven nights a week, I sat like a stenographer at the miniature electric organ whose oozy touch inspired a very specialized hatred. A measure of musical deprivation was that the evening's bright spot was the opportunity to play "A Whiter Shade of Pale," by Procol Harum, with its bass line lifted from Bach's "Air on a G String."

The nights might have been bearable if the days had offered rest or relief. Our lodging, in a gardenlike complex at the edge of town, might have sufficed the mere six of us, but not the mob lured there by rumors of our hospitality. A singer from another band installed himself with an English girlfriend recovering from hepatitis. Members of what was once another band, distinguishable by their wide collars, filled what remained of the furniture and colonized the floor. Unable to share quarters with Ramón and sometimes forced to split the settee I had claimed with total strangers, I moved into the kitchen and staked out permanent rights to an oval of floor next to the garbage.

Two of our guests had special talents. One was a slight but muscular poet named Hilario, who never wore more than a bikini and who insisted on his own greatness to the point that one wished the worst for his verse; to my disappointment he was actually gifted, his recitals of Machado and Lorca were moving, his watercolors graceful, and his personality—once the façade had been pierced—was endearing. Still more entertaining was a heavy-set bohemian from Jerez who captured the Torremolinos scene with a gift for parody that justified his floor space. After establishing himself as a regular, he disappeared. The third morning of his absence his picture greeted us from the front page of a Málaga newspaper: he and a sidekick had been picked up on seven counts of armed robbery. Known as El Pupi, his specialty was to hit banks in the wee hours, avoiding employees, and he was foiled by an early-arriving washwoman whom he was forced to knock out and leave tied in a locked john.

When floor space ran out, the overflow spilled onto the patio furniture, where our guests often snored until noon. Neighbors complained to the manager, who threatened eviction. We told the hangers-on that if the furniture were further abused there would be nothing left for anyone, but they kept coming. When the police showed up to inquire about El Pupi, the manager reached his limit and we were ejected.

We relocated to a larger, more anonymous apartment on the sixth floor of a development behind town. The move shook many of our parasites, but friends of the Jerez guitarists showed up, fresh recruits piled in, and on a grander scale the situation replicated itself. Never returning to sleep until dawn, plagued by constant upheaval in the apartment, chronically exhausted, I felt my health slip away. If I weren't allowed to dream, I could at least read. There were racks of English books for tourists and I picked up *The Razor's Edge*. Leaving Ramón to socialize with our colleagues, I spent restorative hours alone on the beach with that tale of another young American searching for alternatives far from home. It was Somerset Maugham, not Ramón, who was pulling me through.

It was hard to remain amused by a life that was physically breaking me down, but the observer in me still found much to relish until the afternoon I saw Everplay members rifling the possessions of the wide-collared band, which had moved back in with us. I asked them what they were doing.

"Collecting the rent," said the lead guitarist.

"You mean you're stealing from guests?"

"We've been paying these guests' lodgings for a long time."

"These are people who have almost nothing, and you're going through their bags and taking what little they have left. You're going to leave them poorer than St. Francis."

"Spoken like an Andalusian!" beamed the rhythm guitarist. "You're one of us."

I glared, an upwelling of retorts ready to spill forth, but held my tongue. The gig would be over for all if I pulled out. Ramón was amassing money for a new set of drums and amid the general mayhem my own folly was to remain professional. I was not even resentful when the owner of The Band Box cheated us of our last night's wages, having seen it coming.

As soon as we returned to El Puerto and Og had perforated our arms in the snarling ecstasy of our reappearance, the

outside world I'd turned my back on again broke in. On the
Talamantes doorstep there appeared a letter from a nephew in
Connecticut, announcing a forthcoming marriage and inviting
me to the wedding. I hadn't seen family or East Coast friends
for three years and wondered how I would now take the States.
Patrick's parents, meanwhile, had dropped strong hints by updating mail that now was the time to return Og to his co-owner,
to help in the recuperation. If we each owned half of Og, I felt
by this point that I owned the half you fed while Patrick owned
the half that took care of itself—but this was not the moment
to be flip. Pondering the idea of a two-week visit, I went to a
travel agent to inquire about booking myself to New York and
a German shepherd to San Diego. The plan to send Og ahead
of me unraveled when I learned there was no one in Madrid
to tend a dog between flights. Iberia, furthermore, accepted
animals only on shipping flights, not those with passengers. My
only option was to book us on successive flights so that I could
tend Og myself in Madrid, then send Og on to volunteers from
the American Society for the Prevention of Cruelty to Animals
in New York.

I was suddenly frightened to leave Spain, even briefly, on
the chance that my own country in its very brashness might
intervene and engulf me. Ramón, in turn, was panicked,
sensing defection. Was I coming back? Of course; I was merely
touching base with family. The proof was that I was leaving
my most valued belongings with Ramón. He couldn't have appreciated, of course, that my most treasured possession was a
beat-up, out-of-print volume of Spanish synonyms, rather than
the quite replaceable portable typewriter I planned to take.
The only way to reassure him was to pour out my feelings for
him. His efforts to control me were backfiring but I recognized
the love they sprang from, and I pardoned his flaws because I
knew on some instinctual level—or thought I did—what it was
like to be Ramón.

We both knew that he would never see Og again and that it was the end of our little family of three. I felt that loss as keenly as he did and we set about a last desperate measure. Informed of a full-blooded German shepherd in heat, and dreaming of a litter like the one Og had once sired, we contacted the female's owner, an olive oil wholesaler. He agreed to divide the pups and offered his warehouse for the assignation. We led Og through an entranceway into a vast and dank cavern reeking with decades of stored oil, at the far end of which, between the great barrels, we were eyed by the bride-to-be. We wished Og *fuerza* and withdrew for the night. Og was either unattracted, overcome by the stench, or simply objected to the arrangement, for we returned the next morning to find the olive merchant in a rage: Og had jumped through the plate glass window between the storeroom and the office, continued into the entranceway, and had only been stopped from another successful break by a padlock on the outer door. There would be, he was sure, no litter.

As I packed the small bag that complemented my typewriter, Ramón's mother said, "Here's a towel."

"The U.S. is full of towels," I replied. "I don't need it."

"No one can travel without a towel," she insisted, and I packed the thin yellow and purple cloth.

In virtual silence, Ramón, Og and I took a taxi to the airport in Sevilla. Feeling disconnected from my flesh, I ordered Og into a box and saw him carted away by officials from Iberia. Less than an hour later I was airborne myself. As the plane lifted from the runway, I looked down and saw the lone figure of Ramón standing outside the terminal, gazing up at the plane. My heart was breaking.

Part II

18

On the other hand, I was coming back in a month. During the layover in Madrid, I talked my way into the Iberia baggage room, slipped Og food and water, walked him briefly into sunlight, then returned him to the cage where we exchanged a last look on foreign soil. He had arrived in Paris three years before heavily sedated, barely able to rally, but his return to the States had to be taken cold—colder than I could have guessed. When I reached Patrick's parents by phone from New York, Mrs. McDougal informed me that Og had landed at the San Diego airport just as customs was closing for Labor Day weekend, and officials refused to clear him for three days. Labor Day! I'd forgotten there was such a thing. Mrs. McDougal protested that after three flights, one across an ocean and another across a continent, Og would not survive three more untended days in a cage. Under threat of a dead dog on their hands, officials allowed the McDougals to visit the airport daily, to feed and walk Og within sight of the now hateful box. But Og had made it to Patrick's wheelchair alive.

After the demented summer in Torremolinos, my culture shock in the States was less severe than Og's, though the wedding did have its touches. My sister-in-law had adopted the personas of her musical comedy heroines, Mame and Dolly, and when the hired band quit, I took over the piano at her request. The bandleader was immediately at my shoulder. I was to stop.

"You've finished playing," I said.

"This is a union contract," he snapped. "Nobody else plays here."

Propelled by untallied champagnes, I lit into "Dolly." The bandleader slammed the piano lid on my hands. I had never heard of a musician attacking another's chops and was shocked that James C. Petrillos's union in New York, the envy of El Pulpón in Sevilla, made Franco's syndicate at El Oasis look well-mannered. My nephew calmed me by springing a surprise: the apartment he had been inhabiting in the East Sixties was fully paid up for the next two months. He had moved out all the furniture except a hide-a-bed and some cardboard boxes, but it was mine free if I wanted to camp there. "It's right above Maxwell's Plum and down the street from Thank God It's Friday!" he boasted.

"What are those?" I asked.

"The hottest singles bars in New York. The whole town is exploding."

Immediately I set up the Smith-Corona on the kitchen counter, perched on the one remaining stool and began to pour out all my stored-up notes—the Infernal Sphere, Og and the slaughterhouse, my coastal season in hell. After marathons of catching up, I prowled for bookstores and read to satiety on the hide-a-bed. I wallowed in the permanent collections of art museums, snared concert tickets, heard Brahms on the radio. On breaks from running loose in the arts I visited New York friends, who later reported their amusement at my English, saying "I seed" for "I've seen," "I've took" for "I've taken," mistakes I was blissfully unaware of. I hadn't smoked before relatives at the wedding and as an experiment I let my supply run out. In two days I didn't even think about cigarettes and I realized, with a glorious shock, that I wasn't addicted after all.

I even took the elevator twelve stories downstairs to Maxwell's Plum. Customers, in their mid-twenties like me, flaunted regalia, jostled aggressively for position at the bar and yammered like barkers for their own attractions; but the capstone didn't come until years later, when I dreamt I was writing a novel about such types and woke up laughing at the work's title, *Careless Nachos.*

Startled at how quickly I'd stopped being a chain-smoking ersatz rocker, I telegrammed Ramón that I would not be coming back as soon as planned, giving him my address and the phone number for emergencies. Ramón had boasted of having written only one letter in his life, a thank-you letter to his grandmother composed under threat of eviction from home, and I was impressed that he pelted me with letters in which I recognized, beneath stabs at humor in our polyglot tongue, desperation. Then the phone rang. It was Ramón, in bad English. He said it was the only language he could speak under the circumstances. He had hired on as a switchboard operator at the American base at Rota, plugged himself through on a break between calls, and to speak anything but English would blow his cover. I was flabbergasted at his inventiveness, and thrilled. A Danish guitarist had turned up, all we needed besides ourselves. The three of us could play jazz as well as rock. With each musician from a different country, we could call ourselves the U. N. Trio. He and I could resume our life as well as go musically in a new direction, becoming an attraction. His calls, dependent on lulls at the base, came in pleading, sporadic volleys. But I hadn't foreseen the offer of a New York apartment. There were things I needed to finish up.

When my time in the apartment elapsed, I considered booking my flight back to Spain, but it seemed heartless not to fly to San Diego and visit Patrick first. In a car rigged for hand controls, he, Og and I made a nostalgic swing through the West and I lingered with him several weeks. The yellow and purple towel glared like an Inquisitor. But I had one more stop to make.

I had caught up with my Aspen half-sister at the wedding, but for comparative purposes I needed to touch base with that glorious fusion of nature, classical music, skiing and bohemian eccentricity. The Aspen Music Festival sold me an upright piano for thirty-five dollars, my sister lent me a Jeep, and a lodge offered a room for me and the piano in return for ferrying guests. Shortly after arrival I was dangerously comfortable. Ramón, apprised of my every move, dispatched a letter accusing me of having plotted this defection all along. I wrote back, leveling with him at last: I couldn't live without my writing or my music, and he had tried to deprive me of both. Even now there was no one I loved as much as Ramón, nor friends in Aspen as close as those in Spain. I should hand the towel back. Ramón's letters ended and there were no more phone calls. Unconsciously as usual, I had made my decision. Of all the people I have been close to over the years, it was Ramón, ironically, who most furthered my consolidation as a writer, for he demonstrated the central importance of the written word by drawing me away from it until I snapped. But I didn't recognize that at the time. If I had lied to him, it was because I had first lied to myself.

As the personal in its finality receded, Spain the country came to the fore. That three-year unwitting detour had been my life's most consuming experience but where, exactly, had I been? I had washed up in that imploded empire with only the sketchiest notion of the forces that brought it about. I plunged into books with titles like *An Explanation of Spain* and *Felange: A History of Spanish Fascism*. Shortly after I was back, James Michener published *Iberia*, a large nonfiction work brimming with episodic history and cultural explication. Suddenly Philip II and the Carlist Wars, references that swirled through the bars with no more meaning than sherry fumes or saffron in the rice, were stanchions in a huge historical scaffold. It was almost painful to learn that the mysterious blank area on the map at the mouth of the Gualdalquivir—that far bank of vegetation we had gazed at from Sanlúcar de Barrameda, and which my friends had told me was "just swamp, nothing interesting"—was in fact the Coto Doñana, a royal game preserve embracing the most important habitat in Europe for migrating birds. Life in Spain was so involving precisely because I knew nothing of the place or its language and was forced to take it in like a child, but my ignorance had cost me experience as well.

As Spain obsessed my reading life, my actual life kept drifting away from it, finally into a house I purchased almost a year to the day from my return to the States, a three-room Aspen cabin I have lived in ever since. The notes I had taken in and on Andalucía came to rest there, in a deep drawer. My current writing was about Aspen, ran in the town magazine, was collected in a modest book, and its most popular story was about the German shepherd who had lived with me in Spain. Sent to me as a house-warming present by Patrick, Og continued his high profile career, was proposed for mayor, and mastered English so thoroughly that he changed his behavior after logical, gestureless explanations that demanded syntax and a full vocabulary or sheer telepathy—in my awe I could never decide which. My hands were upon him during his last difficult breaths, one evening in his thirteenth year, and those hands had to dig his stony, shallow grave in the backyard during one of the most difficult nights of my life.

Read out on the subject of Spain, out of contact with Ramón, my semi-Andalusian dog now gone, my last contact with Spain was a faithful correspondence with Manolo. Every three or four months I received a letter updating me on Skinny and Sparkplug, on the Bar Central, on smalltown changes. The *pino gordo*, the huge pine in Las Canteras that had engulfed the rungs installed to climb it, had been felled by a fascist mayor appointed from Cádiz; he alleged it was sick but everyone knew that the tree was removed because it was a town symbol. A bridge was constructed from Cádiz to the shipyard at Matagorda, spanning the entrance to the bay, shrinking the forty-kilometer trip to the capital to five kilometers by bus and turning Puerto Real into a virtual suburb of Cádiz. A new toll road from Sevilla to the south now passed behind town, eliminating the transport trucks that had roared through its twin chutes. Inflation was double digit. Weekenders from Cádiz had discovered the dunes of Las Canteras, so ideal for picnics, and sometimes the pine grove was more full of outsiders than locals. Unlike Puertorrealeños, who treasured their park, the crowd from Cádiz left it full of trash. "It is hard to end a letter," Manolo once added, "without sending my best to Og."

The most surprising news was personal. Quite independently the twins began to read of other religions and expelled Catholicism from their systems. Luis wrote me that he had discovered the books of Castaneda and he reread all of them annually, a task that lengthened as new titles appeared; his spiritual leader was the Yaqui shaman Don Juan Matus rather than the Pope. After a passing interest in Zen, Manolo dismissed religion altogether and asked my forgiveness for once having woken me up to convert me to Catholicism. By return mail I apologized for lobbing a shoe at him that unfortunate morning. Manolo's real religion was now literature. Had I read Faulkner's Snopes trilogy? It was required reading, as was every word of García Marquez. Into these exchanges broke the headlines: after thirty-nine years in power, Franco was dying. Or was he? The mock newscaster of the comedy show Saturday Night Live interrupted a skit to announce the death of Franco. He broke into the next skit to announce that Franco only looked dead but was still breathing. So it went for the rest of the show: Franco was dead; whoops, no he wasn't. Finally one morning into these exchanges came the 1975 headline: Franco was dead.

Knowing the Generalísimo was uniformly despised by my friends, I awaited news of alleviated Spain. Many Puertorrealeños, it turned out, had belonged to underground unions and political groups—communist, syndicalist, environmentalist—which now surfaced to give the town a rounded and acrimonious political life. But amid democratic energies the social fabric was shearing. Large new buildings were cutting up the farms and pastures outside town. One Easter a group of fourteen-year-olds killed a collection of exotic animals on the road to Las Canteras. Cocaine and hashish were selling like popcorn. That kind of barbarism, wrote Manolo, typified post-Franco Spain. "The dog has died but the rabies lives on."

Next came the life changes. Skinny married and fathered a brood. Sparkplug retired and lost most of his vision to cataracts. Manolo was engaged, then married, to a woman named Manoli, a combination that reminded me of Papageno and Papagena in *The Magic Flute*. In the photo he sent she looked petite and dazzling. A daughter was born, then a son he named Bruno. "At the campground," he wrote, "didn't we once agree that Bruno is the Spanish equivalent of Bruce? It means dark." Though Bruce is etymologically unrelated to Bruno, I was honored. Another son followed.

As Spain receded in time without shrinking in my consciousness, I became aware of a disturbing phenomenon. When I had been back in the States three years and matched it with the three years I had spent in Spain, it seemed like my time in Aspen was the merest fraction of the time I had spent in Andalucía. A Spain became a personal three-year unit of time. I had been back one and a half Spains, two Spains, three Spains. Even when I had been back three times as long as I had been away, my three years in Spain felt longer. Perhaps I had been wrong to return to the States for a wholly unexpected reason: my subsequent life was racing past as if I weren't living it. Time was said to pass quickly in prison, not because of the

suffering but because of the monotony, and perhaps the comfort of my house was a kind of prison. I did my best to slow my
life down with time-lengthening travel, with explorations of the
deserts of the American Southwest and Mexico, whole seasons
away from home in landscapes I converted to poetry and prose.
But my life kept hurtling ahead. Four Spains. Five. My only life
was careering toward a terrifying limit.

As future lifespan shrank alarmingly, so did language I had
thought inscribed in my circuitry. Was it possible that words
that sowed themselves in a brain so ripe to receive them could
as effortlessly die off? Absorption of new sounds had made me
a participant in the world of their speakers, and being newly
dumb was turning me back into an outsider. I read Manolo's
letters aloud, studied their locutions, tried to clutch some echo
of Puerto Real. On forays to Mexican deserts I made small
talk with every rancher, mechanic or salesman who might answer back, but found my mental processes balked, my mind
filling with plaque. Once a spontaneous speaker, I planned
my sentences ahead, then stumbled as I tried to deliver them.
I thought of my condition, in wrenched rhyme, as language
anguish. In 1975, eight years after I'd been away, Manolo
wrote, "I've realized with some distress that with every letter
it's harder for you to write Spanish. Are you aware of it?" The
distress was mine.

The final link with Spain was beyond language, and welled
up warped and fractured in dreams. In one version, Puerto
Real was surrounded by a freshwater lake; in another, the pop-
ulace was living in a wall of cubicles like large storage lockers.
In an elaborate transformation, the chutes through town were
parallel tunnels whose cross-streets were a kind of pedestrian
subway system that emerged into seaside terraces full of restaurants and cafés. Sometimes Puerto Real was welcoming and
took me in; on other nights I could not understand Andalusian
and was ordered away.

Once in Baja California, a friend asked me to play "Manha do Carnaval," which Starfis played nightly at El Oasis, referring to it as "Orfeo Negro" after the movie that introduced it, *Black Orpheus*. Given a near infallible memory for music, I was surprised not to remember how the tune went, a frustration that gnawed at me. That night I dreamt I was asked again for "Orfeo Negro," and after some fumbling I began to play it. Yes, this was it; I had the music back. As I played, I slowly began to wake up. When I had fully come to, I went over the dream and the tune I had rescued from my unconscious—and it was gone again. Furthermore, I realized that my dream mirrored the story of Orpheus himself, the demigod of music who went to the underworld to rescue his love, Eurydice, and was warned that he would lose her again if he looked back to assure himself she was following. He looked anyway and she melted back into the depths. Spain was Eurydice, the lost music, fleeing as I tried to catch hold. It was a figure that entered one of Puerto Real's convex mirrors for traffic, swelling until it loomed out of proportion, then winking out. It was Cádiz, the white city, glimmering across the bay like an imaginary reef, half seen, then blanked into mist.

After I had been away for sixteen years, I received a phone call in Aspen, person to person, from someone named Ray in London. Asked the operator, "Are you Bruce Berger?"

"I am, but I don't know any Ray in London."

"Will you speak to him?"

"I'm sure it's some mistake."

"You don't wish to speak to me?" interrupted a clipped British voice.

"International calls are expensive. I don't want to waste a stranger's money."

Said the operator, "Since you're already speaking, I'll put you through."

"Why won't you speak to me?" persisted the voice.

The name was common enough but I couldn't think of a single Ray. "Where do I know you from?"

"El Puerto de Santa María."

I gasped. "Ramón!"

"Raymond. Ray. I'm now a British citizen."

I had to get us out of English because I couldn't connect this Oxford don with the Ramón I had known. My French was now worse than my Spanish, so I said, *"No tenía ni idea que fueras tú!"*

"I no longer speak Spanish," he replied. "I can't remember how it goes."

"How strange to be talking after so many years."

"I called to ask you why you never came back."

"It's truly what I said in my last letter." I repeated that I couldn't remain with someone who denied me my music and my writing. Writing was my identity, and I wanted him to know that even if he didn't read. "I have some books out. Give me your address so I can send them to you."

"I move a lot but I'll give you the one I have now."

What had he been doing since our last contact, I asked. Spain wasn't right for him and he had moved to Britain. He had married a couple of times but it hadn't worked out. His father had died, then his mother. He used to go back to Spain but he no longer had ties there. He asked for my own news, then said, "You're right, international calls are expensive. I should ring up."

The call from Ramón was the most distorting, unsettling dream of all. If Spain was ultimately a three-year diversion in my own life, for Ramón it was a way station in his transformation from Spanish Moroccan to Englishman. I sent books to the address he gave me but never heard from him again.

I had shied from returning to Spain because of the intensity of my time there and fears I would no longer understand or be understood. But now I realized that the real impediment had been Ramón: to go back would have been to see him again face to face, to come to terms with the life we had lost. With that barrier removed, I needed to know what Spain felt like after Franco, to see what time had done to my friends and to expose my own changes to them. I didn't mention this resolve in my letters to Manolo. Then the moment was ripe, and a week after answering his latest letter I wrote a second one, advising him of my arrival date. He wrote back, "When I got a second letter so soon after the first one, I was baffled, for it was my turn to write. I set it in front of me and looked at it. Suddenly I realized it was because, after eighteen years, you were coming back. Opening it and reading only confirmed what I already knew."

A full six Spains after I unwittingly left, I deplaned in Málaga.

Part III

19

My heart raced as I cleared Chiclana and then San
Fernando in my rental car, then caught the dark windswept silhouette of the pines of El Pinar—my own private pine grove—cresting the hill like hair combed
backward, a shape like no other. But what was that
white shimmer behind them? The horizon dissolved into
limestone palisades, pale verticals not quite legible in
the clearing mist. It wasn't until I was upon them that
they turned into apartment buildings—solid squared-
off blocks, three and four of a kind, four and five stories
tall, massifs in what had been fields and the ranch of ill
repute. At home and yet unmoored, I pressed on to town
and was funneled through on one of the twin chutes. A
new interchange spun me around, then shot me back
through on the other chute. With relief I abandoned the
car by a new apartment building and my feet got me to
the Bar Central.

I walked in to laughter and shouts, all aimed in my
direction. "You're eighteen years late!" cried Manolo
through his *abrazo*. He and Luis, both in horn-rimmed
glasses, looked less like twins, age seeming to elongate
Luis's brainy forehead and round Manolo's brow and
brushy moustache. Out of the bar's new feature, a booth
for selling lottery tickets, stepped the diminutive, radiant
Manoli. Because it was still morning Manolo poured me
coffee, with a splash of *coñac*. Setting my cup by the

lottery papers he was working on, he reached for the telephone, made a couple of quick calls, lurched back, knocked my drink onto the papers, then poured another. Deep into our catch-up, I felt a tap on my shoulder, turned to look, found no one, then looked the other way. It was Skinny, who was now rotund. I'd forgotten that old trick of Skinny's. One drink later an older and slightly built man peered in the door, one eye behind a frosted lens, the other misted from within. It was Sparkplug. After nearly two decades, our social quintet was back together. Only Og was missing, and our first full quorum toast was to him.

Informed that today Manolo had to work straight through and couldn't take me to food and bed until the bar closed, I made frequent sorties, to pace myself as well as to reacquaint myself with the town. The owners of the Bar Gallego were stunned at my reappearance—and at my request for coffee. The tight grid of Puerto Real, more fixed up here, more dilapidated there, was virtually unchanged except for the waterfront, which was overwhelmed by a long, imposingly modern building labeled Pabellon de Deportes. Manolo informed me that it was an enclosed basketball court, convertible to other uses, that held seating for hundreds and had hosted matches between Spain and foreign teams. The sports pavilion, pronounced Luis, gave outsiders their first reason for coming here since Napoleon coveted Puerto Real as a springboard for attacking Cádiz. Fortified by a bar sandwich, I walked around it with respect. These prowls rested me from my re-immersion in Spanish. I was relieved that I would not be kicked out for not understanding Andalusian; this was the way Spanish *ought* to sound. My grasp was half guesswork, my speech balked and patched, but I was already getting better as the day wore on—better with every drink, in fact. I had forgotten that one of the secrets of fluency, particularly in the early stages, was never to be caught quite sober.

I felt I had overlubricated my speech by the time Manolo and Manoli piled into my Ford Fiesta and directed me out past Las Canteras to an apartment complex. In a two-story suite of rooms, over more beers, we downed snails and potato omelet prepared by Manoli. I met the three children too blearily to take in their individuality. Manolo, wound up, talked and showed me books until one-thirty, apologizing that he had to get up four hours later. I apologized that I would not be getting up with him, and let him lead my jet lag to an upstairs bedroom.

Midmorning I awoke surrounded by dolls. Now I remembered: they had moved the five-year-old Noa in with the three-year-old Bruno and the two-year-old Hugo. The apartment proved empty, so I completed the tour. Between two other bedrooms lay a bath as large, with dancing space between the sink and the tub: the cult of the bathroom had struck. Downstairs progressed from entranceway to livingroom, kitchen and outdoor utility area. By any standard this was a well-planned, well-appointed apartment and I was impressed. Soon Manoli poured through the door with the charges she had removed so I could sleep. Mentally I settled in: this was the new Spain I had come to experience.

Obsessive with questions about life after Franco, I was answered by chance events. With Manolo or *en familia* we strolled the apartment complex's concentric and connecting ovals, a labyrinth of gardened walkways and red tiled buildings I never quite mastered, but all paths led to a kiosk where we stopped for beers. Placed where walkways crossed, this stand drew neighbors to newspapers, cigarettes and lottery tickets and each other, and permitted kids to wheedle candy from the fathers they summoned to food. The layout was civilized, harmonizing the private and the social.

Bearing knives, we dropped in on a neighbor couple. The men had bought a two-month-old slaughtered goat and Enrique

had already peeled it to a slim pinkness except for the still
hairy head, which stared wild-eyed that this could have happened amid middle-class domesticity. Home for a nightcap
after the evening's goatfest, Manolo suggested I carry my three-
year-old namesake up to bed. Bruno was still small and the
request was ceremonial, but I paused to consider my history
of back problems, complicated by a ruptured appendix that
had delayed the trip itself. Remembering advice from aikido
to center your weight two inches below the navel, I rose from
a well-centered squat with the sleeping Bruno, bore his evenly
distributed weight up the stairs, lowered him into bed without
stooping, and returned downstairs, pleased to have done everything correctly.

The next morning, as I rose from the john, there was a jab in
my spine like a nail driven the wrong way. I broke into a chilled
sweat. I hid my panic as I drove Manoli to the Bar Central, but
as I stood having coffee and coñac I felt my upper torso pull to
the right. Skinny arrived for a walk around town and I stepped
slower and slower beside him, constricted and shuffling, until
we nearly stopped. "A spasm like this can last for days," I told
him.

"Let it," he said. "What's your hurry?"

The next morning, Manolo told me, "The doctor's on his
way."

"On Sunday?"

"It's the day he's free from the sports pavilion."

After bawling me out for not doing exercises every day, the
nattily dressed young doctor asked me to hold a metal bar attached by cord to a battery-operated meter the size of an electric
razor. He placed a series of needles in my ear, asking me how
each felt. Nothing hurt but there were degrees of tenderness,
reports he correlated with the readings on the meter. He considered a moment, then placed two needles in one ear and one
in the other. "The two needles relax the lumbar area," he said,

"and the other is for the body's general wellbeing. They need
to be in for an hour before I give you the rest of the treatment."

"Then let's go to the kiosk," said Manolo.

Once we had beers in our hands, the doctor told me that
during the Cultural Revolution, the continuity of acupuncture
was lost in China and the Chinese had to recover it later from
the French. Was current acupuncture French or Chinese? It
was a debatable point. Needles, in any case, were only relax-
ants, not cures; they loosened muscles and allowed the back to
regain its own position. As I stood at the apartment kiosk listing
to starboard, needles sticking from my ears, sipping beer and
discussing the provenance of acupuncture while Manolo introduced me to neighbors who didn't register anything unusual, I
thought, *so this is post-Franco Spain, half bourgeois, half sur-
real.* When we returned to Manolo's, the doctor removed the
needles, had me lie on my stomach, performed minor adjust-
ment that was half massage, applied some cream, and wouldn't
hear of accepting money. The next morning I was stunned to
discover that my back was straight.

When I visited Skinny, his wife and four children in one of the
cement slabs on the way into town, I realized that Manolo's
curvilinear housing was the exception. Skinny's family's four-
room suite was one of four clones that replicated on each floor
of each stairwell of each duplicate building. Amid high-gloss
furniture, armadas of framed snapshots, built-in chandeliers
and industrial lace we stuffed on chicken with vegetables and
potato salad, then ducked out to the complex's equivalent of
the kiosk. Every complex provided a twenty-four hour pharmacy and an enclosed bar called the *club social.* Because of
the lack of spending money, the *club* was surprisingly sober;
here the men gossiped, played dominoes, bet on sports events
and bought lottery tickets, preferring gambling to drinking because it was more like investment, less like dissipation. Skinny

and many other men were on the boatyard payroll, but their turn to work often came to no more than a couple of months a year. Said Skinny's brother, looking up from dominos, "I'd rather loaf, even if that means coping with the boredom."

"If everyone's living out here in apartments," I asked Skinny, "what's going on in the middle of town?"

"Remember where I used to live? Come see it now." We finished the beer he wouldn't let me pay for and we walked a half-kilometer to the courtyard of packed humanity I knew so well. "Welcome to Dracula's Castle," he said, pushing in the door with a cinematic creak.

On the floor of the courtyard steeped a pool of green water, backed by a heap of refuse. A shriveled and ancient woman sat by the first door, her hair tied back so tight it stretched the skin taut over her cheekbones. "I'm so happy you've come," she cried, pulling Skinny toward her and kissing him on both cheeks. "I hate to see anyone, hate to be seen. I've been hit by cars, motorcycles, bicycles, everything. And look at this place! Everything is falling in." Skinny answered in vain as she fussed with a small electric device in her lap, tried to install the hearing aid to which it was attached, then gave up and chattered on without listening.

Skinny made his getaway and shoved open the door at the back of the patio where his family had lived, and where I had been overwhelmed by too many people to meet at once. Through the gloom I could make out only heaps of fallen plaster. As we withdrew, a substantial and well-dressed woman in her sixties emerged from another door and invited us in. "I've got the only three livable rooms left here," she said. "Come see." Her quarters were filled with solid oak furniture, adorned with family photos and religious pictures, spotless except for the plaster dangling beyond reach from the ceiling. When we got to the bedroom, she jabbed a finger at a portion of the ceiling that had fallen in. "That happened only last week." She took us back to the kitchen and poured us each a shot of *anis*. "And now there are rats. That's the only thing that really scares me. I've set traps and captured one. Another ran out to the street when I went to market the other day. This place is a ruin," she boomed, sounding plucky, even bravely amused by the decay.

"Does anyone else live here?" I asked.

"There's one elderly couple upstairs. But they're out now and I couldn't tell you where it's safe to step."

Where were Skinny's brothers and sisters living now, I asked when we were back in the street. Of the nine, seven were married and had apartments of their own and the other two were living with their mother in her own new apartment. Each of these new apartments was larger than the one that had once held them all.

"Are all the old courtyards in the same condition?"

"No. Some of them have been bought by single families, which are fixing them up. But that takes more money than we've got." So here was Puerto Real's surprising fate: gentrification.

One morning a bearded young man wheeled his bicycle into the Bar Central, rested it by the door and began handing out a flyer from city hall, department of parks and gardens:

Given the importance of our pine grove, Las Canteras, its use as a park located near important cities, its beauty due to natural soil with many hills and slopes, and the old specimens of pinos piñoneros, *the best alternative is to construct an enclosure around the entire perimeter of the park for better control and vigilance, for reforestation, and to provide a system of irrigation and fire prevention.*

As a first step during the study period, the Environmental Delegation is conferring with the Agricultural Delegation of Cádiz, the organism in charge of sick and dead pines and underbrush.

The Delegation is at the full disposal of anyone with environmental concerns.

Luis spoke up when the young man left: "The paper is from the government but the young man is the force behind it. He bikes all over, looks into environmental problems and organizes people to do something about it. This plan to enclose the pines is mild. Some people want to see it barricaded for ten years and the public banished so vegetation can come back and people can be educated in how to take care of it."

"Is it really that bad off?"

"I need a break. Let's go look."

When we got to the tracks at the edge of town, Luis began to point out the changes. "They put in this underpass after a kid was killed by a train. Right away the tiles were swiped, and because there was a spring where they dug, it was always wet and the place stank. They installed a pump, but every time it rains, the pump fails and the tunnel fills."

"They could stock it with inner tubes so people could float across," I suggested.

"Through the garbage? Good luck."

I noted without comment that the bar where the old man danced and never paid was now shadowed by a vehicular overpass. Luis nodded toward Puerto Real's pair of modest Italianate villas, in ruins, with only shards in the windows. Never fully occupied, they had been taken over by drug addicts. The Silesian school across the way, where I had taught English to the monk who fell asleep saying *probably probably probably,* had been replaced by a grander structure. Its roof leaked, the wiring was dangerous, the project supervisor had taken off with the funds, and the monks were bunking elsewhere until it was all redone. Just beyond it the pines still soared from red earth, their trunks inky in the filtered, misty light, the dunes overflowing with foliage. It wasn't until I got close that I saw them: fistfuls of brambles in the sky, trees dying from the bottom up, entire dead trees. Complementing cracked wood overhead, in the crisscross of hollows where people walked, were streamers of garbage, blown newsprint, toilet paper daubed with shit and, here and there, the tossed syringe. "I've had my break," said Luis. "Let's go back to the bar."

As for El Pinar, I returned on my own. Overcome by the same seediness, its clearing was full of weeds and the storage tank that passed for its pool, which had seldom held water, now looked incapable of retaining it. The pastures, once ragged with goats, cows and patched buildings in back had been leveled for smooth fields and farm machinery; the trail to town was choked off by apartments; barbed wire severed the campground from the railroad; and the miracle was that the campground existed at all. Yet here it was, full of tents. The empty restaurant, swamped in foliage, still stood, and so, almost eighty, did Bernardo. He summoned me to a table outside his house and poured us glasses of Valdepeñas, boasting that his liver had recovered and the doctors told him he could drink all he wanted. I noticed that he actually drank very little. My old room was no longer habitable but he had a trailer for me, if I wanted to move in. He then recited me verses about the neutrality of justice, saying he had composed them only last week.

"Do you really think Bernardo wrote those verses?" asked Skinny.

We were laughing about Bernardo as Skinny drove me and two of his brothers to the Rio San Pedro to fish the next day. He and the brother in the front passenger seat pulled shoulder belts across their torsos without attaching them, as if they were ornamental sashes. As soon as we were out of the car, I asked about the pink sky that had mystified me all morning. Hanging in pale salmon folds, a net of silk wobbling horizon to horizon, the scope and strangeness of the effect were menacing. "That's sand from Morocco," said Skinny's brother, Joaquín. "It blows across with the *Levante*."

"You mean that's part of the *Sahara Desert* hanging in the sky?"

"That's exactly what it is."

It was as if the northern lights were trembling over a sunny stretch of Andalucía; I had remembered no such thing and wondered whether some new environmental calamity was brewing. We crossed the railroad tracks, followed strips of pickleweed and saltbush between canals that had been dug as traps for fish, and reached a footbridge where three men were already fishing. "The fish hang out in the shadow under the bridge," said Skinny. The brothers were carrying cane poles with bare hooks attached by string, and I was curious to see what kind of bait they were going to use. None, it turned out. They lowered the hooks into the water and Skinny sprinkled bread. When fish surfaced through the green murk to eat, the brothers jerked the poles violently upward. "The object is to snag part of the fish," said Skinny. "Any part." The men on the other side of the bridge, baiting their hooks with lunchmeat, were pulling in a few small silver fish, but our group caught none. "We're not having any luck today," said Joaquín after an hour. "Let's leave."

Offered the front passenger seat on the way home, I tried to attach my shoulder belt, then realized there was nowhere to do so. "They fine you if you're not wearing your belt," said Skinny. This was the Puerto Real I recognized.

So much past to check up on! One morning I drove to El Oasis and found the building intact, but the bar and garden I so admired had been covered by a low-ceilinged tin barn. Peeking in, through purple light I made out posters, bus seats, trash barrels and graffiti. Ghetto chic? High Grunge? In disgust I continued to the Puerto de Santa María waterfront, parked and continued on foot to the family bodega of Javier and his brother. They wielded the telephone and soon we had assembled a group of almost every rocker I had played with. All, without exception, were married; some had two kids, others four. I was particularly struck by Paco, the bass guitarist struck by polio, whom I had remembered as a dour personality; now completely bald, he seemed the brightest, most buoyant spirit of all. One ex-rocker worked in a mattress factory, another had a windshield repair shop, another was a bookkeeper at the American base. "I work in a casino in Cádiz," said Javier. "Gambling has been legalized in a few government-run operations. But there's no point in your visiting me there. I'm not allowed to recognize anyone I know. I'd have to look right through you."

Most, to my astonishment, were members of the Communist Party, which had ridden to power in the city elections. Carmelo, the Simbroni singer who had recruited me for the Infernal Sphere, was Minister of Culture. With the death of Franco, the Puerto-born Rafael Alberti, best known living Spanish poet, had returned from exile in Chile, and Carmelo had become his secretary. "I'd introduce you, but he's away in Madrid," said Carmelo.

"Don't worry about their all being Communists," said Javier's brother in a private moment. "They don't know anything about politics. They think they're Marxists but they're really just middle-class consumers."

Before the evening was out, someone said, "It's too bad Ramón couldn't have been here. You two were so close." How far from the mark that was, I thought; it was a case of our being together permanently or not at all. When the rest went home, I wound back several streets and stared up at the balcony, so appropriately Moorish with its sheath of wood and glass, where he and Og and I hung over the market with our irreplaceable life.

I strayed next to Jerez, not to see anyone in particular, merely to walk the streets. Five minutes after I had parked, a man a generation older than I stopped me in the sidewalk. "Welcome back!" said this stranger. "I remember seeing you play in the spring fair."

"That would be in 1966," I said.

"Sounds right."

I was just recovering from that surprise when I was stopped again, this time by a young man with wild hair: "Bru!" I didn't recognize him either and had to ask. He was the younger brother of an Everplay guitarist. "You were in and out of our house all the time."

"How old were you then."

"Eleven. I'm twenty-nine now."

"And you recognized me!"

"People from Jerez never forget. I'm delivering a picture to a bar owned by the gypsies. Come with me."

Soon I was in a dark bar with Boni the framer. For two hours he wouldn't let me buy a round of our beers. The owner unwrapped the newly framed painting and hung it over the bar: a gypsy wagon was headed to El Rocio, the annual celebration of the Virgin in the delta of the Guadalquivir. The wagon was passably done, commented Boni, but the colors of the flag were off. After Franco, he whispered when the owner stepped away from the bar, the government tried to integrate the gypsies with the rest of society by setting them up in businesses like this one. But gypsies were gypsies and the bar was selling dope out the back. Boni was doing this job as a trade.

I got back to my car just as a cop was writing a ticket for overstaying. I talked him out of it, then began buckling my seat belt. The cop stopped me. "You don't have to wear the belt in town," he said. "Just on the highway."

I hadn't planned to venture as far as Sevilla, but someone in El Puerto told me that El Pulpón, the musical agent, was still in business. I couldn't imagine accepting any job he had to offer, but couldn't resist inquiring.

Warned that Sevilla was now full of thieves, I pulled into guarded parking even though it was the middle of the day. I took an elevator to El Pulpón's seedy four-room office, its only concession to décor a spider plant on an air conditioner. The great man, with his large flared nose, heavy features and swept-back hair, greeted me floridly. "How am I not going to remember you? Be seated. I just need to take care of a few clients."

He talked of job possibilities to several men in their late twenties, simultaneously fielding repeated calls from a party who wanted to rent three dogs for a parade and needed assurance they were tame as well as distinguished. When El Pulpón looked up and saw me still there, he appeared startled. "How's the job situation?" I asked.

"*Hombre*, all the nightclubs have been turned into discothèques and they're not hiring live musicians."

"I saw what happened to El Oasis. How about tour boats?"

"They've all been replaced by airlines." He named all the shipping lines that had succumbed. "Every year it's worse, and I can't even employ the people I've got. Live musicians are on the way out. Come back Monday and maybe I can get you something for the fair." I recognized this as an exit line and made my farewell.

When I returned to guarded parking, I found that a back window had been smashed and a daypack containing my camera, binoculars, passport, cash, spare prescription glasses and notebook had been hauled up from the floor.

I now saw more of Sevilla than I cared to: rental car agency, police station, American embassy. The agency replaced the glass that afternoon but I had to return for the paperwork. In my new passport photo I looked like someone whose passport had just been stolen. I completed the police report and passport application and sped back to Puerto Real. The next day the Bar Central received a call from the embassy. The passport had been found under a bus seat in the town of Dos Hermanas: the thief didn't want to be caught with it. I sped to Sevilla one more time and kissed my passport with its photo that was merely unpleasant.

I thought often of the old joke, if Franco is at the helm, the *Guardia Civil* is on the prow, the priests are on the poop and

the ship sinks, who is saved? Answer: Spain. Franco was ten
years gone and his corpse was still being happily kicked. A
man came into the Bar Central with a fake identity card, sup-
posedly signed by the *caudillo*. "Fascist!" screamed the other
patrons. "Swine! *Cabrón!*" Amid laughter they grabbed him
and pitched him bodily to the sidewalk. Streets that had been
named for Franco's cronies regained their previous names:
Puerto Real's pedestrian street, formerly Primo de Rivera, was
now Calle de la Plaza; El Puerto's Calle General Mola, about
which I'd written the poem about the dove being pelted with
stones, had reverted to Calle Cielo.

The other two institutions lived on, circumscribed. The
Catholic Church had lost its monopoly and locals were now
evangelized by a gamut from Protestants to touring gurus. Said
Manolo, Jehovah's Witnesses were a particular menace. In
reaction to their own education by nuns and priests, Manolo,
Manoli and other young parents were banding together to found
an alternative primary school. Without state funding, parents
themselves would have to teach in rotation, as well as raise
a suitable building if they couldn't find one, but they were
determined their children would grow up without religious
indoctrinization.

As for the *Guardia Civil*, all over Spain they had been banished from the cities and in the countryside they operated under
severe new restrictions. Puerto Real successfully faced them
down when some public housing at the edge of town, promised
to the locals, was appropriated by the *Guardia Civil* for a barracks. Bands of citizens demonstrated, occupied the buildings
and refused to come out despite threats of tear gas and forced
dispersals. They were backed by the mayor, and after weeks of
riots and mutual threats the police backed off and the citizens
won. The *guardia* were even turning into nostalgia. Manolo
played chess with a friend who carved his own set on a *Guardia
Civil* vs. gypsies motif. On the fascist side, the pawns were the

Guardia Civil, the knights were thoroughbred horses, the rooks were military barracks, the bishops were church bishops, the king was in full military dress and the queen was in black for Holy Week; on the opposing side, the pawns were gypsies with moustaches and sashes, the knights were burros, the rooks were hovels, the bishops were branch-bearing *curanderos*, and the king and queen were decked out for the spring fair.

But if that triune ship went down, was Spain—or Puerto Real—saved? I was struck by the town's loss of cohesion, the shearing of its social fabric. Skinny had answered Manolo's summons to my arrival almost instantly, but the time since they had last seen each other was measured in years—they couldn't remember how many. In the guise of my visit, friends were having reunions among themselves. Puerto Real was a small place, with everyone within walking distance, but its residents were losing track of each other.

A leading indicator, trivial as it seemed, was the collapse of the movie culture that drew the citizenry almost nightly to the one indoor and two outdoor theaters. The coming together and the post-mortems compensated for the films themselves, worn out as they were from repeated viewings, and the evening's new plot lines were those traded by the audience. Movie-going was now about movies, for the opening of the bridge to Cádiz made it easy to board a bus and take in first-run films at a large and comfortable theater. No one familiar need be encountered. But even trips to Cádiz were the exception, for everyone now had a TV, and when they felt the urge to see a movie they just popped one into the VCR.

Full of fond memories, Manolo retained strands of the movie tradition at the apartment. Remembering that I had gone three times to see *Shane*, he rented it and we chanted the dialog. His kids were receiving a traditional upbringing, for the picture they lived by was the town favorite, *Seven Brides for Seven Brothers*. Even as I took a more jaundiced look at this musical

comedy based on the *Rape of the Sabine Women*, group abduc-
tion choreographed by Agnes De Mille, Noa, Bruno and Hugo
threw themselves into it like the audiences I remembered. "My
heart was throbbin' throbbin' throbbin . . .," sang Howard Keel.

"Trobbin' trobbin' trobbin'," sang the kids.

"And I was sobbin' sobbin' sobbin'," sang Keel.

"Sobbin' sobbin' sobbin'," chorused the kids.

The kids laughed when they sang "sobbin'" but cried when
the movie was over. They had named seven of Noa's dolls for
the seven brothers. "And the brides?" I asked.

"Brides?" said Manolo. "They don't care about the brides."

This was a continuing *cachondeo*, but it took place in a
darkened room in one apartment. No number of brides could
now pull the town together.

The reason uniformly cited for Puerto Real's new dysfunc-
tionality wasn't the bridge or TV; it was drugs. Some ten percent of the adolescents were addicted, Sparkplug's two sons
among them. When I left, in 1967, the use of drugs was more
or less confined to the tourist enclaves of the Mediterranean
coast, where marijuana and *kif* from Morocco was scored with
pounds and marks. I had expected marijuana to make its
way to Puerto Real, and cocaine for those who could afford
it. Cocaine, in fact, had not made it to Puerto Real, and the
drug of choice was heroin. The crime rate had soared. The old,
victims of repeated muggings, no longer ventured out at night.
The able-bodied circulated normally, remaining vigilant, and
I never personally felt unsafe. But as a vital social center, the
sidewalk had lost ground.

Other factors drove people apart. High unemployment left
little spending money for activities that drew friends together.
The boatyard at Matagorda was still the leading employer but
business had fallen drastically. With the reopening of the Suez
Canal, European ships could reach Asian boatyards more
easily and Spaniards could not compete with Japanese wages.

The great hope was a new General Motors plant that manufactured parts for assembly in Barcelona. Puertorrealeños rushed to take jobs, then found themselves unfit for this new kind of work. In Matagorda the work rhythm was keyed to specific tasks performed by hand, separated by natural breaks for coffee, beer and cigarettes, easing workers through the day. At General Motors the employees were appendages of machines and had to perform repetitive maneuvers straight through from nine to five, with a quick lunch and brief supervised rests. Most simply couldn't adapt. Some quit right away, some were fired for unproductivity, some went to the doctor with headaches and other new complaints. Poverty and unemployment started looking like the healthier alternative—along with the lottery. Sparkplug, who had played all his life without winning a peseta, took the bus to buy tickets in Cádiz on days when they didn't sell them in Puerto Real. The lottery was taken very seriously, even though odds were nil; its practice was almost a form of prayer.

Another social disruption was the dispersal of the population from the tight grid that was Puerto Real to the apartments that ringed it in receding formation. Beached on a private sofa, watching endless shows and venturing only as far as the complex's *club social*, the formerly centripetal citizen had exploded outward, each into his own scattered niche. The gain in personal space was enormous, a relief to people like Skinny's family, who had been packed so tight that it was hard to have a private thought. But private space was also space between people and Puertorrealeños had been freed into isolation. I had seen them congested and economically miserable, but never before had I seen them bored.

Modernity itself, held at bay by Franco, had done the rest. Street life was reduced to the vehicle and the human being; gone forever were donkeys ridden by men from the country, burros hauling carts, goats like the ones that leapt on my car to screw. Gone, mysteriously, were the country people themselves,

small, leathery, wizened, dressed in grey and black. Where did
they go, I asked.

"Nowhere," answered Manolo. "It's just that their children
didn't turn out like them. They had more to eat and as they
grew they filled out. Town people and country people now look
the same."

Grey and black, the colors of threadbare propriety, were
also gone. Individuals and the common culture were now at liberty to blush like chameleons. The sidewalks were flamboyant
with track suits, sweat suits, sneakers and jeans, T-shirts and
ballcaps of all hues, beards, buzz cuts, hair natural and dyed
from sixties shoulder-spill to eighties blow-dry, plumage for
any shopping mall in the world. And those in the turquoise
nylon jogging shorts actually jogged. Even as adolescents took
up heroin, many in their twenties were on a health kick and ran
in Las Canteras, or on their own treadmills if they could afford them. More, they were giving up cigarettes. With eighteen
smoke-free years behind me, I had dreaded Spanish interiors
and I was stunned that Manolo, Luis and many more friends
had given it up. To complete my shock, Manolo and some of
his friends had gotten *vasectomies*. Amid all the degeneration
there were countersigns I never expected.

What most encouraged me, however, was continuity, the
way the spirit of Puerto Real still flourished through the cracks
of its own disrepair. When I accompanied Manolo on an errand to City Hall, a lean-faced man in grey genuflected to a
potted palm, stood gazing up with his hands folded in prayer,
crossed to the door for tax payments, dropped to his knees and
crossed himself, turned and stood with closed eyes in the sun
streaming through the skylight, genuflected to the information
window, rose again to let the light bathe his face, then walked
out the door. I was the only one who followed his movements.
"Did he think he was in church or was he doing the Stations of
City Hall?" I asked Manolo in a low voice.

"He does this everywhere," said Manolo, "including in the middle of traffic. His mind is almost gone and he spends his day thanking God for the light. The nuns took care of him until he fought with them. People protect him and make sure nothing happens to him."

This care for the unfortunate was no more than Manolo did himself. Every day an old man left his middle-aged son, who was epileptic and somewhat retarded, in the Bar Central, where employees and clientele took care of him together. The kidding of carousers sometimes got a bit rough, but he defended himself as an honorary member of the gang until his father returned, asked how his day had gone and took him home. I couldn't help comparing that treatment to his probable fate in the United States, where he would have been locked up or turned out in the street.

My general impression, from observation and rigorous bar talk, was that Franco had kept the lid on so tight that no one knew what to do with liberty when it struck. The police had been banished, for good reason, but drugs and crime had exploded into the vacuum. I cheered the death of Franco, and also realized that my car wouldn't have been robbed in Sevilla if he were still alive. As for Puerto Real the microcosm, I remembered my dream that its citizens were living in rows of storage lockers. Puerto Real had turned into a walled city and its inhabitants were living in the walls.

Now that the barrier has been overcome, I have returned to Puerto Real—first every five years, then with increasing frequency. I watched Manolo's kids grow up, followed the phases of my namesake. As a grade-schooler, Bruno was a parody Andalusian. Feet planted apart, gravel-voiced, gesturing like a stand-up comic, he told stories in lowlife slang, cracked one-liners and would have made a decent warm-up act for the Infernal Sphere. The next Bruno was from Madrid—even

pronouncing the esses of his plurals, exclaimed an awestruck
Manolo. I missed the adolescent Bruno, for he refused to study
or work and had vanished into a distant apartment of young
drifters. "If Bruno doesn't shape up," pronounced Manolo,
"I'm going to buy him a one-way ticket to the Pyrenees." The
young adult Bruno, veteran of assorted jobs loading trucks and
ships, his phases outgrown, turned out to be so warm, genuine
and loving that I was proud that he bore, after a fashion, my
name. The older generation fared less well. Manoli got cancer,
went through chemotherapy and radiation treatment and was
in remission. Manolo and his friends all went back to smoking.
Sparkplug died.

In 1991 I became a contributing editor at *American Way*,
the magazine of American Airlines, and had the features editor
send me to Spain to do stories—on the art scene in Madrid,
on a physics conference in Mazagón, on offshore banking in
Gibraltar. When the art story didn't pan out, I substituted a
piece on Puerto Real. With a more clinical eye I tracked the
battle between waterfront preservationists and those who favored creating a beach by hauling tons of earth from the Río
San Pedro. I dragooned Skinny into taking me to the boatyard,
which I had never actually seen after all these years. We stood
by a drydock so large it seemed a natural catastrophe, and I
gasped as steel beams swooped menacingly by cable to a half-
built oil tanker. "Make it quick," Skinny grumbled. "This is
the first time I've come here without getting paid."

A couple of months after I was back, I received a letter from
Manolo that began, "*Tan estrechas son las calles de Puerto Real,
tan claustrofóbicos sus cruces, que el pueblo parecía una suerte
de tamiz para atrapar al ser humano . . . .*" I was baffled by
these phrases, so familiar, yet displaced, then recognized the
opening of my essay. Some Puertorrealeño had taken a flight
on American, was flabbergasted to find a story on Puerto Real
proclaimed on the very cover, and whisked it straight to the

Bar Central, where Manolo took it to a pair of translators from Madrid who chanced to be working in town. I hadn't yet received my own copies of *American Way* with the piece in English, and was stunned at the swiftness of this. There followed a copy of the town magazine, *Calle Ancha*, which ran the piece with old photos of the Bar Central, a shot of me and Manolo's brother Luis at the campground in 1965, and a view of the town through a curved mirror. Then I received a congratulatory note from the mayor. I felt like a homeboy who made good.

Having gotten the feel of post-Franco Spain as represented by Puerto Real, and having acquitted myself in a magazine, I now felt free to follow it mostly in the niche within a microcosm that was the Bar Central. That was where my host spent his days, and where scraps of the outside world came as if to a magpie's nest. Once I arrived to find that the clientele, which had never shown the least interest in other languages, was salting its speech with phrases from Lakota, having bused themselves to Cádiz to see the film *Dances with Wolves*. Manolo, reading up on the tribe, had encountered a Spanish-Lakota glossary in the back of a book and photocopied it for his customers. I could now make journal entries on such curiosities on the spot, for the Bar Central had converted its upstairs into a private office with sofas, a desk where Manoli did the lottery tickets and the bookkeeping, and a manual typewriter for my own use. Someone who watched Hemingway write *Across the River and Into the Trees*, not his finest work, remarked that it could be more accurately titled *Across the Street and Into the Bar*. My writing situation eliminated that hazardous walk.

But my notes were less and less bacchanalian. I had arrived to a culture of sherry drinkers and there were fewer of them with every visit. Drinkers kept reducing their sherry in proportion to beer, muttering that they "mustn't overdo it" when they had an *amontillado* or a *fino*. This cutting back pertained to more than sherry, for those who could no longer tolerate Manolo's perfectly aerated drafts now drank non-alcoholic beer from bottles. *Tapas* had been curtailed because of cost. Gone were the miniature rations of goulash or potato salad or cod; the Bar Central's selection was down to olives, anchovies with breadsticks and cubes of cheese on a toothpick.

But it was the collapse of sherry drinking that most stunned me. In El Puerto, the wife of a Starfis guitarist told me that at the spring fair she drank her sherry cut with soda. The hallowed beverage turned into a spritzer? A purist might blench but it helped her maintain. The town's proudest institution, Fernando A. Terry's ancient bodega, meanwhile, had been bought out by Domecq and now turned out only coñac. It was hard to believe: the leading sherry maker of El Puerto de Santa María, one of the three great sherry towns, no longer made sherry. In Puerto Real, the Bar Central's copious selection of sherries had been reduced to a token barrel, retained for atmosphere. It felt as if Spain itself were being phased out.

Over dependable drafts—of beer—our core of friends discussed how the rest of life had gone flat. Buildings had so filled the countryside that there were no separate towns anymore, merely a homogenous dribble of apartments interrupted by historical centers. The perimeter of the Bay of Cádiz, once a cloudy embankment of pines and marsh and dunes, was now a snarl of tall buildings, bridge struts and construction cranes. People shopped at the Carrefour, a French chain in El Puerto de Santa María, buying from strangers in company uniforms instead of from lifelong friends. Fairgoers from the Puertos complained that no one dressed in regional costumes anymore—and the fact that they themselves only went in street clothes was an irony so bald that it seemed bad taste to mention it. Sighed Skinny, "It's not like before, when we grew up outdoors pretending we were Indians, chasing lizards, trapping birds. Now kids stay at home with their video games and

TV." I thought a childhood of boredom in an upscale suburb had given me a corrupt taste for picturesque backwardness, but it was they who voiced the nostalgia. They missed the animals in the streets, the little shops that sold only shawls and candles, the absurd rivalry between towns of no consequence, the inventions of people with no one to entertain them but each other.

Said Manolo, looking at me directly, "When you were here was the intensest time of our lives." I was taken aback, having always assumed that it was a new place, new people and new language that had brought me to a burning focus, expanding those three years until they overwhelmed all the ones that followed. But perhaps that fervor was not so private. In showing me their world, they had explored it more thoroughly themselves, scouring the map for the unknown, then packing the food and wine. Even when they showed me the overfamiliar, they imagined how I received it. Perhaps my presence among them had allowed Manolo and Luis and Skinny and Sparkplug to ingest their homeland afresh, through foreign eyes. That was an intensity we had created together.

I answered with a question I'd been waiting to ask: "Manolo, there something I don't get. This is the sherry-making center of the world. Sherry was invented here. It's what we all lived on. For better or worse, it was our life's blood. To me, it's always been this place's own flavor, its very symbol. Now when we go to the spring fairs, which are celebrations of sherry, no one drinks it anymore. No one drinks it here at the Bar Central either. Even you don't drink it. How come?"

"Can you take the undertow?" asked Manolo.

"No," I confessed. "I can't drink wine at all any more. Even with meals I now drink only beer. So I'm personally relieved that people aren't buying sherry for me and expecting me to drink it. But that's just me, and I still love the stuff."

"Sherry has up to six percent more alcohol than other wines, depending," said Manolo. "People finally got fed up with the shoving and shouting and fighting that extra percentage provoked. Andalusians joined the rest of the world in drinking regular red and white wines with meals, with maybe a sherry as an aperitif or a sweet one as a dessert wine. Young people associate sherry with the older generation and they consider us all heavyweights. They don't drink it at all, so there are no new sherry drinkers on the way. If you'll recall, Og never drank it either. He saw what was coming and stuck to beer."

"But sherry is the very symbol of Andalucía, and even you have given it up."

He leaned forward over the bar to whisper: "Sherry is poison."

Bruce Berger is best known for a series of nonfiction books exploring the intersections of nature and culture, primarily in desert settings. The first of these works, the essay collection *The Telling Distance*, won the 1990 Western States Book Award, and its contents have been widely anthologized. It was followed by *There Was A River*, whose title piece is a narrative of what may have been the last trip on the Colorado River through Glen Canyon before its inundation by Lake Powell, and by *Almost an Island*, which recounts three decades of exploration and friendships in Baja California.

Mr. Berger was born in Evanston, Illinois, and attended Yale University and the University of California—Berkeley. In addition to his books, his work has appeared in *The New York Times, Orion, Outside, Barron's, Sierra* and many other publications. For three years he was a Contributing Editor at *American Way*, the magazine of American Airlines.

In October, 2008, Mr. Berger was sent by the Department of State to represent the United States at the Mussoorie International Writer's Festival in northern India, followed by a week of readings in New Delhi and Mumbai.

List of Aequitas Books

Note: *Aequitas* is a non-fiction imprint of Pleasure Boat Studio: A Literary Press

The Blue Moon Boys: The Story of Elvis Presley's Band ~ Ken Burke & Dan Griffin ~ $19.95

Illuminations: Memorable Movie Moments ~ Richard Pepperman ~ $15

The Pitcher's Kid ~ Jack Olsen ~ $18.95 and $28.95 (casebound) ~ memoir

Among Friends ~ Mary Lou Sanelli ~ $15

A Passionate Engagement ~ Ken Harvey ~ memoir ~ $18

Speak to the Mountain: The Tommie Waites Story ~ Dr. Bessie Blake ~ $18 / $26

Listening to the Rhino ~ Dr. Janet Dallett ~ $16

Falling Awake ~ Mary Lou Sanelli ~ $15

Way Out There: Lyrical Essays ~ Michael Daley ~ $16

The Enduring Vision of Norman Mailer ~ Dr. Barry H. Leeds ~ memoir/criticism ~ $18

Rumours: A Memoir of a British POW in WWII ~ Chas Mayhead ~ $16

When History Enters the House: Essays from Central Europe ~ Michael Blumenthal ~ $15

Available from your favorite bookstore, from amazon.com, from bn.com, or directly from the publisher at
www.pleasureboatstudio.com
or, via email, at
pleasboat@nyc.rr.com.